Blue Sky 04/05

September 2004 – Annu Palakunnathu Matthew & Magali Nougarède
October 2004 – Critical Mass
November 2004 – Jim Cooke & Allen Maertz
December 2004 – Martina Mullaney & Adrain Chesser
January 2005 – Thomas Roma & Bob Thall
February 2005 – Soody Sharifi & Germán Herrera
March 2005 – Charles Traub
April 2005 – Charles Cohen & Gregory Gorfkle
May 2005 – Simon Norfolk
June 2005 – Douglas Levere & Jindrich Streit
July 2005 – Nina Berman & Jeffrey Milstein
August 2005 – Paul Seawright

In any given year Blue Sky Gallery produces approximately 22 exhibitions of the very best photographic artists working around the world. From 1975 through 1992 we documented these shows with about 150 posters, many of which still adorn our office. For the past 13 years we've been producing catalogues several times annually instead, to provide both our artists and supporters with a more substantial record of these exhibits. Now, in an effort to expand on that idea, the time has come for another transition.

In this inaugural issue of our Blue Sky Annual Yearbook you'll find a year's worth of imagery from artists throughout the U.S. and Europe, tackling a wide array of subjects and concepts. From Annu Matthew's striking exploration of cultural and historical stereotypes, to Thomas Roma's masterful portraits of the people and landscape of Sicily, to Germán Herrera's view of the interior of self, to Simon Norfolk and Paul Seawright's troubling yet poetic portrayals of complex issues surrounding two countries grappling with the effects of war... these are all personal images with universal messages. You'll also find the top ten vote getters from Photolucida's *Critical Mass* competition, who were selected out of 600 entrants by an impressive panel of 50 jurors to earn a spot in a traveling show that was launched at Blue Sky and is now touring the country.

We need our artists now more than ever to reflect a different kind of mirror on the world. We offer this collection, this book, in honor of them.

Kirsten Rian
Executive Director

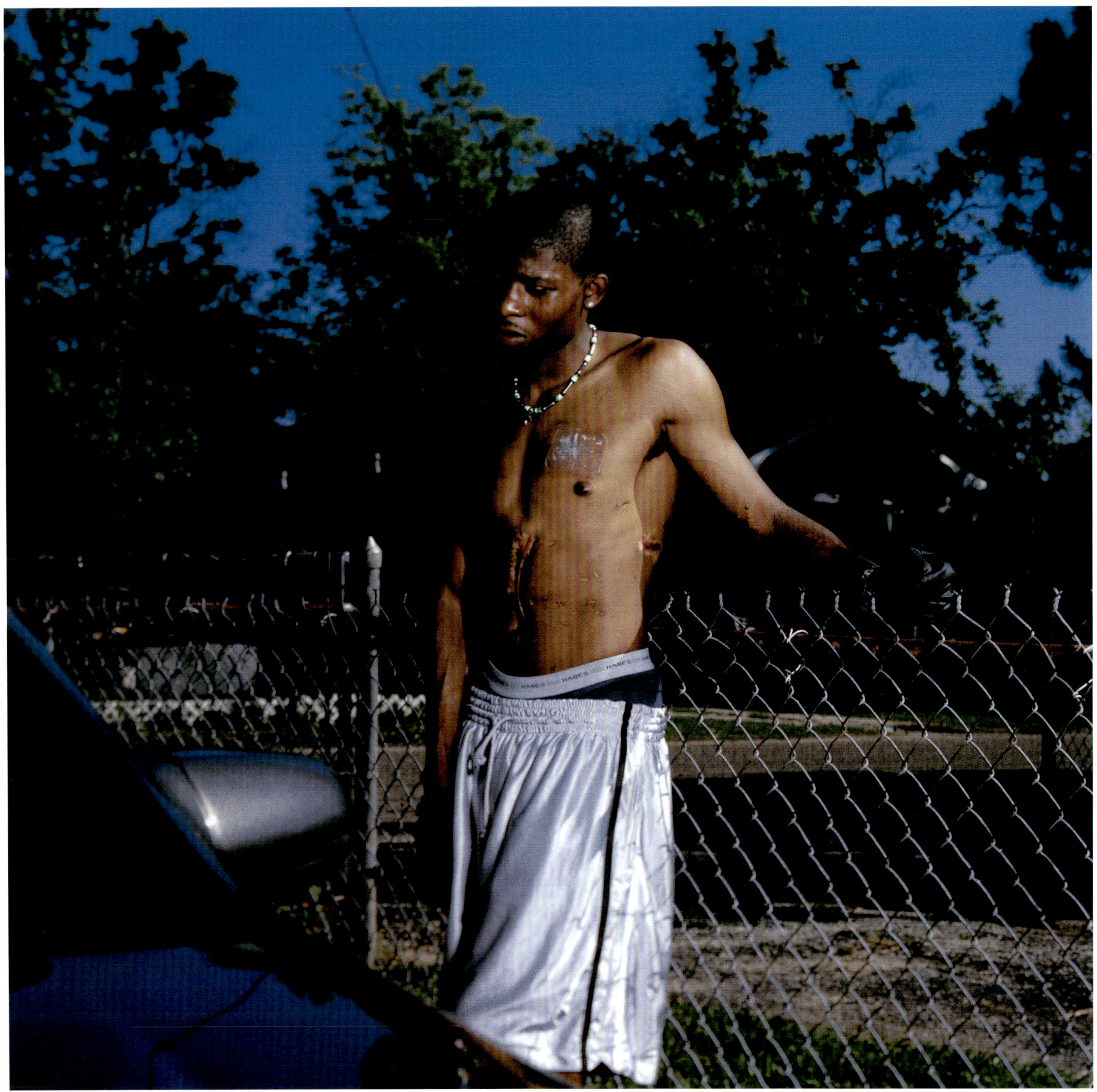

Cpl. Tyson Johnson III Nina Berman

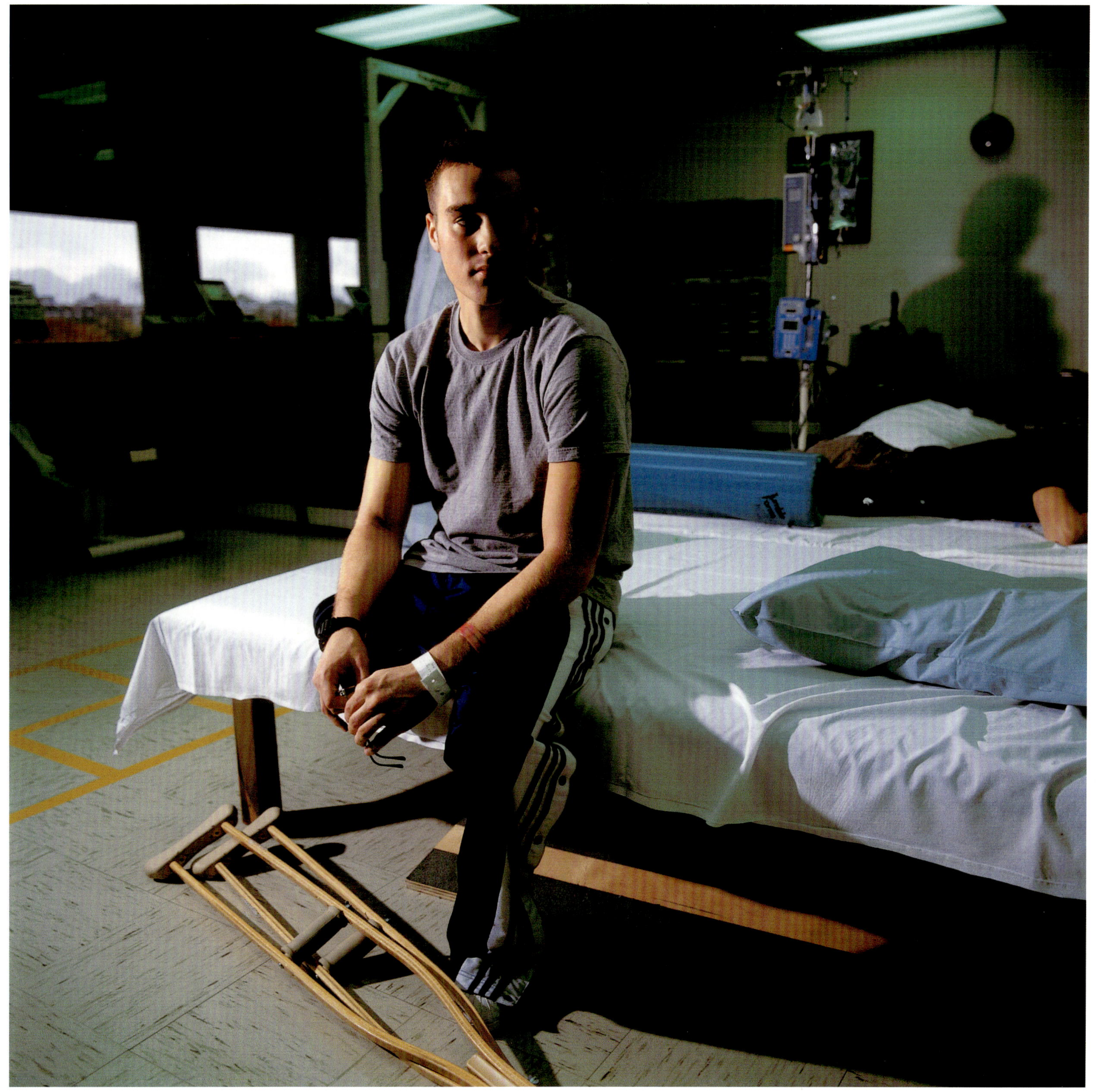

Pfc. Tristan Wyatt Nina Berman

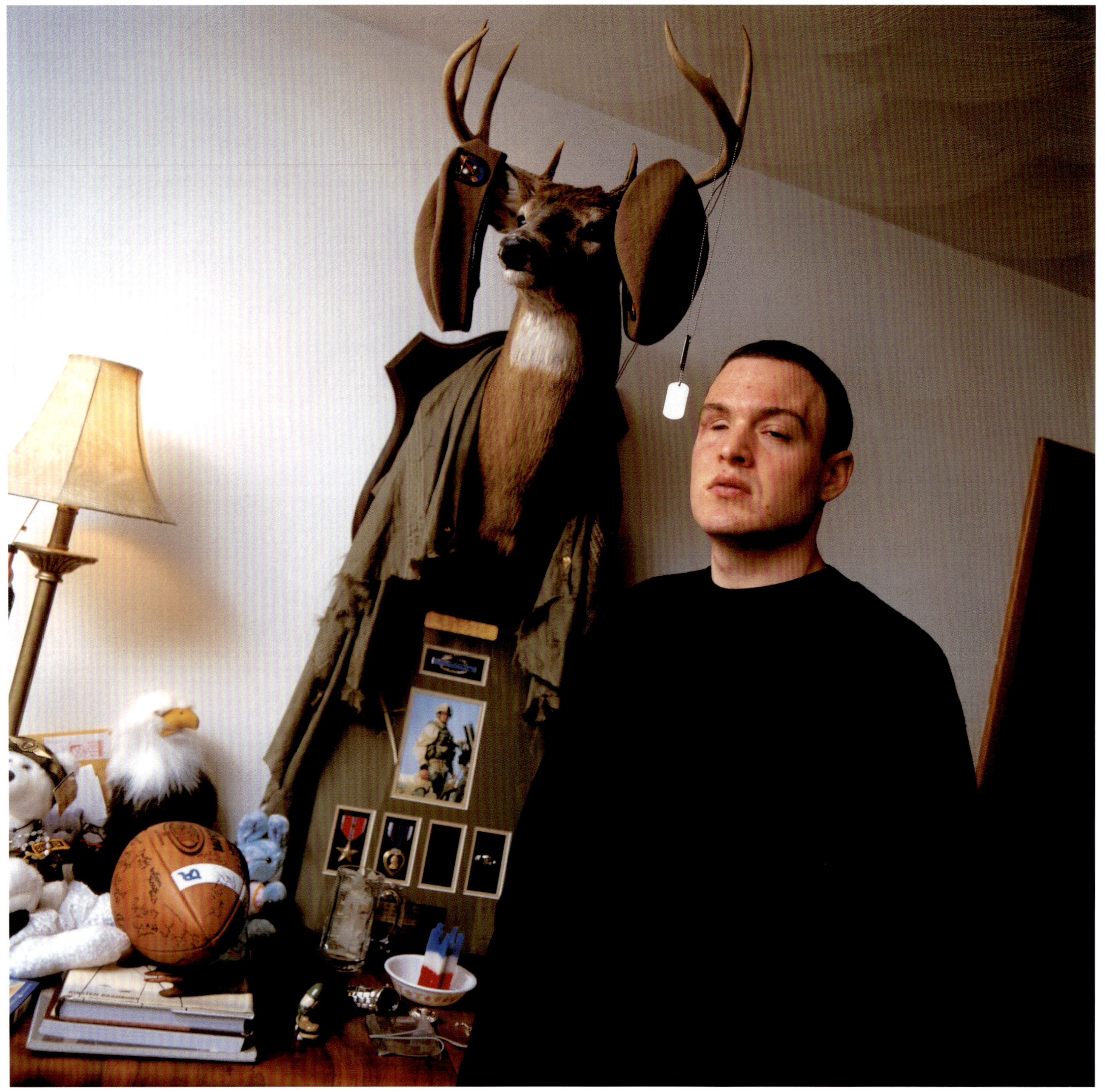

Sgt. Jeremy Feldbusch Nina Berman

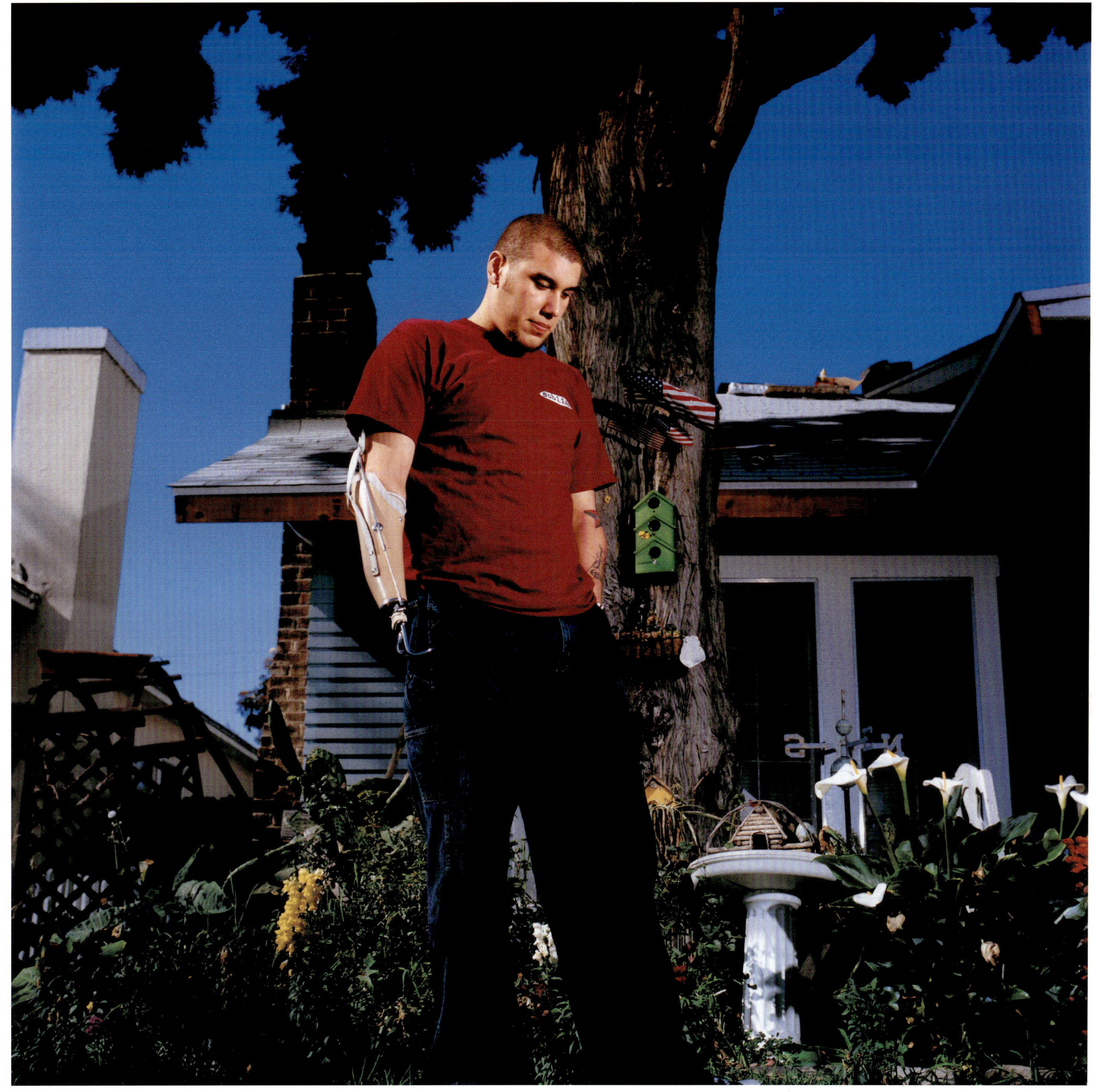

Spc. Robert Acosta Nina Berman

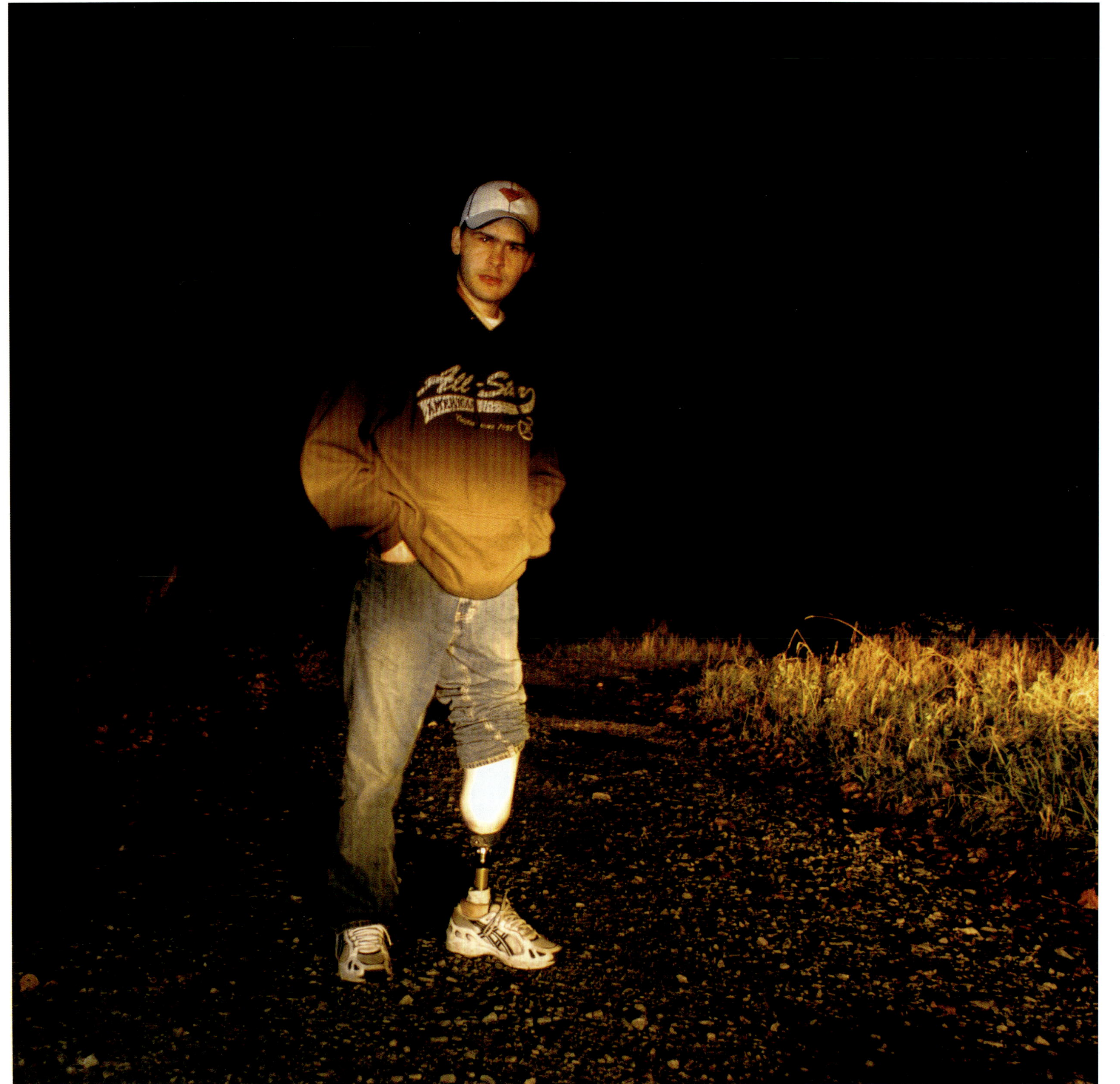

Spc. Sam Ross

Nina Berman

Purple Hearts

An image of a wounded American soldier is one of the few pieces of documentary evidence the American public can see to begin a process of separating propaganda—that war is quick and bloodless—from truth.

Since October 2003, I have been making portraits and conducting interviews with Americans who were wounded in the Iraq War. I seek them out at their homes after they have been discharged from the military hospitals at Walter Reed in Washington, D.C. and Brooke Army in San Antonio, Texas. I stay away from the homecoming parades, the VFW initiation events, the yellow ribbons and appearances with politicians. I want to see the soldier alone as each confronts his or her loss and considers the experience of war and life ahead.

These portraits are not sentimental; if anything, they are detached. They are done in a formal manner in that the person is aware of being photographed. The process takes a few hours and always begins with a taped interview in which I ask questions about life at home, the recruitment process, the injury, what he or she liked about the military, and the experience in Iraq. Lately, I've been asking them for their definitions of freedom and democracy, a question that often leaves them puzzled.

When viewed together, the words and photos make for a complex, sometimes contradictory portrait of American youth; the values, dreams, the lack of opportunity facing them after high school, the culture of violence and drugs which many tried to escape by enlisting and the myths of warfare which helped influence their decisions to join.

When I started this project, I wasn't prepared for the physical damage I would see. I remember the first soldier I photographed was completely blind. His world is black from morning to night. Titanium plates hold his brain together. He has seizures and mood swings and needs frequent naps. I photographed him in his bedroom standing next to a giant deer that he had killed when he was 16 years old. Dangling from the antlers were the soldier's dog tags and his army ranger berets. Below the deer was a picture of the soldier in uniform. This young man, tall and strong, a university graduate, and first in his class of 228 rangers, trembled at the sound of the camera's shutter.

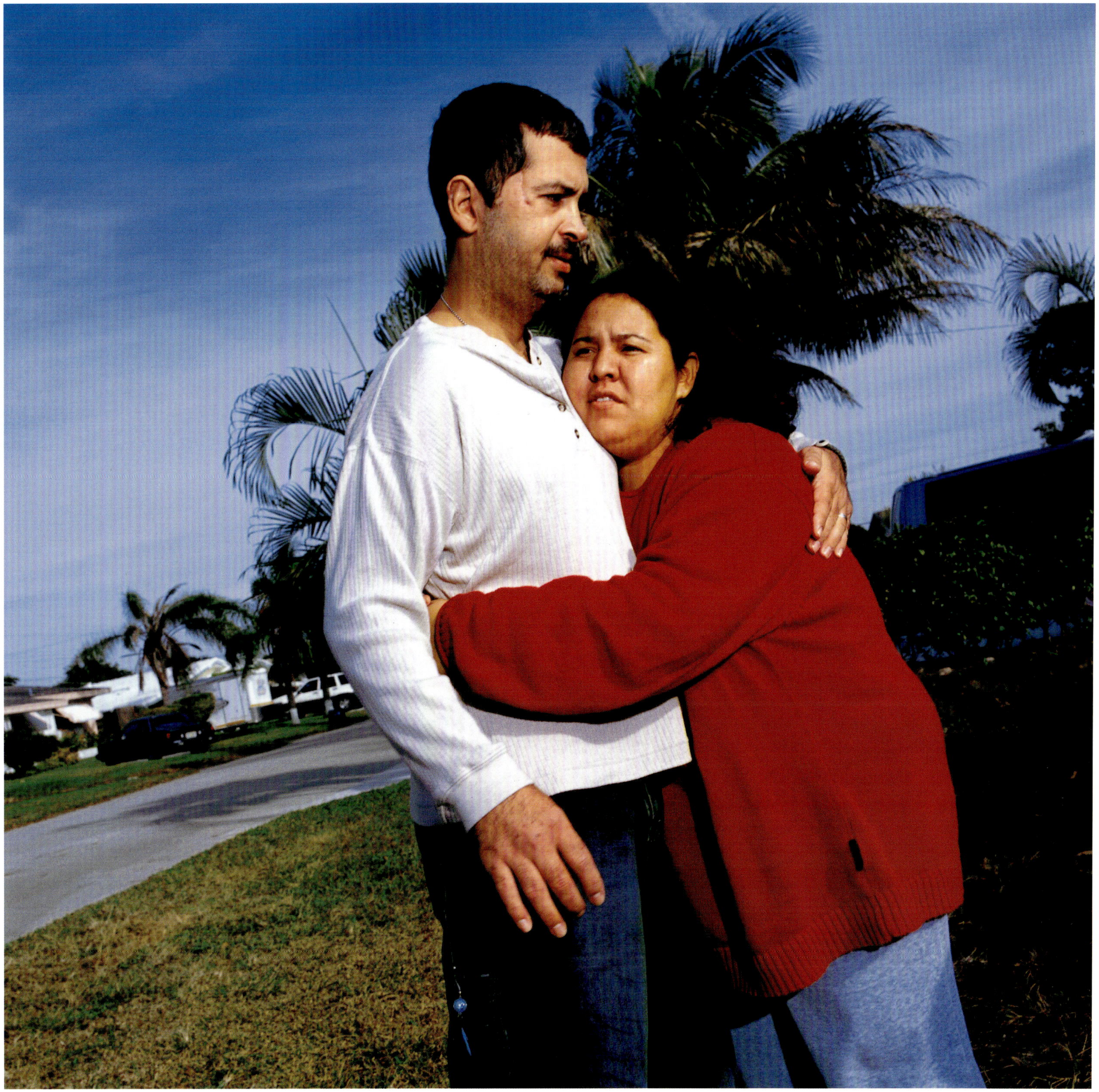

Sgt. John Adams Nina Berman

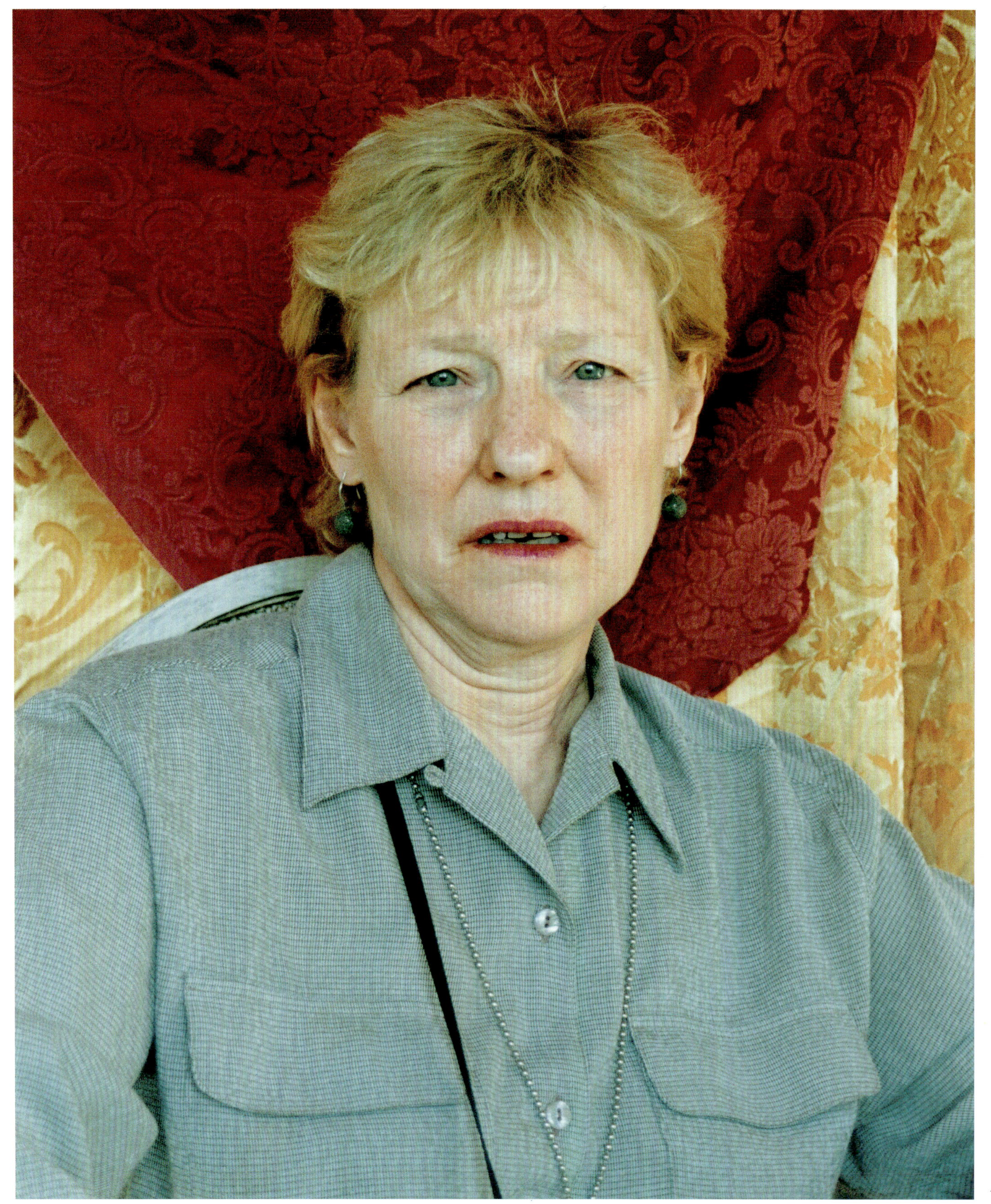

Adrain Chesser

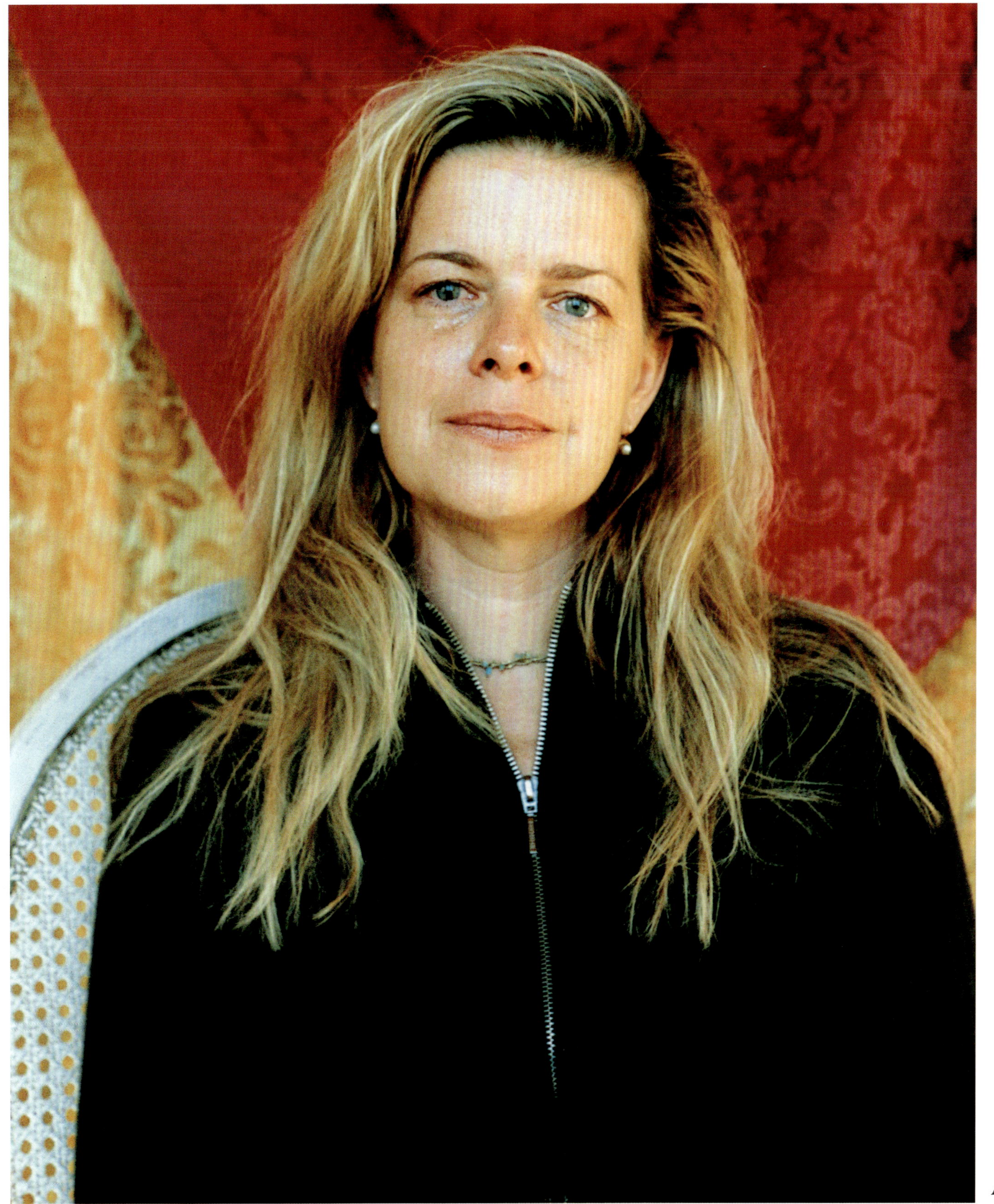

Adrain Chesser

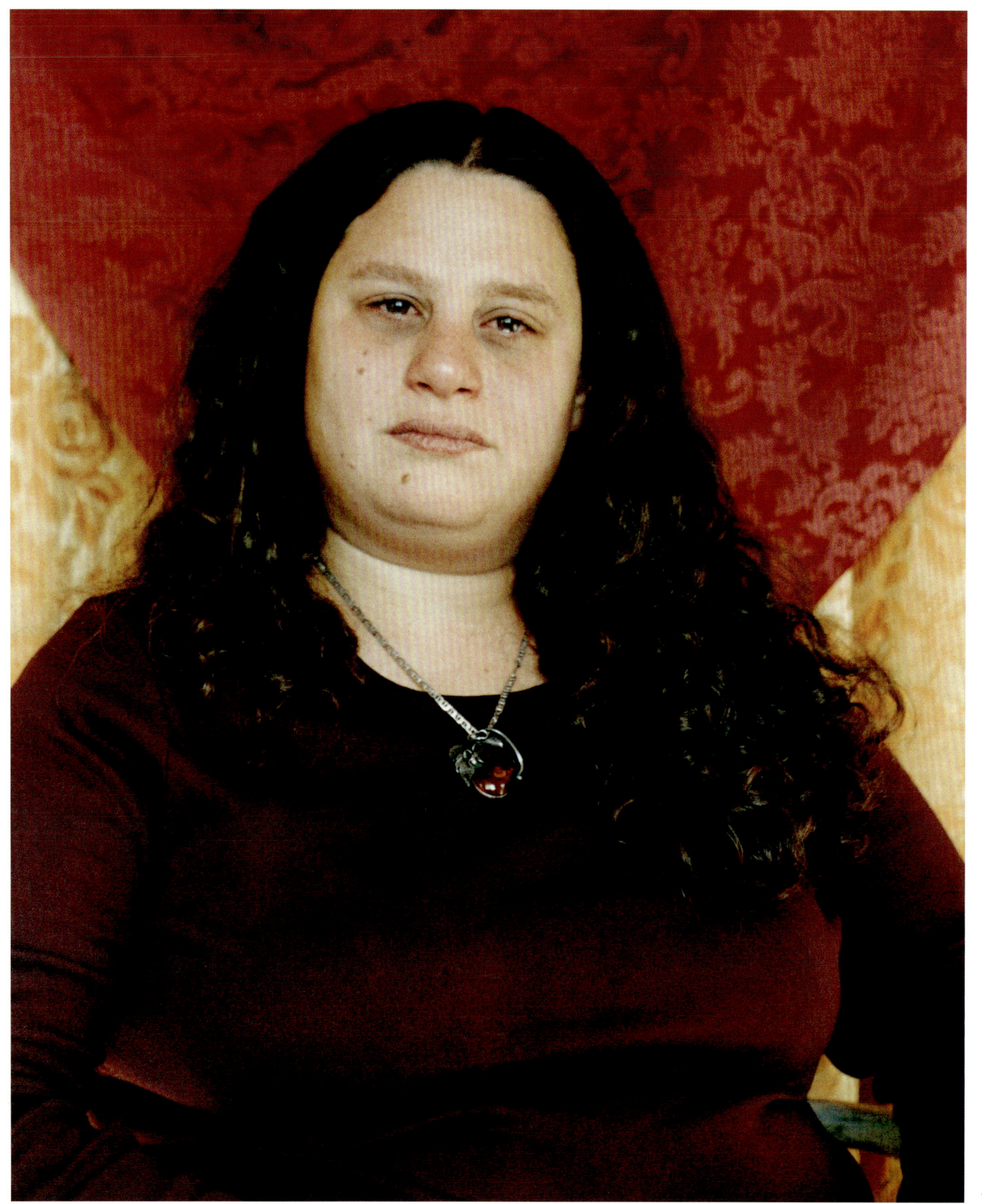

Adrain Chesser

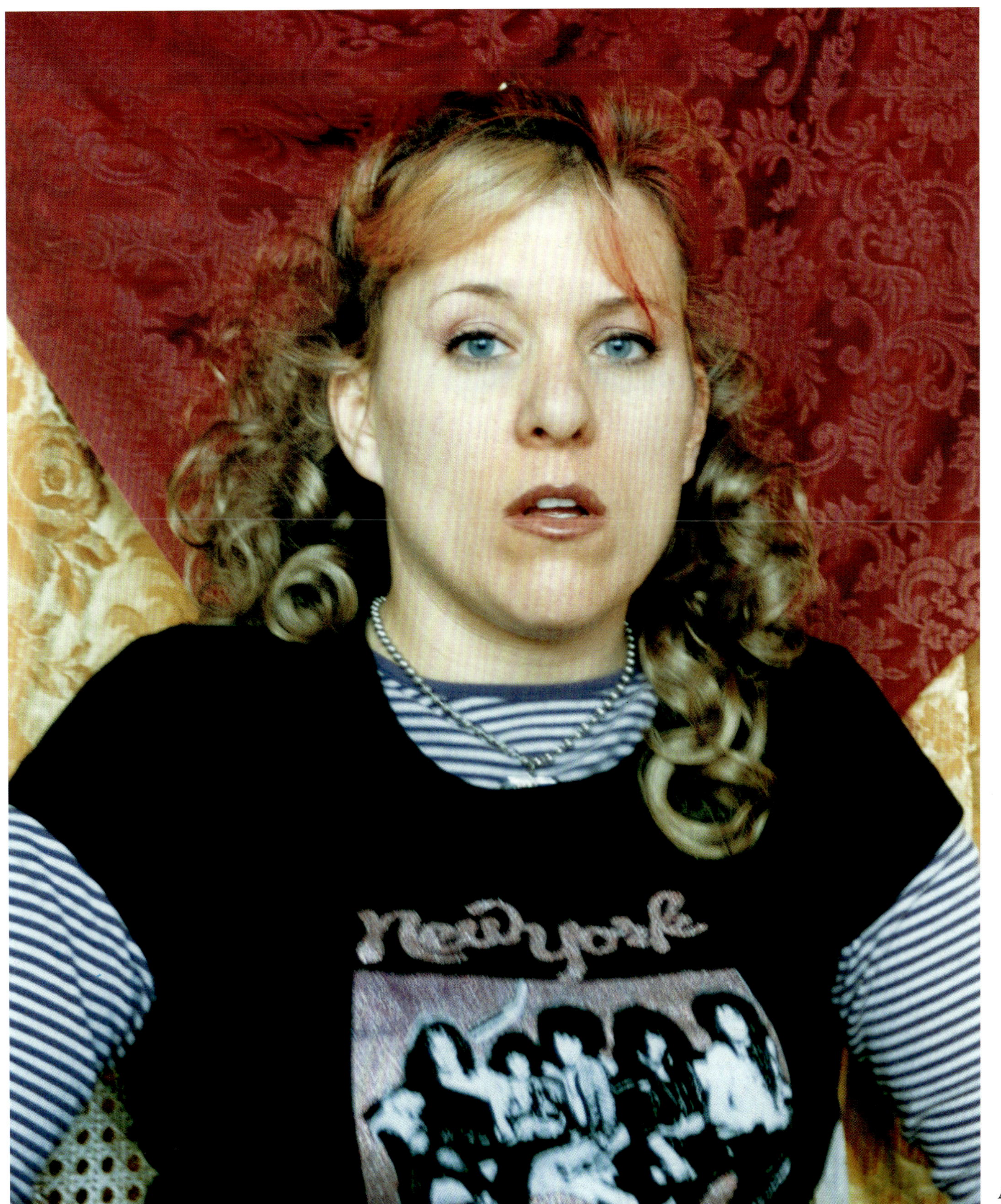

Adrain Chesser

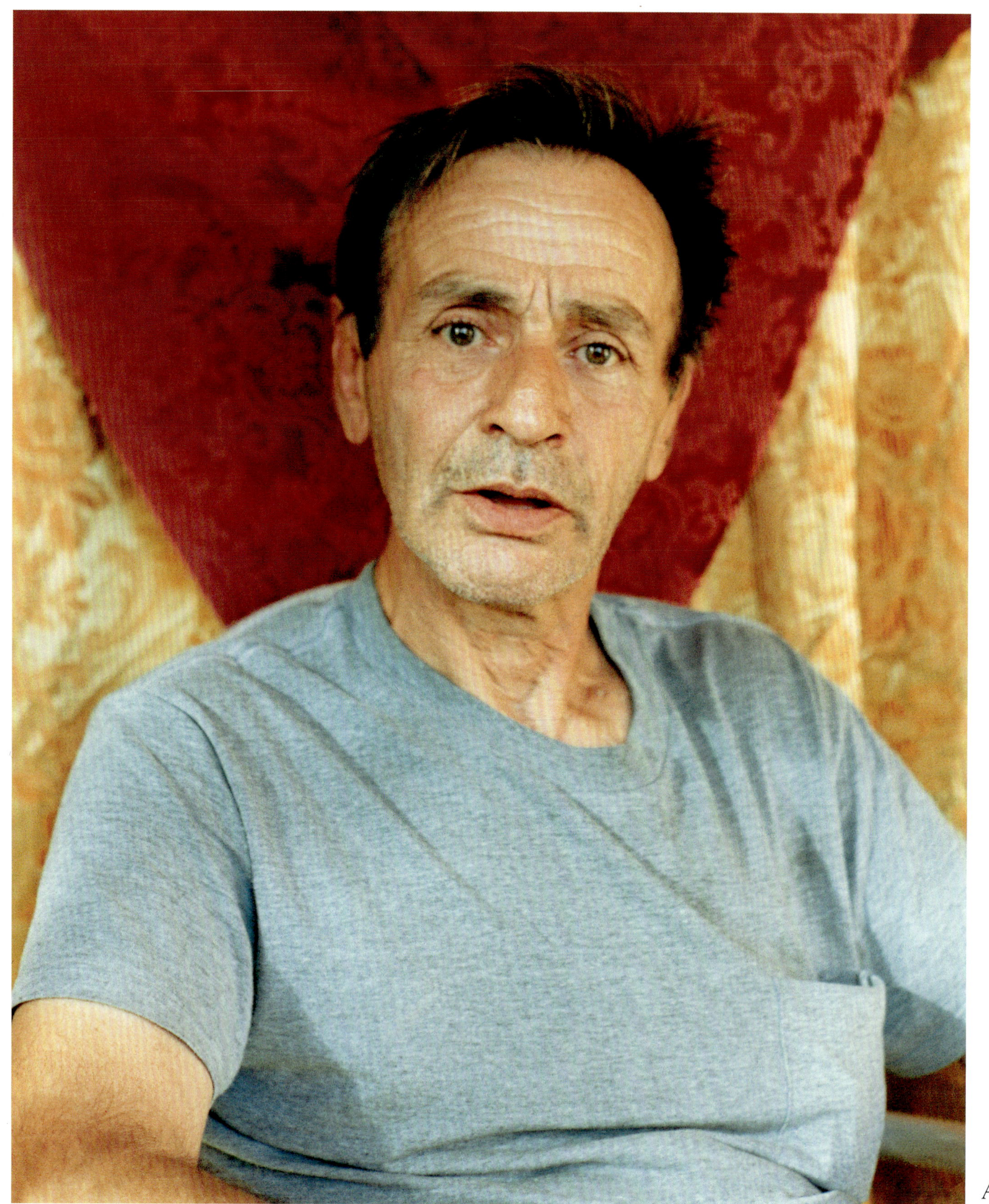

Adrain Chesser

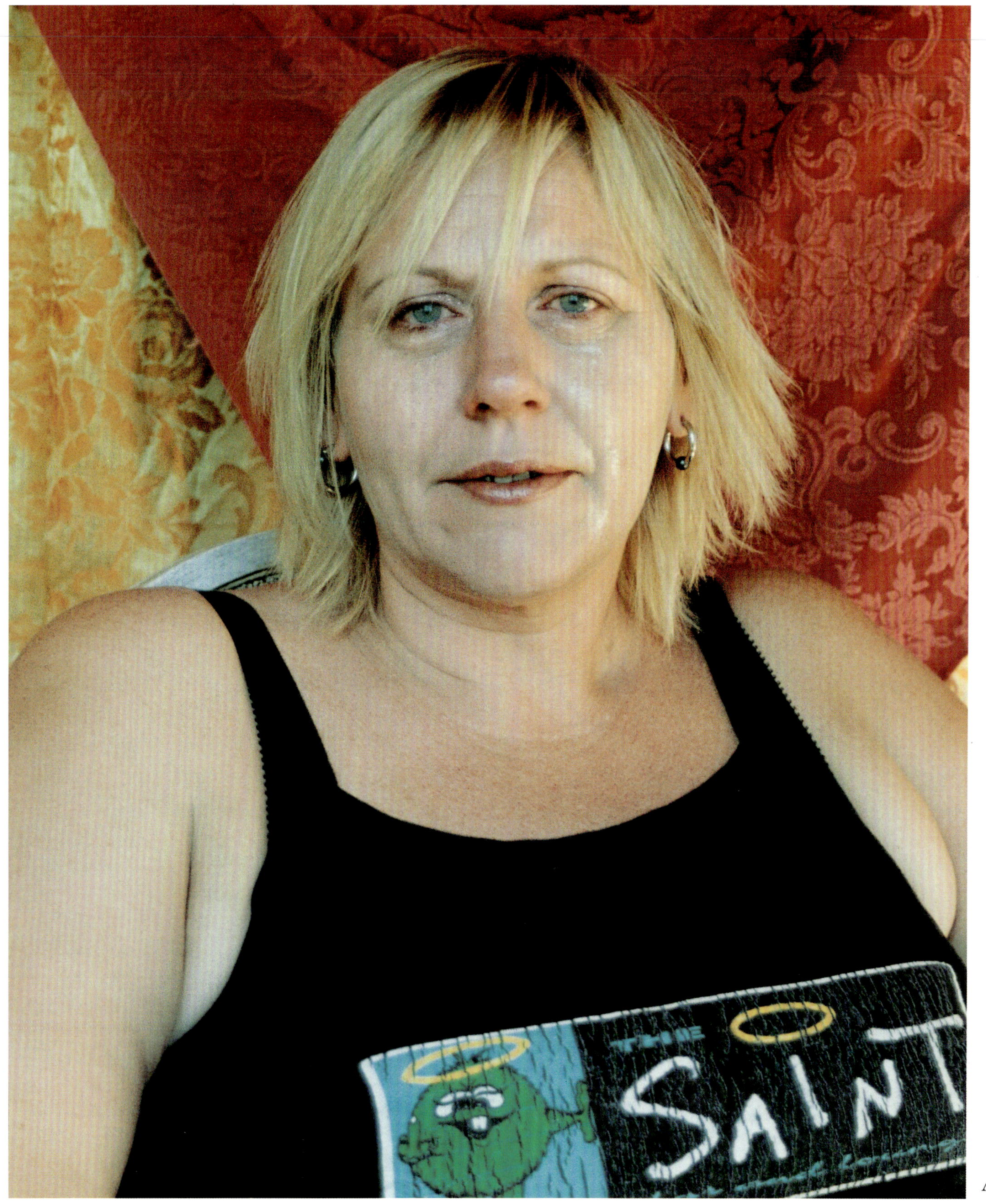

Adrain Chesser

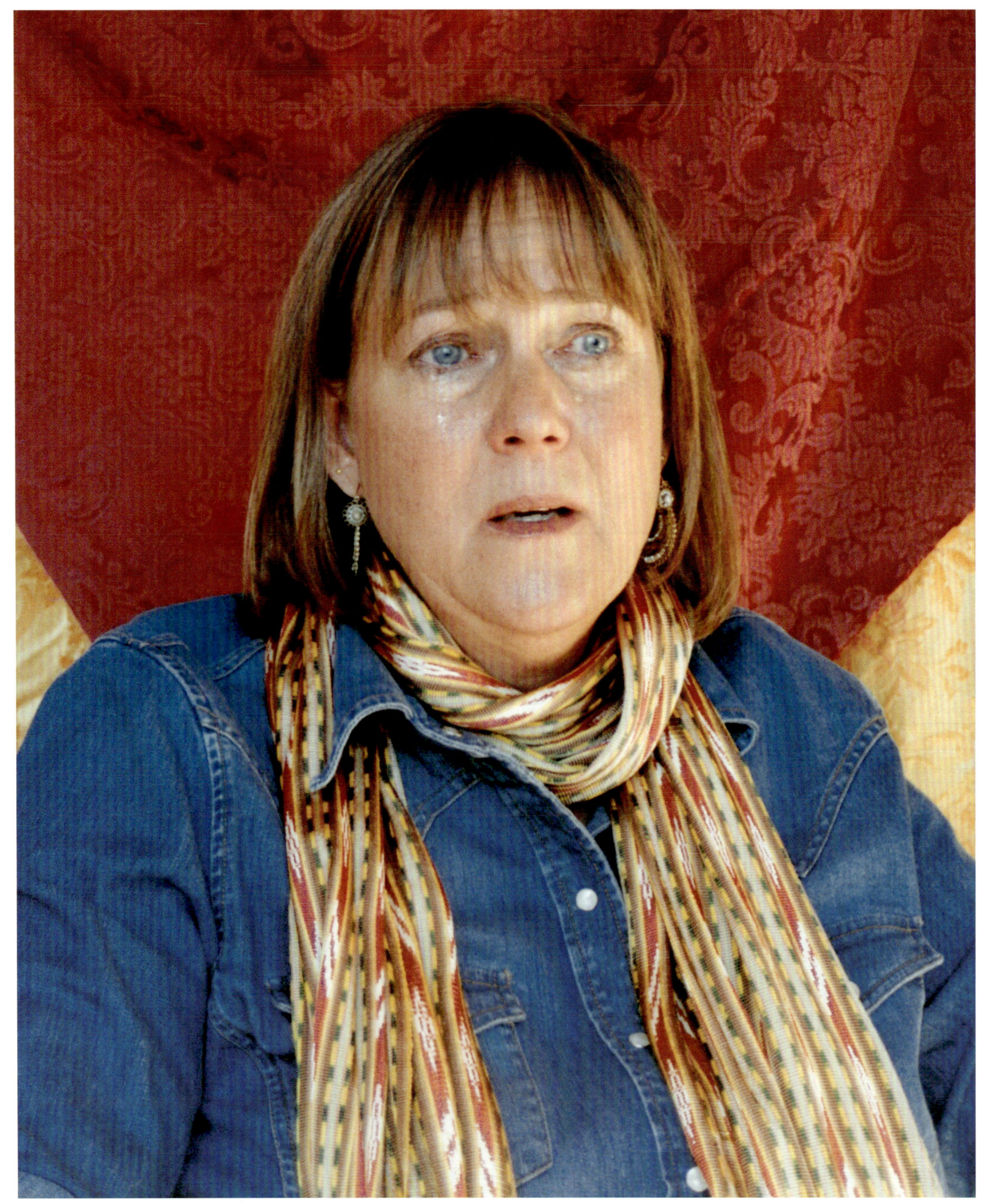

Adrain Chesser

For beauty is nothing but the onset of terror we're still just able to bear.
– Rilke

I have always felt that one of photography's greatest allies is memory, whether it is personal or collective, real or imagined. The illusion of the realism of photography has the potential to access emotions bound to memories, sometimes causing extreme physical reactions, at other times a nagging unease or the warm sensation of pleasure.

When I tested positive for HIV and was diagnosed with AIDS, I had an extreme physical reaction whenever I thought about having to tell my friends and family. Looking at this reaction more closely I realized that it was the same reaction I had as a kid whenever I had to disclose something uncomfortable to my parents, fearing rejection or even abandonment if larger secrets were revealed.

It occurred to me that it might be possible to overcome this paralyzing fear if I photographed my friends as I told them about my diagnosis. I invited each friend to come to my studio to have their picture taken, a simple head shot, for a new project. They weren't given any other information. For a backdrop I used the curtains from the living room of the house I grew up in. I put everybody through the same routine, creating a ritual that would prove to be transformative. At the beginning of each shoot I would start by saying "I have something to tell you."

Each sitter's reaction was unique, depending on their own experience of loss, illness and death. But as a collective, the body of work speaks to a more universal experience. The phrase "I have something to tell you" is often the preface for life-altering disclosures, pregnancies, deaths, love affairs, illnesses of all kinds, winning the lottery. The phrase becomes a kind of mile marker in a life, delineating what came before from what comes after.

I printed the photographs on glossy paper for several different reasons. First because the surface is reflective and will often give off a glare that distracts from seeing the actual image, not unlike what we do as humans creating facades to distract from what lies beneath. Also the surface is extremely fragile, scratches on the surface are like scars on a human body speaking to the experiences of life that a photo has as an object. The scratches gently reinforce the knowledge that, like this human experience, a photograph will not last forever.

While these photos are probably the worst pictures ever taken of my friends, they are undoubtedly the most beautiful.

Adrain Chesser

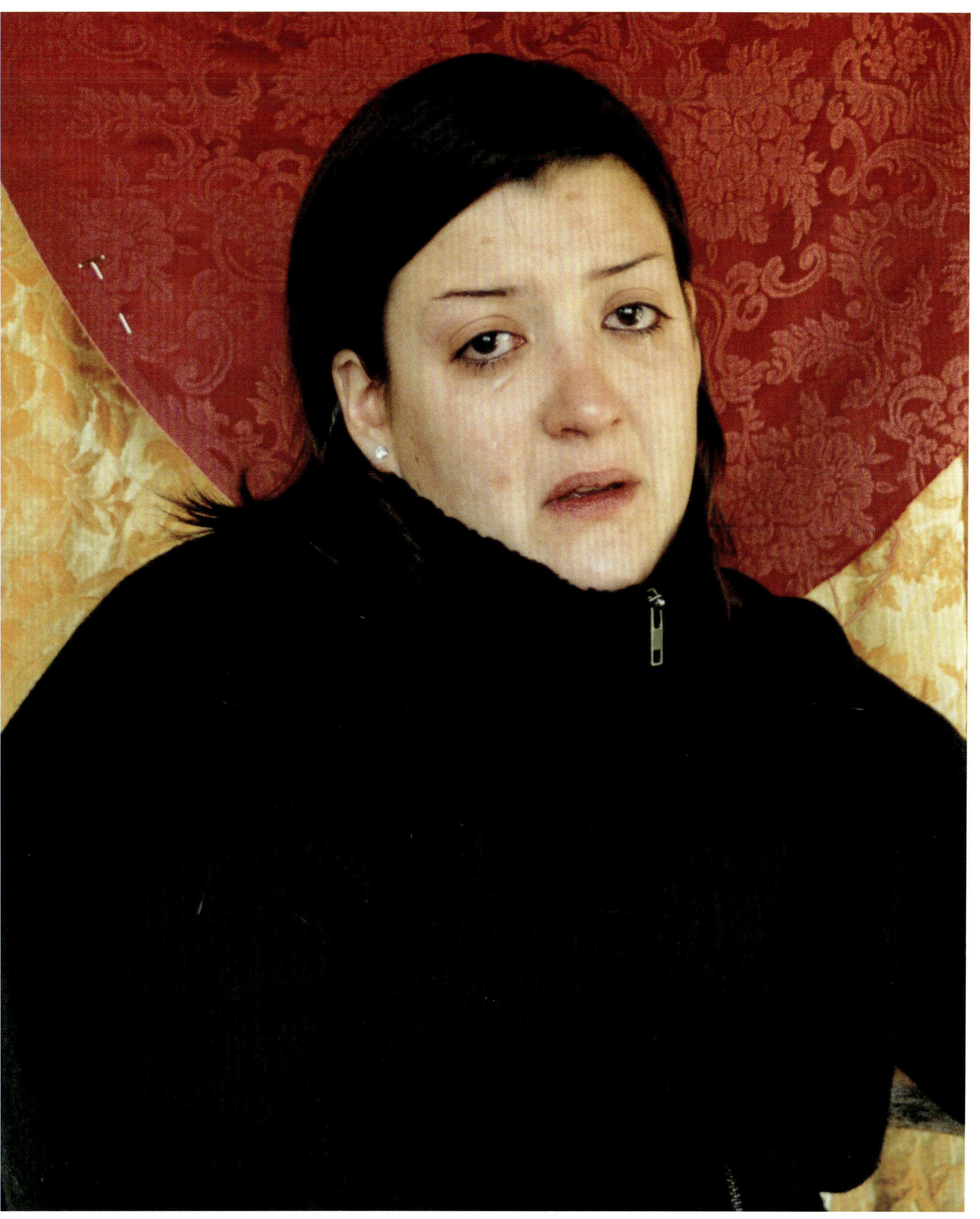

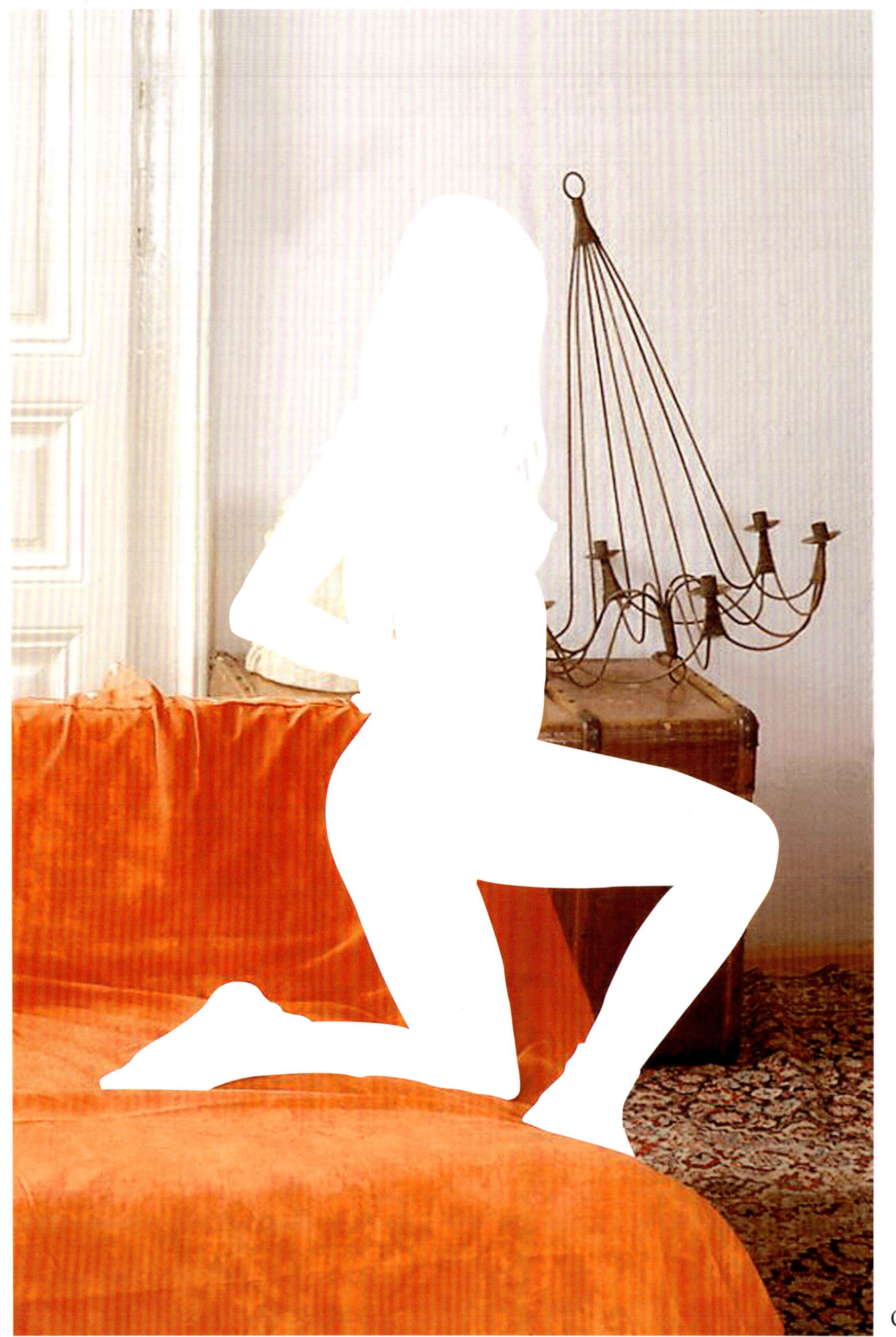

Charles Cohen

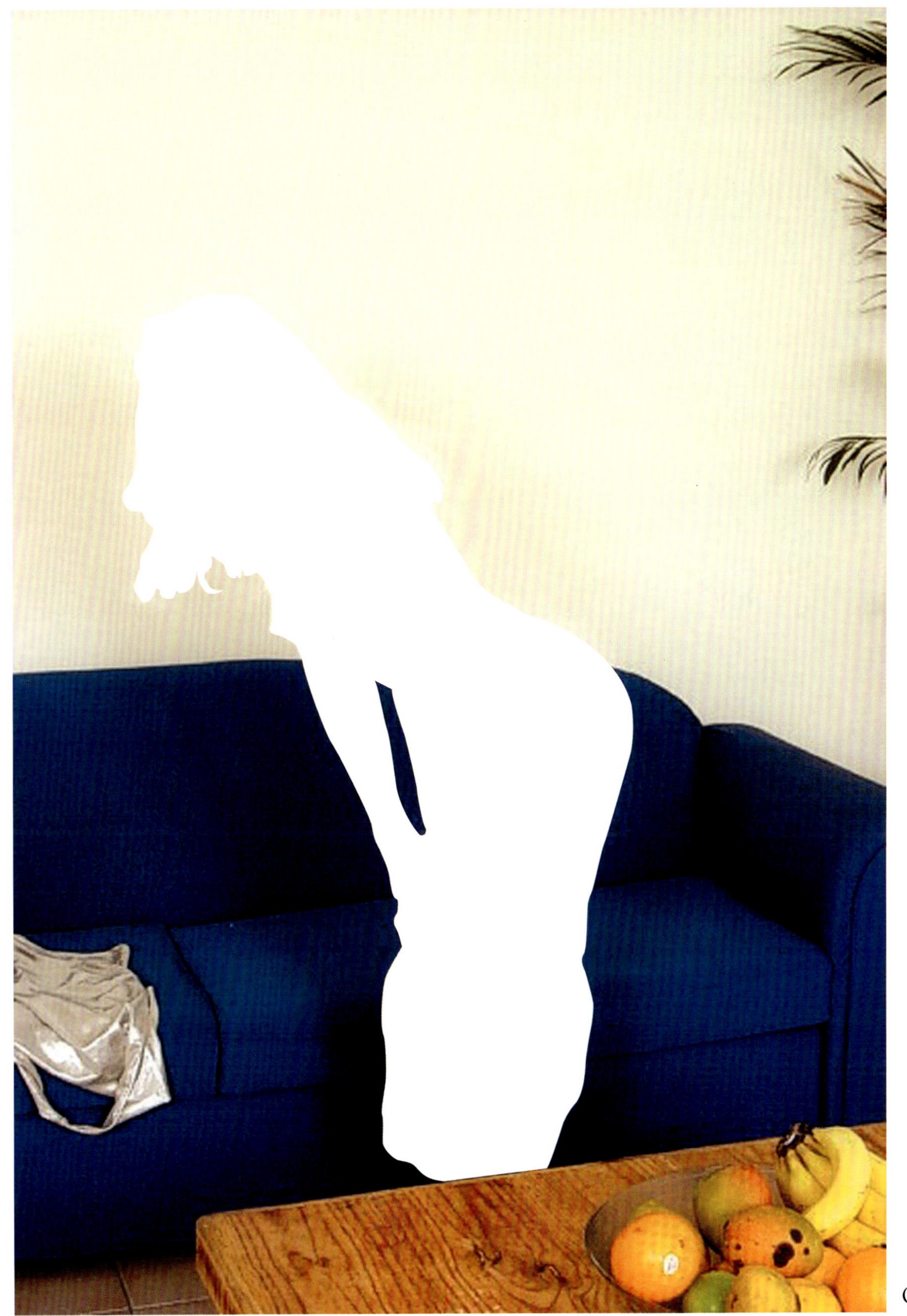

Charles Cohen

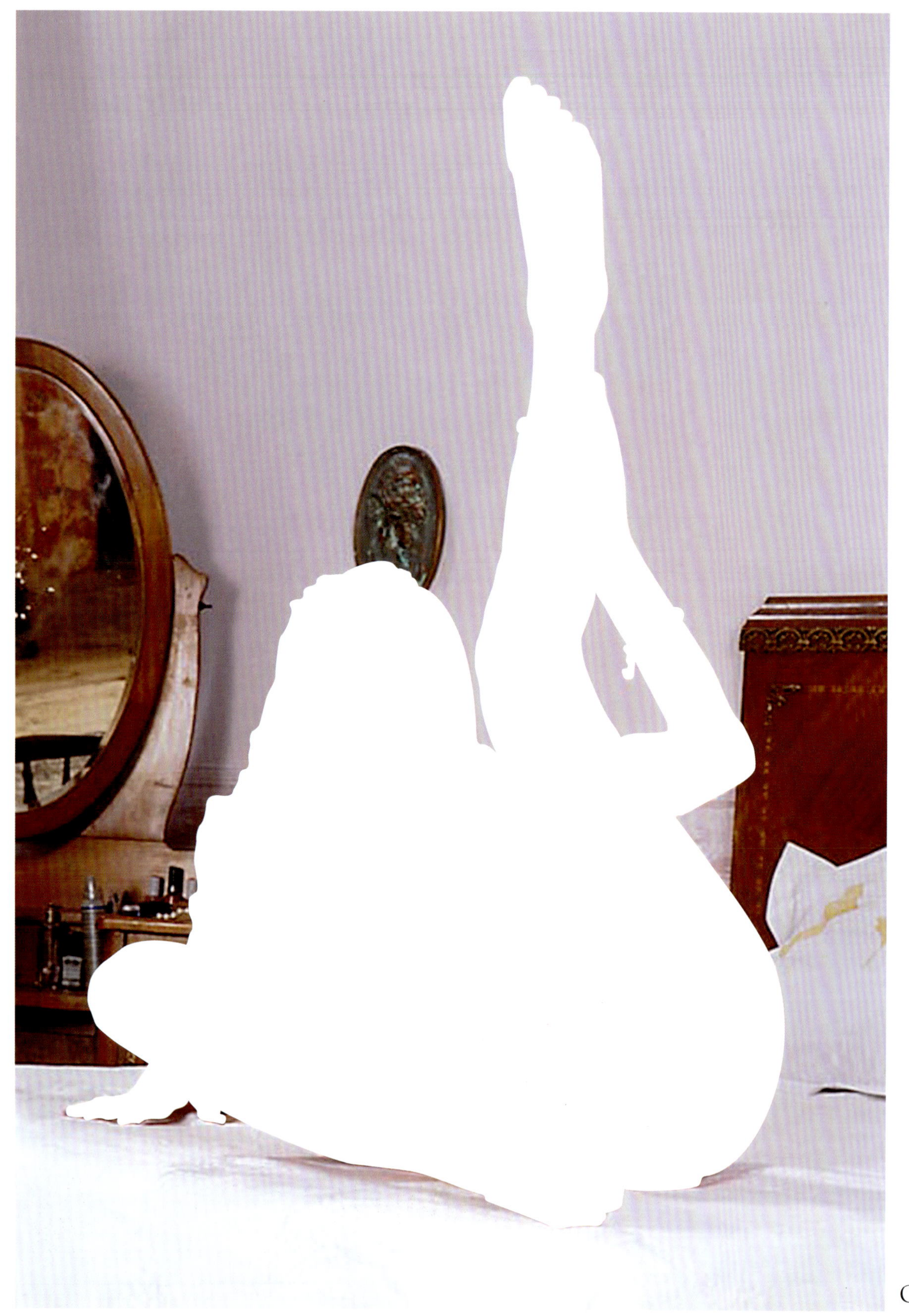

Charles Cohen

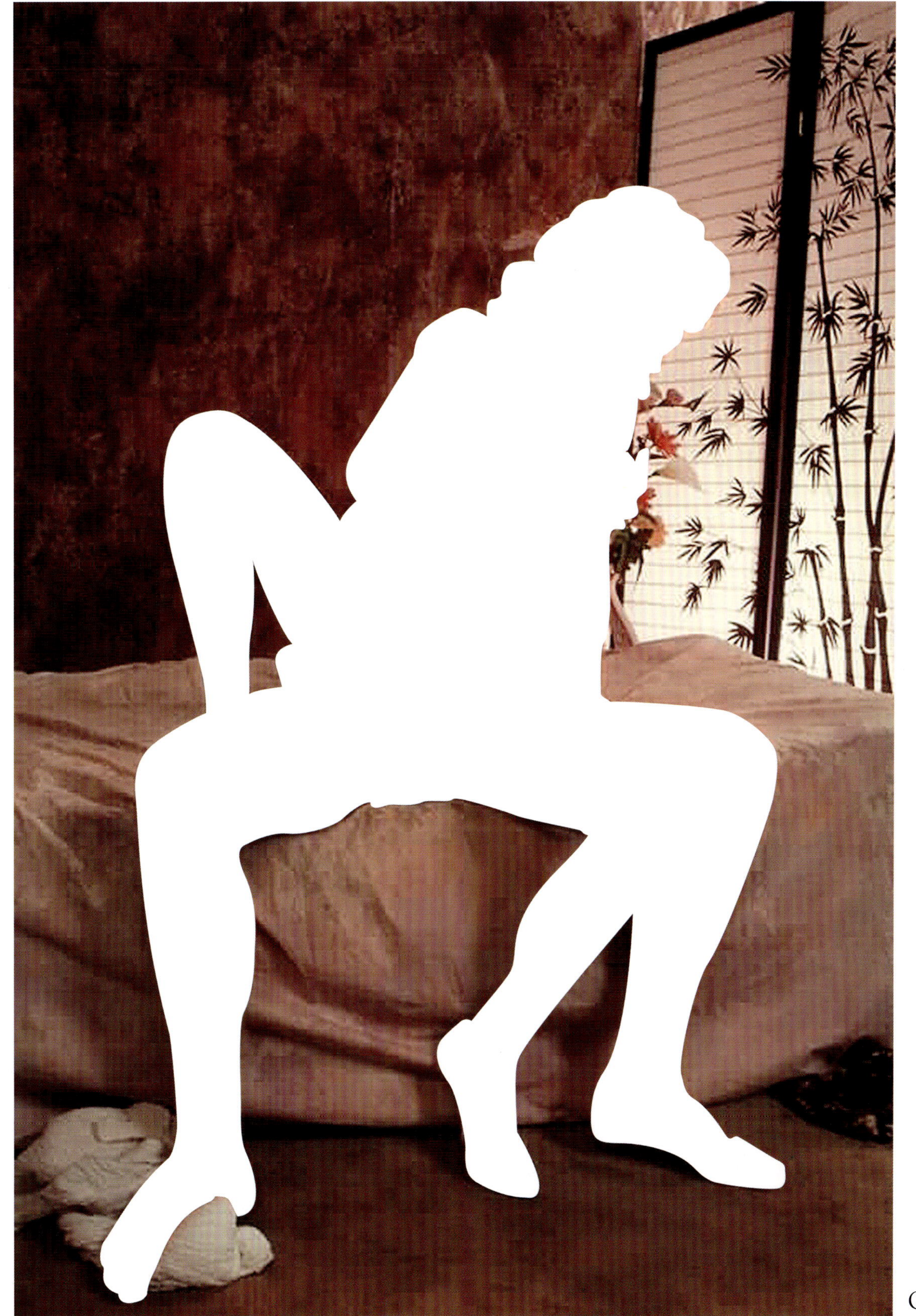

Charles Cohen

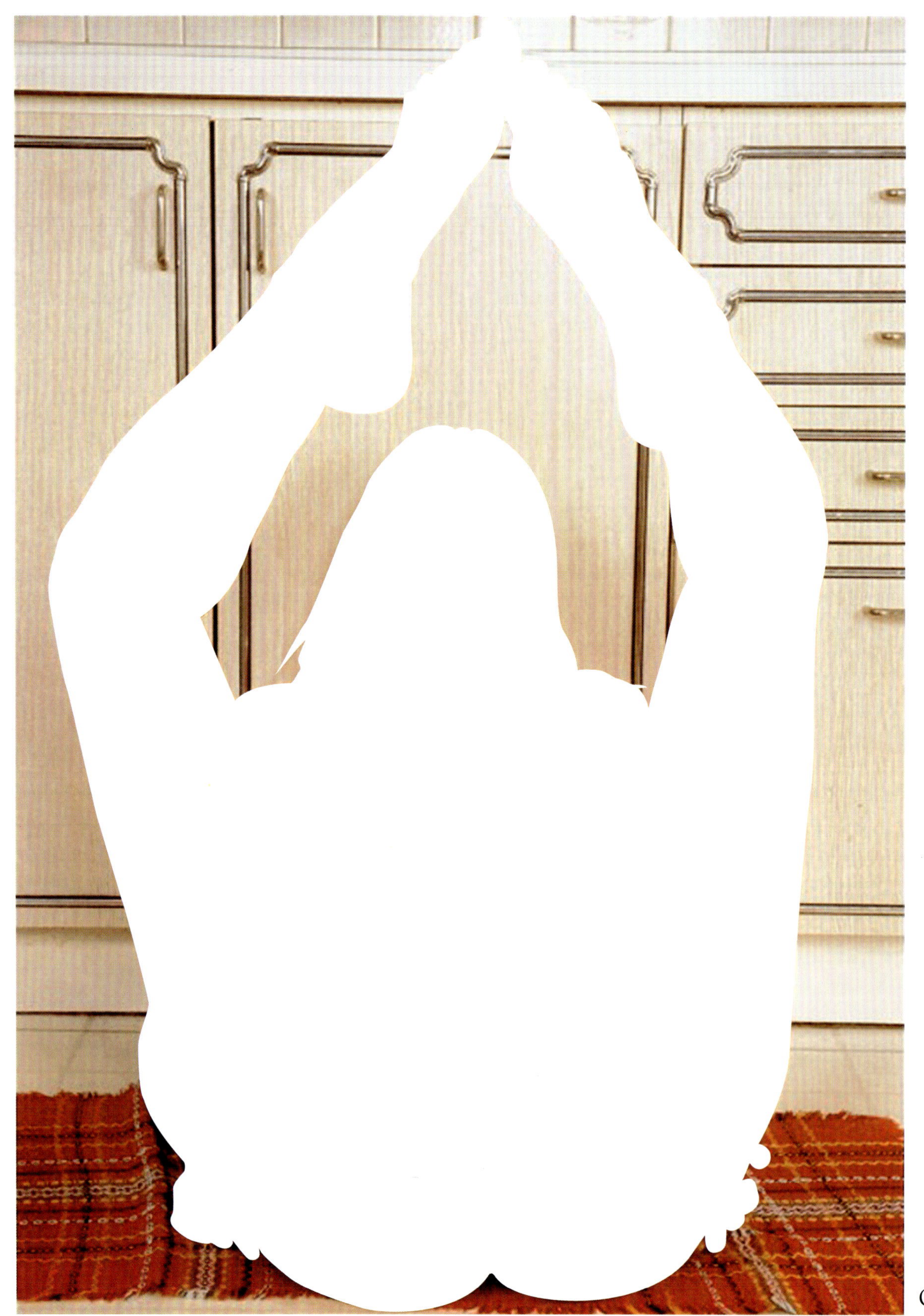

Charles Cohen

Buff

What we no longer have is complicated by the way we remember it. A pervasive sense of longing ultimately indicates a link between the present and what is lost, what is missing, as well as, perhaps, what is regrettable. We are surrounded by absence. One only needs to alter perception slightly to see how present it is.

The transformation is simple. In this case, the commonplace is rendered abstract by denying the image its original function. A void replaces what ought to be present, or rather, what is expected. Buff does not have to be based on pornography, but because its intended function is simple and explicit – to entertain the voyeur – it is thus easily manipulated. Ironically, it is because pornography suggests participation that we can observe the phenomenon of stimulation in a more heightened fashion. This is the process of abstraction.

While in most cases the pictures are still clearly erotic, one finds oneself appreciating the image in ways not common to pornography. This is the effect of abstraction. The color palette, the interaction of light and shadow, negative space, and references to art history contribute to an unexpected beauty. Several dualities become apparent and are changed: the background and the subject (foreground), the refined and the crude, the private and the public, the perceiver and the perceived, and the present and the absent, among others. The relationships between these themes find a dynamic equilibrium dependent on the viewer.

It is the spirit that the participant lends to an object that makes it more than the sum of its parts. If one chooses to react to Buff the way one would to pornography, perhaps one might welcome the opportunity for insight into one's own relationship to the images. The little bit of abstraction that I introduce is intended to alter a conditioned response just enough to draw attention to the preconceptions that we bring to the act of observation as well as the process of abstraction itself.

Abstraction does not only occur when we cannot identify elements of a piece. To the contrary, when any given program, image, or object is reduced to its separate components, and one is removed or emphasized over another, the interruption that ensues is the wedge that allows us to find intellectual pleasure and beauty where we do not expect it.

Buff is one case study in abstraction as it may exist in the realm of the mundane. Abstraction does not reside in any particular experience, let alone in any one artistic medium. The reward for appreciating the diversity within abstraction is the ability both to communicate an internal experience that is beyond common language and to bond with our own individual meanings and memories that we are entitled to project on the medium of everyday life.

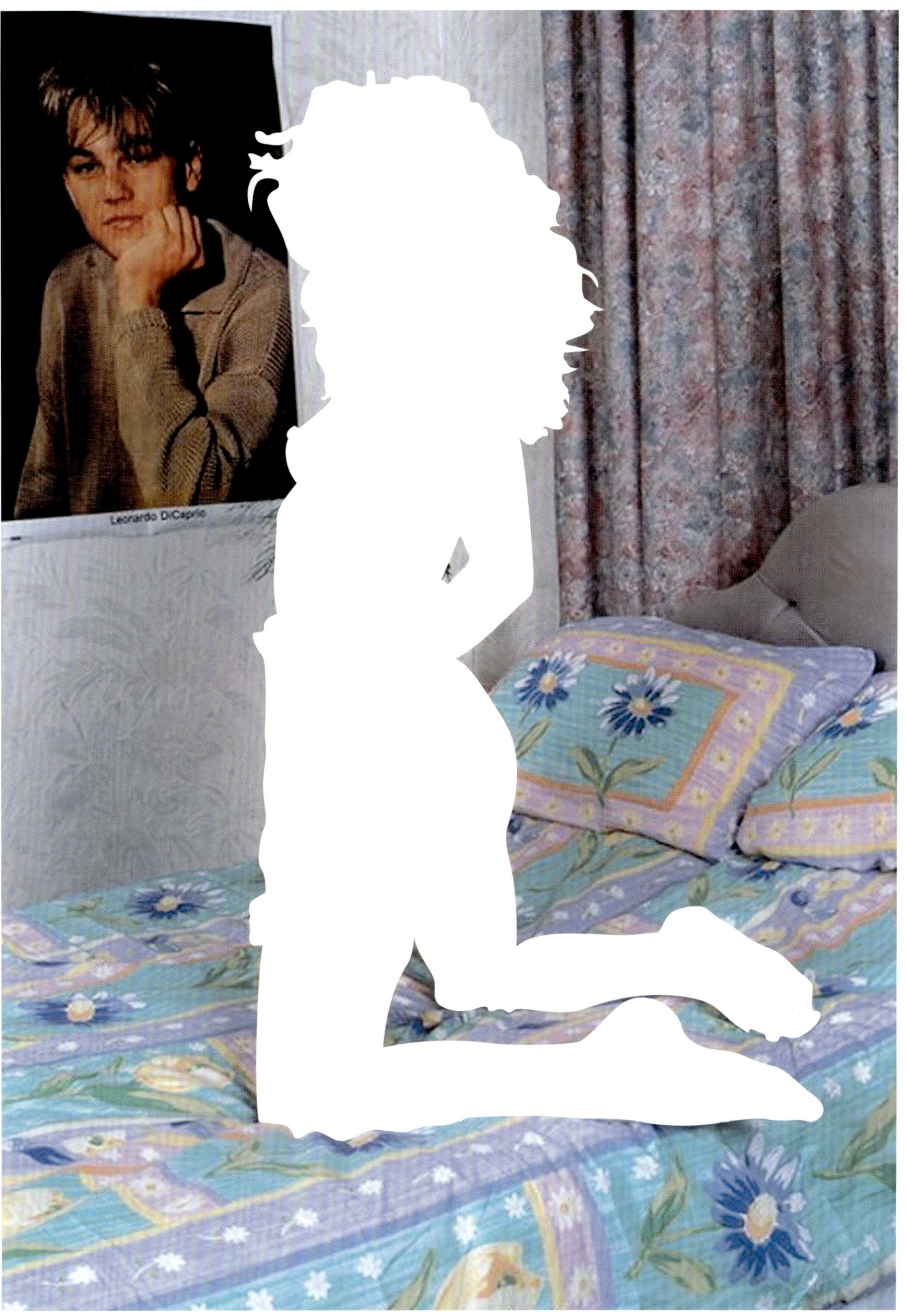

Charles Cohen

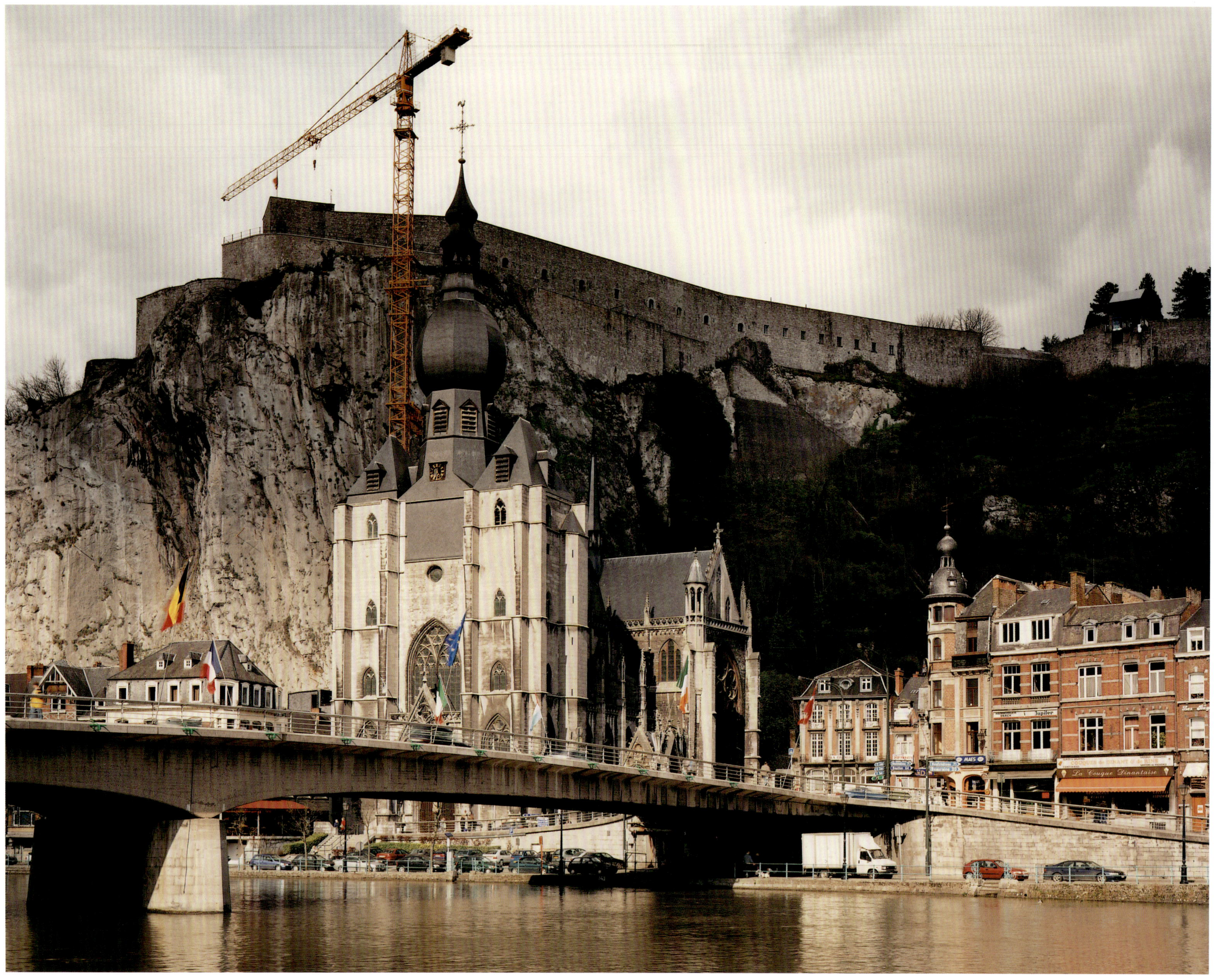

Dnant, Belgium, 2000

Jim Cooke

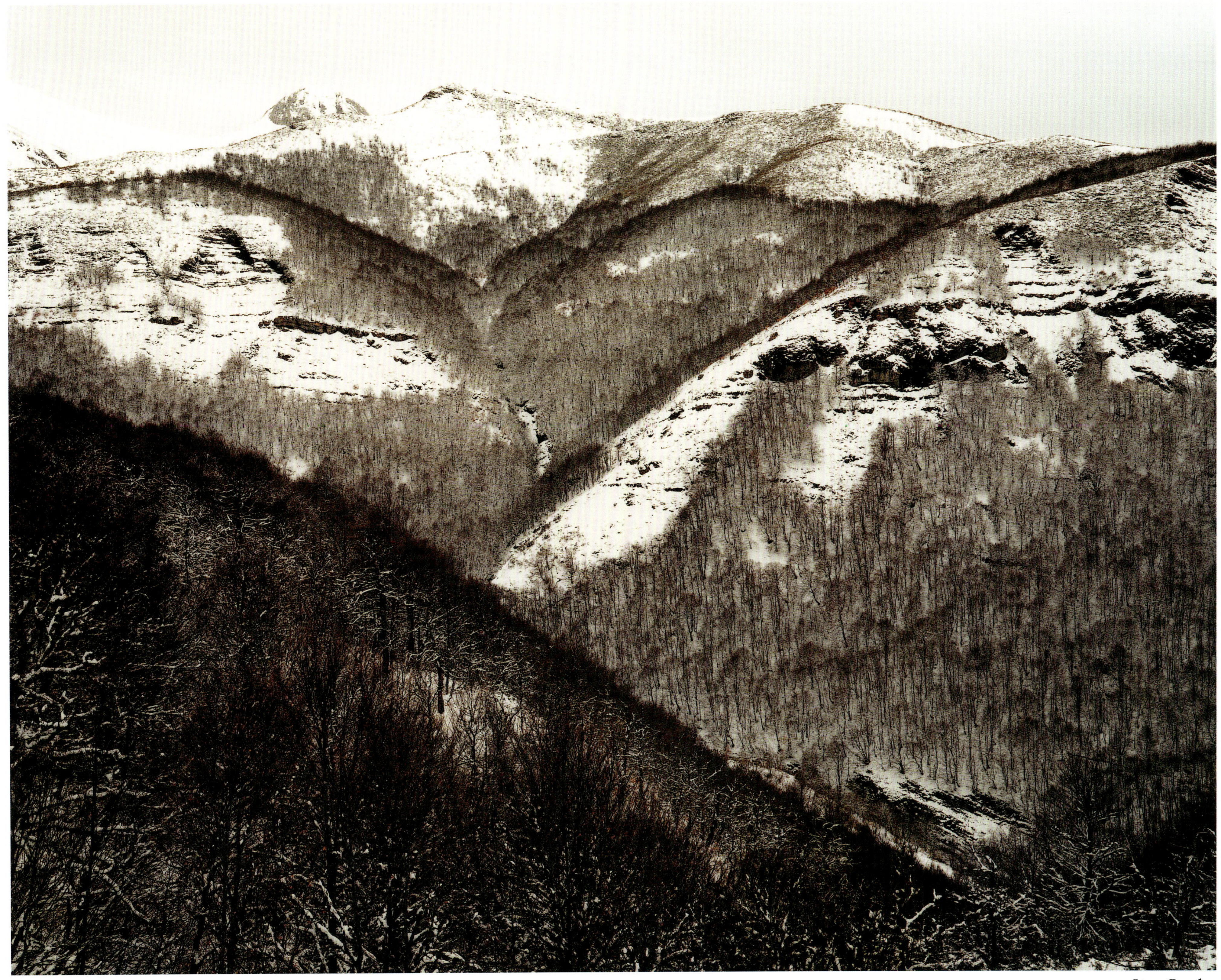

Picos de Europa, Spain, 1999 Jim Cooke

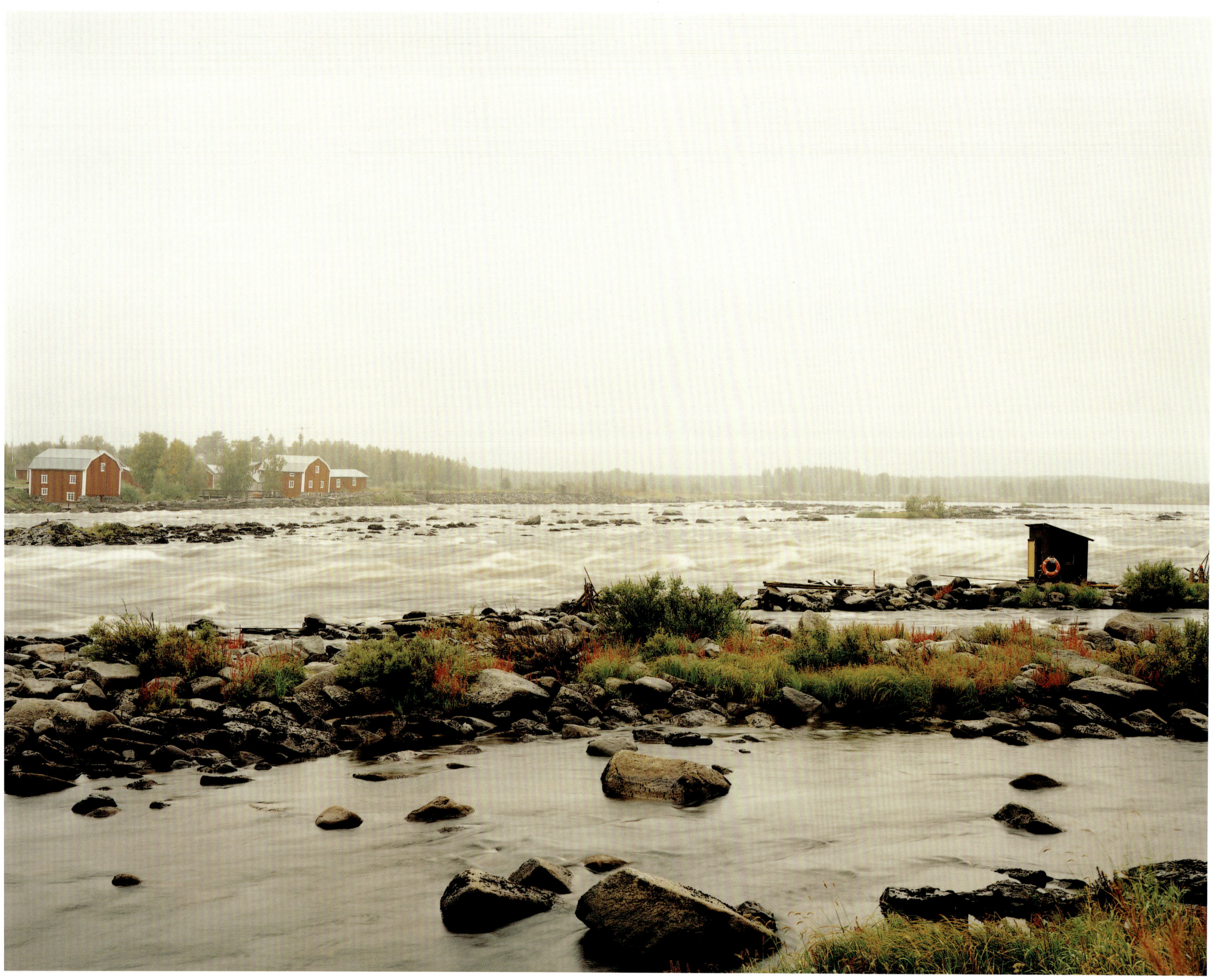

Finland – Sweden border, 1999

Jim Cooke

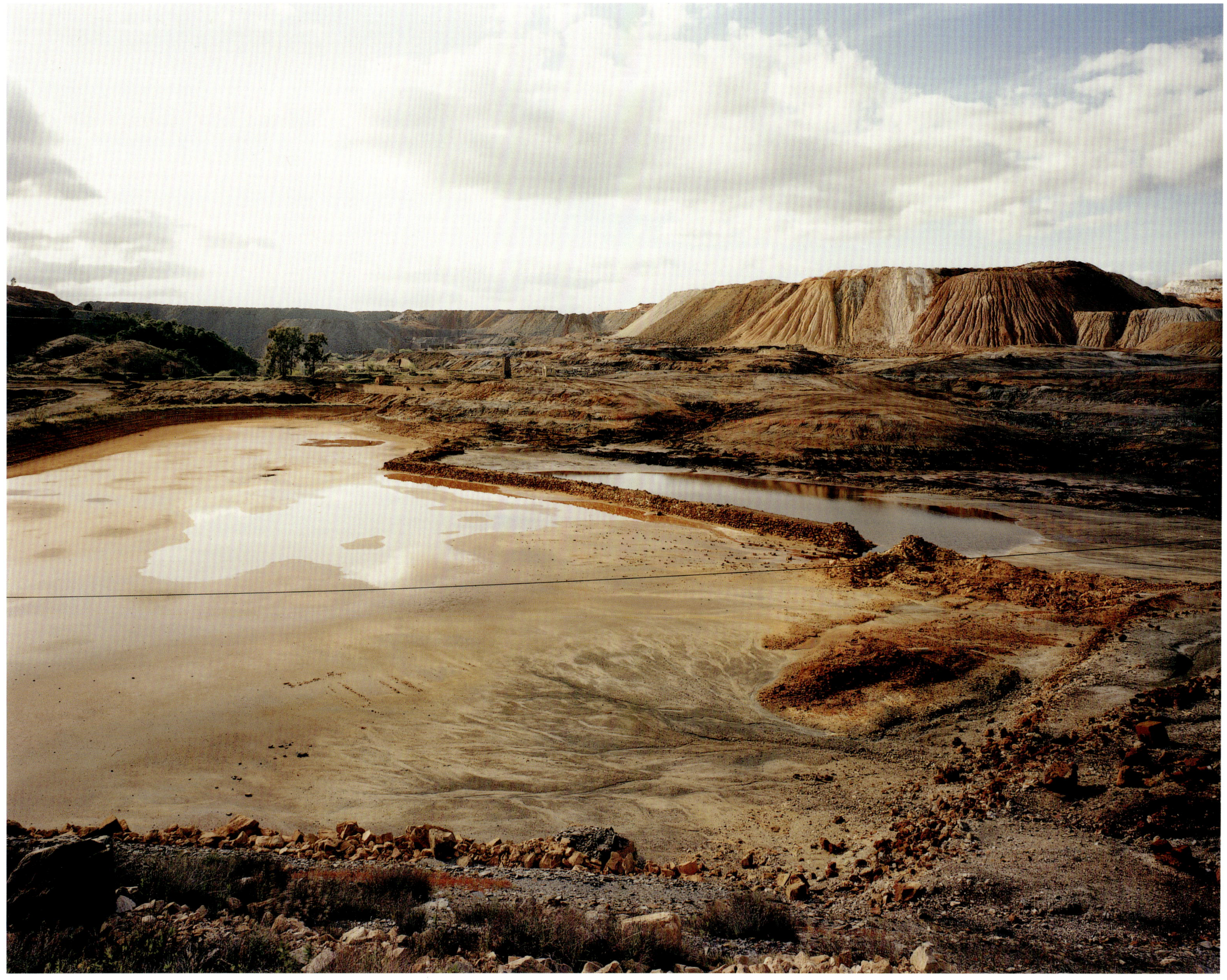

Rio Tinto, Spain, 1999

Jim Cooke

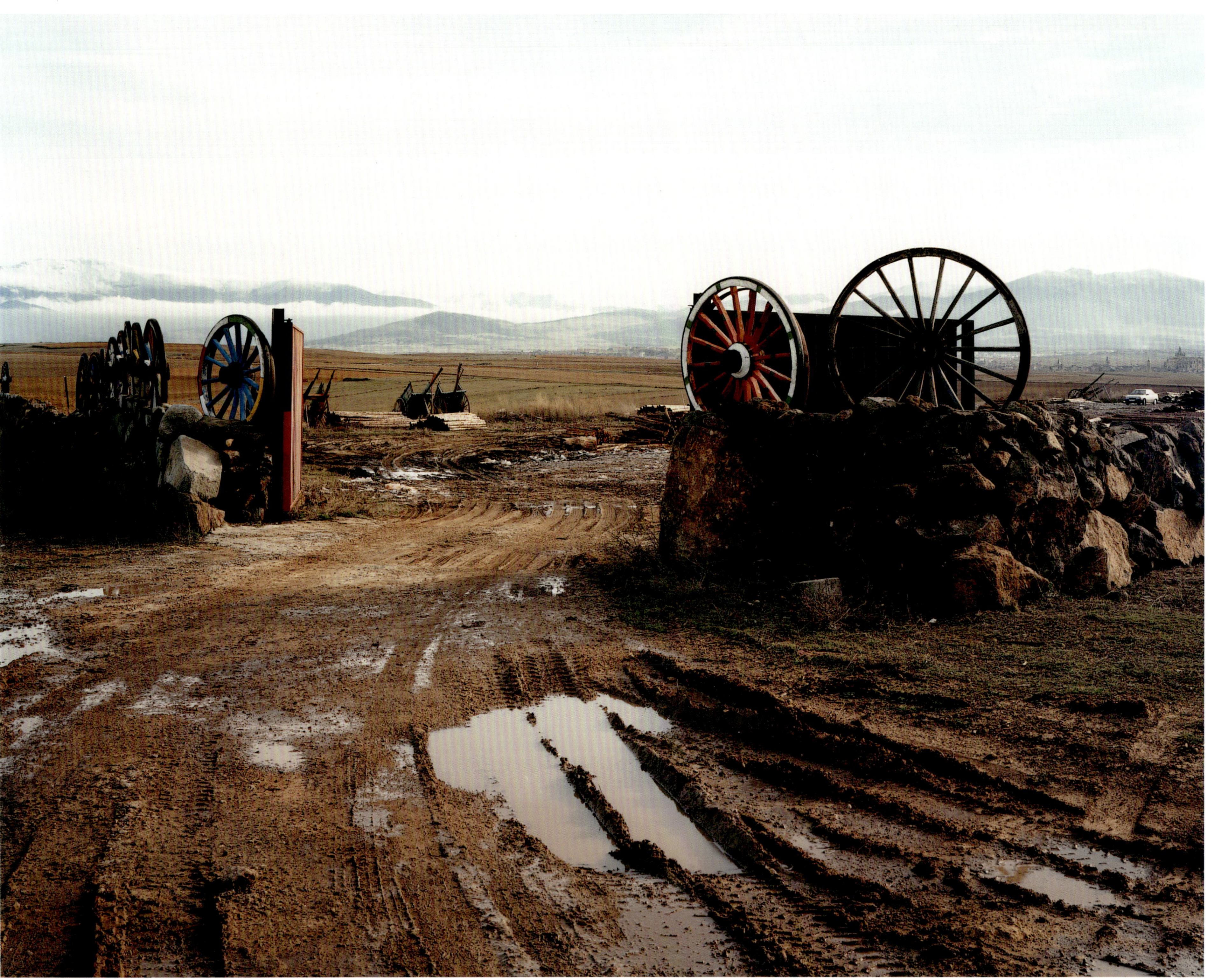

The formative scheme behind Jim Cooke's new work was to consider Europe at a time of rapid transformation, as the fabric of an old industrial culture makes way for a new, post industrial and technological landscape. This is the story of an old rustic arcadia reshaped by industrialisation whose monumental structures then themselves fall into ruin, to be replaced by the endless modular systems and soaring towers that technology makes possible. This sense of unfolding epic sagas, each with its own claim on the sublime, is the underlying theme of Cooke's work.
– David Chandler, from his essay *'Being There'*

Segovia, Spain, 1999

Jim Cooke

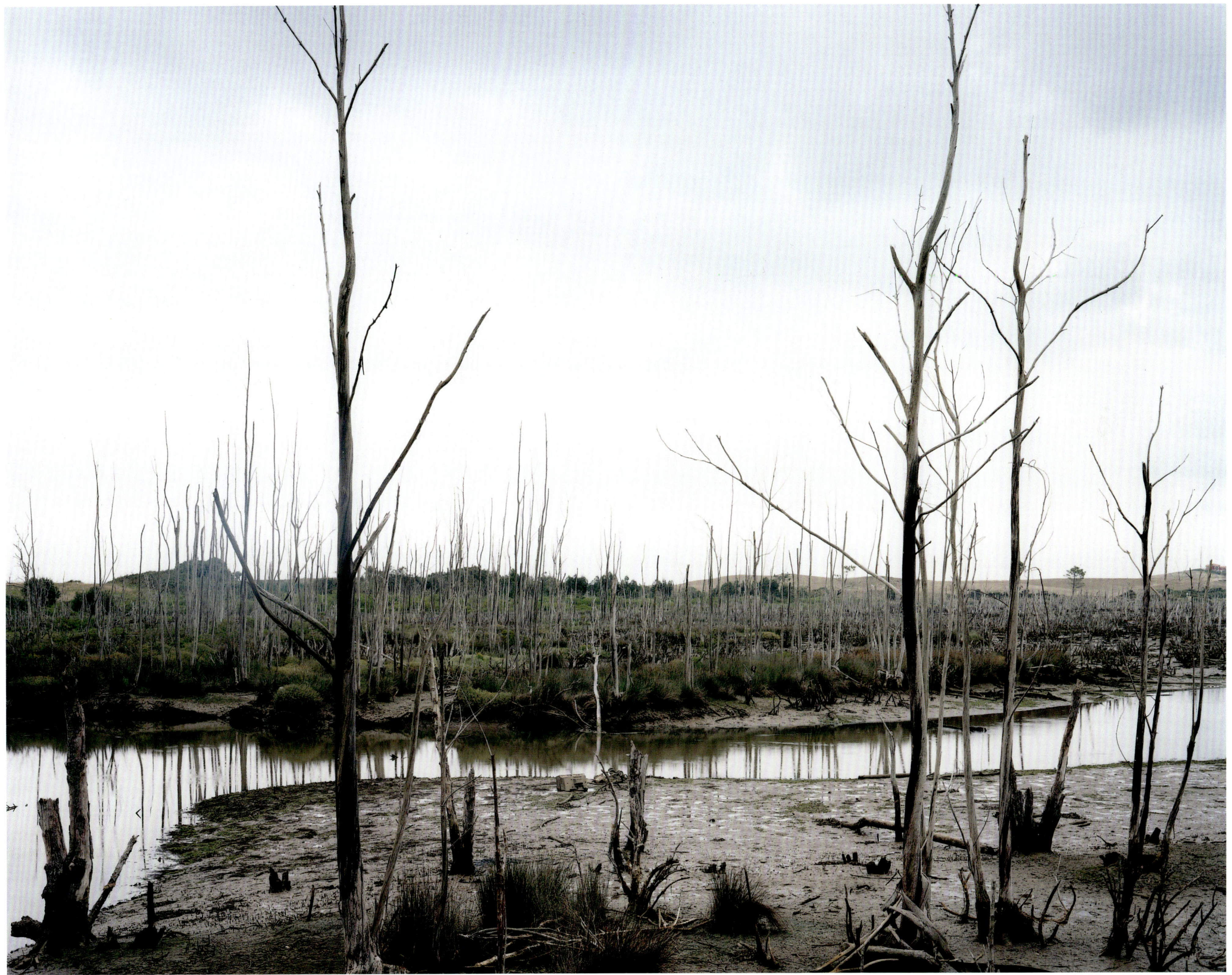

Northern Spain, 2001

Jim Cooke

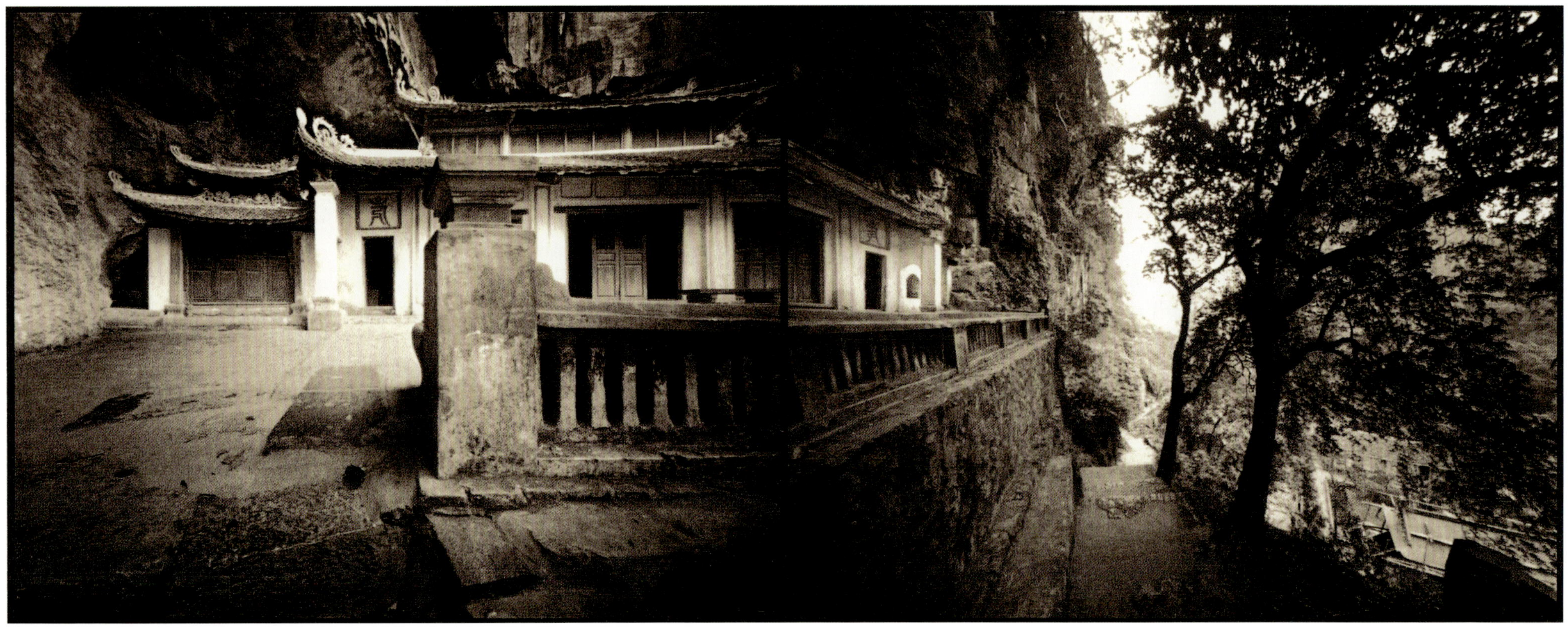

Ghosts in the Landscape: Viet Nam Revisited

I began returning to Viet Nam early in 1995. My intent: photographing, writing and learning about the land I first saw as a combat Marine many years before. Full of youthful ignorance upon my initial arrival in Viet Nam, saddened and still ignorant upon my departure, I returned home with more questions than answers and more anger than I care to admit. This time, older, gentler and more mature, I hope for a better understanding. Carrying vivid memories - some good, some not so, all intense, all needing clarification - I navigated each day through the landscape of my emotions. Following, I share a journal entry:

The lack of discernable change is jarring at times. Memory runs deep in my veins as I wind my way along narrow dirt paths and bamboo groves, past straw houses and barking dogs. More than once, as I wander the small hamlets, I have felt on patrol, the weight of my pack reminiscent of those days and the tripod feeling like a weapon. but now I'm searching for images instead of "Charlie." These moments are disconcerting but I do not brush them aside. I am trying not to brush anything aside, I want to embrace all that comes along.

Yes, there is a major contradiction between journal entries such as this and my images, but one has to remember, that while I was in Viet Nam during the 1960's the events of the moment were happening in the lush landscapes you see before you. We patrolled rice paddies and quaint villages, all seemingly quiet and pristine only to turn the corner and step into hell, turn another corner and return back to quiet and pristine. The dichotomy was constant. As I worked in Viet Nam during my return trips, this was the flow of my mind ... quiet landscapes accompanied by a torrent of memories that never fade.

Craig J. Barber

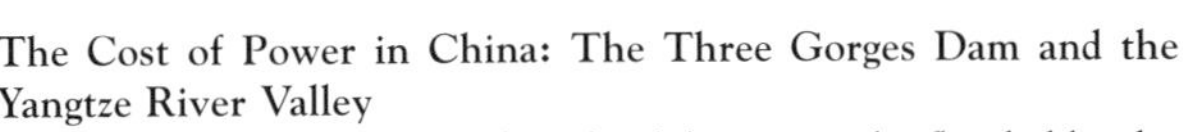

The Cost of Power in China: The Three Gorges Dam and the Yangtze River Valley

My purpose in traveling the length of the area to be flooded by the Three Gorges Dam, from Chongqing downstream to its construction site, was to create a lasting photographic document of a part of the planet destined to disappear; and to honor the people of this mythic valley that has inspired poets, artists and philosophers for countless centuries. It is also my hope that this body of work will function as a warning to future generations.

The desire to build a dam across the Yangtze River, 610 feet high and 1.3 miles long, creating a reservoir 50 miles longer than Lake Michigan in a densely populated area is an example of how flaws in our perceptual system can cause immeasurable harm. This immense dam, the largest concrete object on the planet, will ultimately force more than 2 million people to vacate their ancestral homes and disrupt the lives of the 30 million people living in the reservoir region. In addition to this social cost, the reservoir will cover 8,000 known archaeological sites, 250,000 acres of China's most fertile farmland and 1,600 factories, which have been burying toxic materials in the ground for the past 50 years. Scientists fear that lead, mercury, arsenic and dozens of other substances, including radioactive waste, will leach out into the reservoir destroying aquatic life. It is disturbing to consider how quickly human activity can transform fresh water, a source of life, into poison.

75 million people depend on the river for fishing and farming.

On June 10th, 2003 at 10:00 pm the reservoir filled reaching a depth of 425 feet in spite of the fact, that in 1999, 100 cracks were discovered running the full height of the upstream face of the dam. The cracks had been repaired only to reopen. Chinese engineers say this is common in large dams, but others suggest it is the result of improper curing of the concrete. In 2009 the reservoir is planned to reach 575 feet completing the flooding of 13 cities, 140 towns and 1,352 villages.

What was intended to be a grand proclamation of China's emergence into the modern world is rapidly becoming a monumental problem due to poor planning, inaccurate or falsified estimates and statistics, construction problems, high sedimentation rates, severe residential and industrial pollution, rampant official corruption and growing civil unrest.

"The Mountain Goddess, if she is still there,
will marvel at a world so changed".
– Mao Zedong, from his poem, *"The Lake Among the Gorges"*

Critical Mass

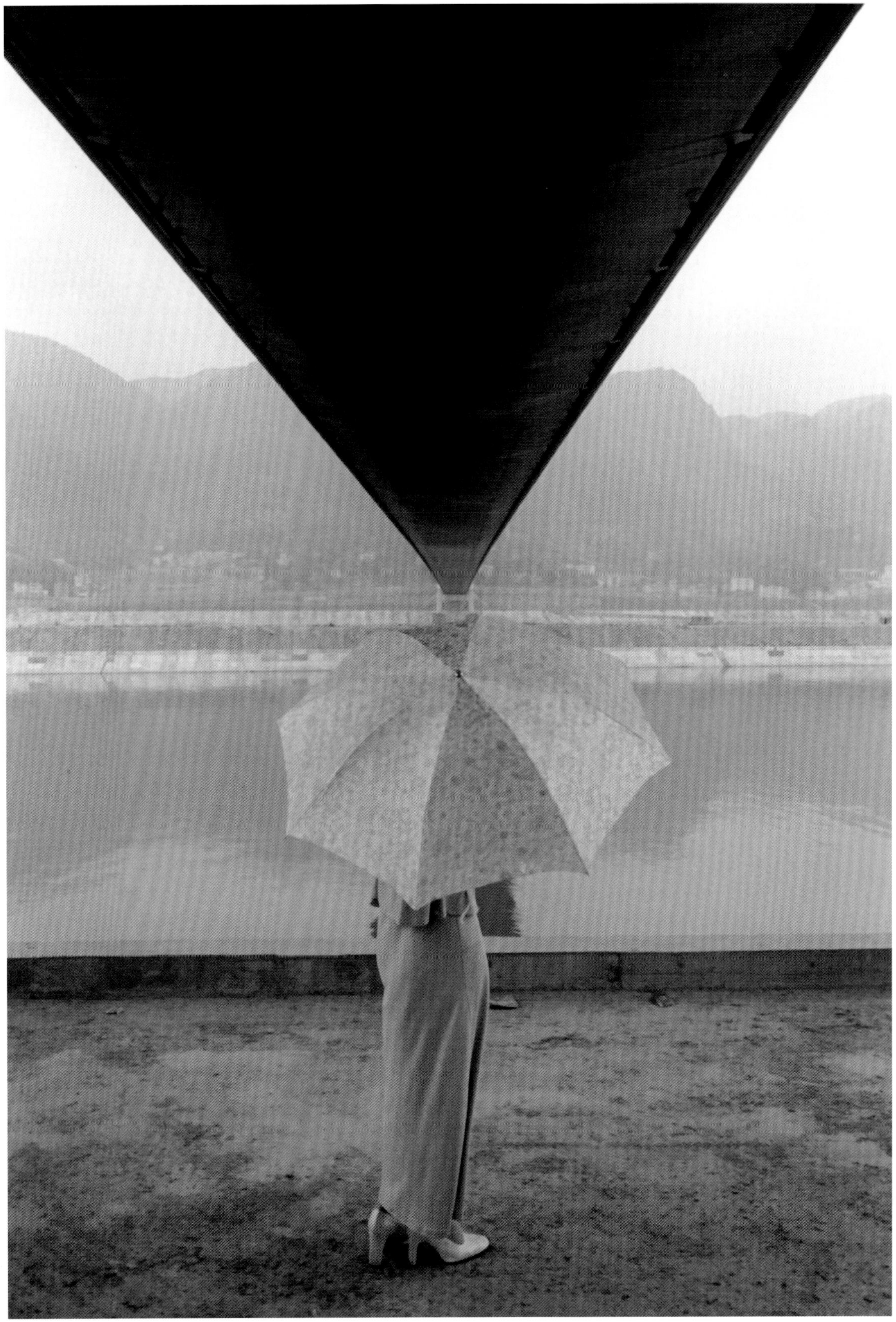

Steven Benson

Roses

"Roses" is a major body of work that this closely-knit husband-and-wife artist team has been building up since 1998. Their efforts have yielded several series of photograms - images cast by the sunlight alone as it touches the light-sensitive paper surrounding the carefully chosen objets trouvés placed upon it by the artists. Here, photography is reduced to its simplest but most immediate expression. Omitting the camera, the Cartiers achieve a quasi "material" likeness of reality, at the very time when the images and world seeking to apprehend it are dematerializing before our very eyes, evanescing into the virtuality of pixels and bytes - be they mega, giga, or otherwise.

In their photograms - each of which, by the way, is a one-off image - Françoise and Daniel Cartier combine an archaic photographic technique with objects that are part and parcel of contemporary life and modern consumer society: lingerie, doll clothes, handkerchiefs and bathing caps on the one hand and, on the other, skeletal doll outlines, X-rays, strands of hair and self-portraits. The objects are almost all bathed in a rose-pink color of varying degrees of transparency, each boasting an aura of its own. While present in the traces, indeed almost tangible marks, they leave on the paper, they are at the same time absent, slowly fading away in the manner of an afterimage behind closed eyelids.

– Martin Gasser

Curator / Swiss Foundation for Photography

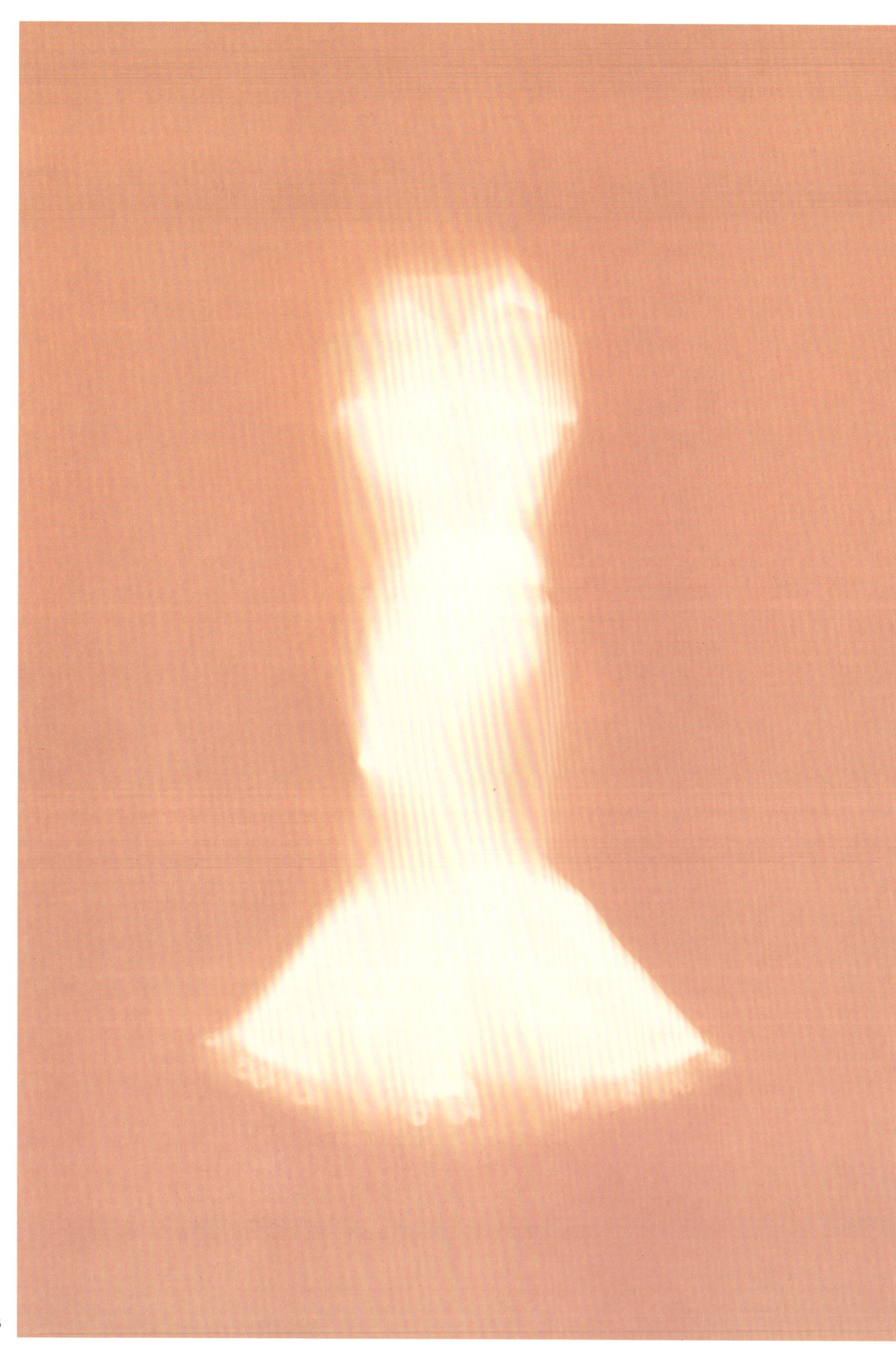

f & d cartier

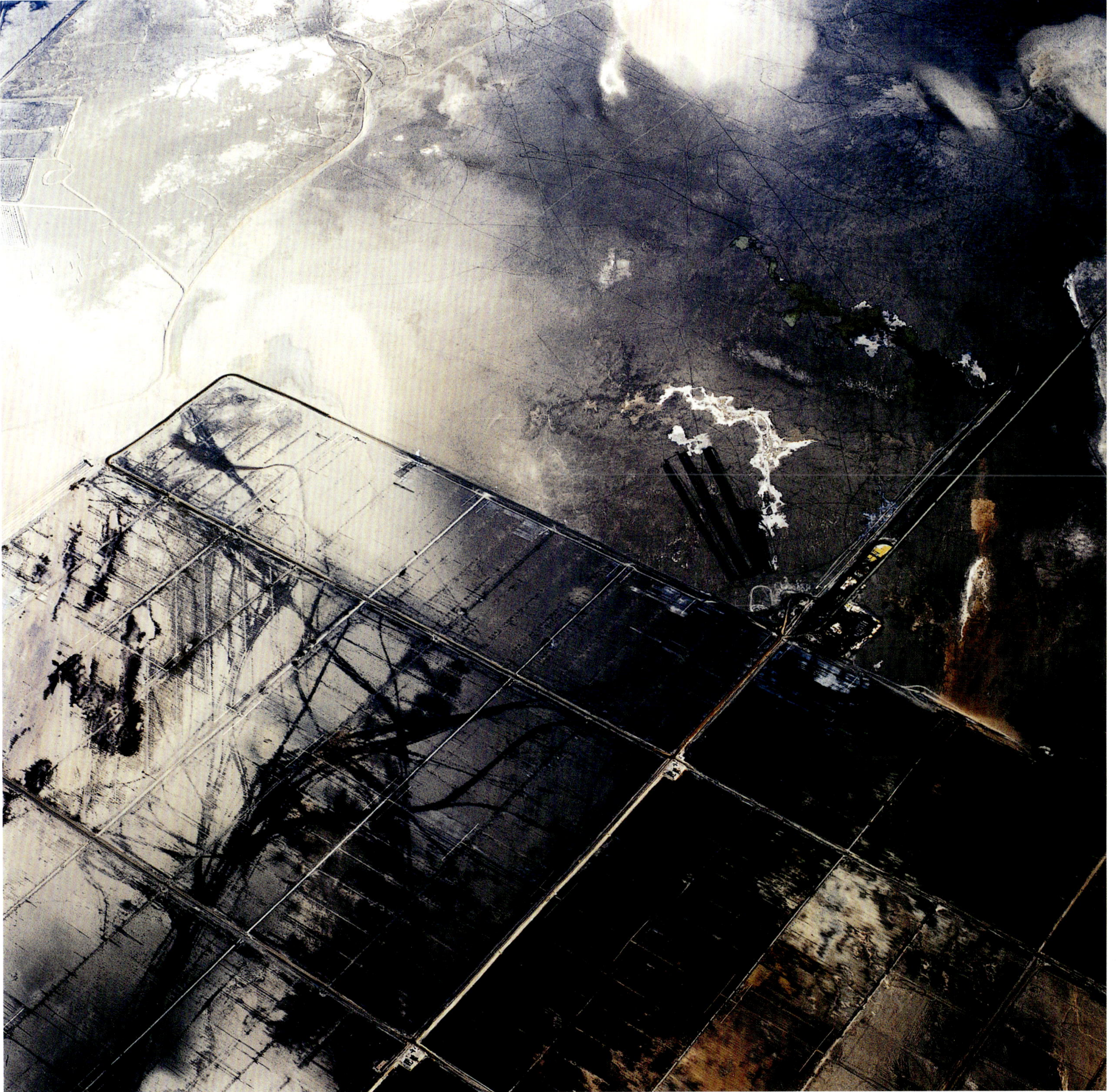

Critical Mass David Maisel

The Black Maps Project

Black Maps comprises aerial photographs of environmentally impacted landscapes. These images have as their subject matter the undoing of the natural world by the wide-scale intervention of human action. The depiction of these damaged wastelands, where human efforts have eradicated the natural order, is both spectacular and horrifying. Although these photographs evidence the devastation of these sites, they also transcribe interior, psychic landscapes, spaces, and structures that are profoundly disturbing-for, as otherworldly as the images may seem, they depict a shattered reality of our own making.

The Black Maps project has unfolded in chapters, focusing on such subjects as strip-mines, clear-cuts, leaching fields, tailings ponds, firestorms, the drainage remnants of Owens Lake, and other manipulations of the natural world. The photographs in this series are presented as either 29"-x-29" or 48"-x-48" color C-prints. The prints extend to encompass the viewer's peripheral vision, and in the process their lushness and strange beauty become psychologically demanding as well as visually exhilarating. The forms of environmental disquiet and degradation are here made to function on both a documentary and a metaphorical level, and the aerial perspective enables one to experience the landscape like a vast map of its own undoing.

These images are meant neither to vilify nor to glorify their content, but rather to expand our notions of what constitutes landscape and landscape art. I am not attempting to make literal records of environmental destruction. Rather I seek to reveal the landscape in something other than purely visual terms, the photograph transcribing it as an archetypal space of destruction and ruin that mirrors the darker corners of our consciousness.

Two sisters watch the exhumation of their mother and four small siblings. The sisters were present that day in August of 1982 when soldiers shot their relatives, but they managed to escape. They spent fourteen years in hiding in the mountains with the CPR of the Sierra, before resettling in a new community and later requesting the exhumation. Near the village of San Francisco Javier, Nebaj, Guatemala, 2000.

This image is from a series of some 150 photographs spanning over ten years which was published by powerHouse Books in September 2004 as Our Culture is Our Resistance: Repression, Refuge and Healing in Guatemala. Turner Libros in Madrid & Mexico City simultaneously published a Spanish language edition.

The images were made in the context of my decade of work as a human rights advocate and occasional freelance photographer in Guatemala. As a whole, this body of work, and the resulting book, are intended to shed light on the struggle and survival of the Maya indigenous peoples of Guatemala who were uprooted and terrorized during their country's protracted civil war. These photographs were taken over the course of the six months in 2000 and 2001 that I worked as staff photographer for the forensic anthropology team of the Office of Peace and Reconciliation in Quiché, Guatemala.

Within the context of a country on the path to peace many survivors of the violence want to search for and reclaim the remains of their loved ones who were massacred or disappeared. The exhumations allow the survivors to begin healing, giving them the opportunity to mourn, as well as the right to expose the truth of what happened, and in some cases to seek justice.

These images speak of the recent tragic history of Guatemala: the repression and genocide carried out by state security forces in the 1980's and the work for justice, truth, and reconciliation being pursued today within a continued climate of fear and impunity.

These are stories of life and death, of hope and despair, and of struggles for survival, respect, and truth. Twelve years ago, in the profoundly beautiful mountains and jungles of Guatemala, I joined my passions for photography and social justice.

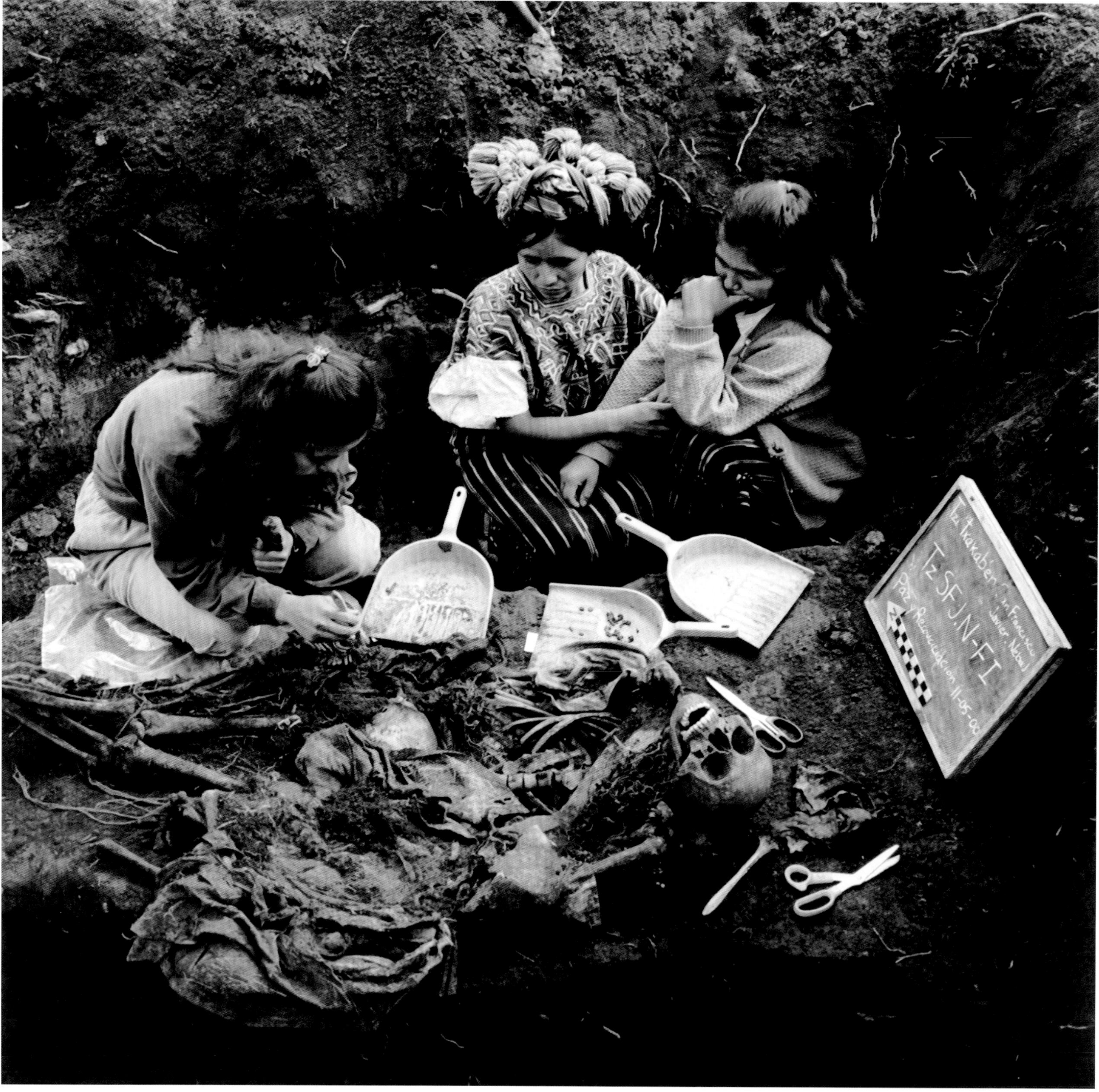

Jonathan Moller

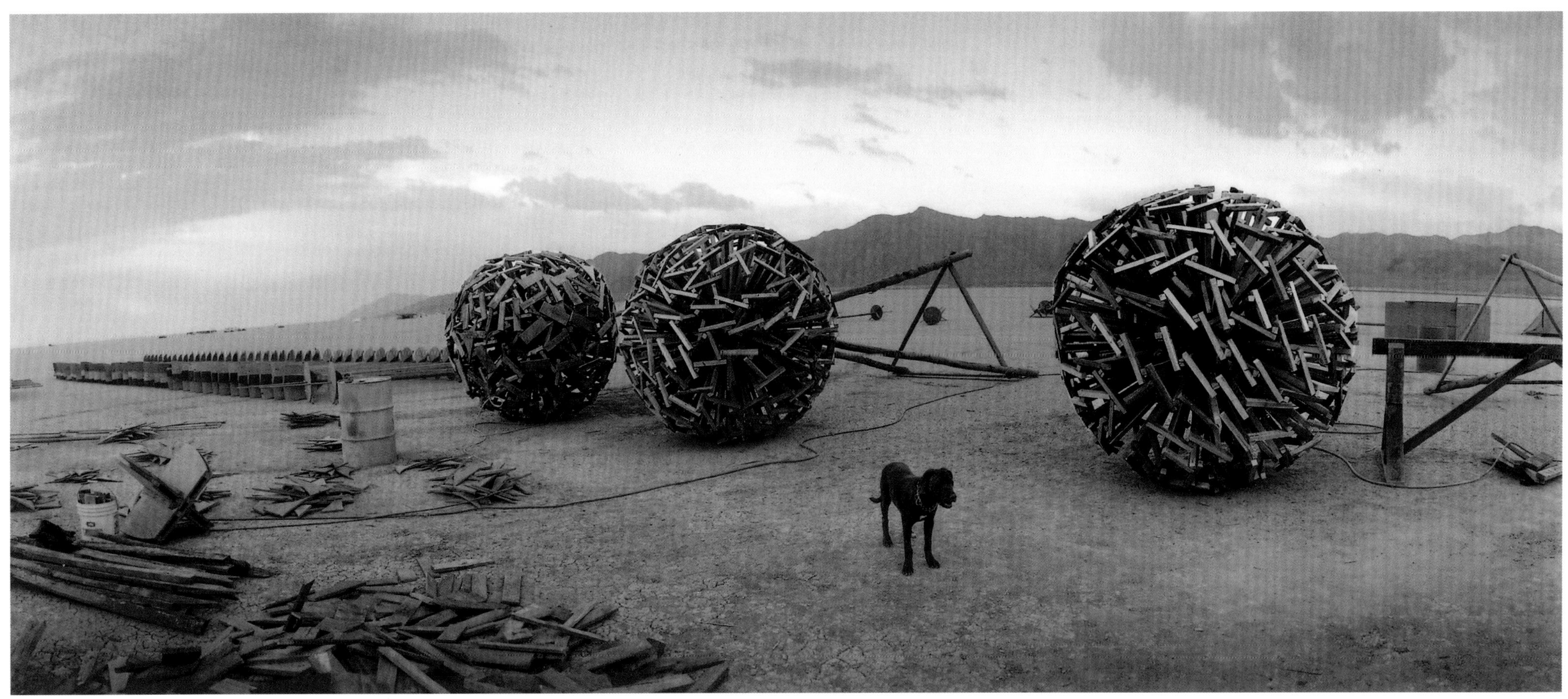

The search for authenticity has led a group of artists out into the Nevada desert. There in the harsh white (and blank) expanse of a dry lake-bed, they are able to make machines that define a new movement in art. Some are robotic, most are built from salvaged industrial cast-offs, and almost all somehow use fire, or should I say FIRE, as their primary means of expression.

I came upon this loose knit group while doing a project on alternative communities. I was so moved that it became apparent that the project I had started no longer interested me. I buried eight years of negatives in the confines of my file cabinet(s) and haven't looked back since.

There is an honesty and defiance that exists in the work that compels me the way that love strikes. Often leaving us involuntarily disoriented. The world that each of us lives in often doesn't make sense. The din and static of mainstream society invades every corner of our lives and many of us are just sick of it. Enough celebrity culture. Enough of every-one airing their dirtiest laundry in exchange for a buck or time in the spotlight. There's something noble and moving in watching someone express a vision as a state of being, in a remote place. Where the audience is often limited to a few friends who have been willing to make the trek a hundred plus miles out into the desert.

So here it is. The media has found Burning Man, but largely missed the soul of the event. Seduced by the nudity and spectacle, but lost to the profound subtlety of the experience. My only wish is that through this expanding body of work, you see what I see.

Critical Mass

A. Leo Nash

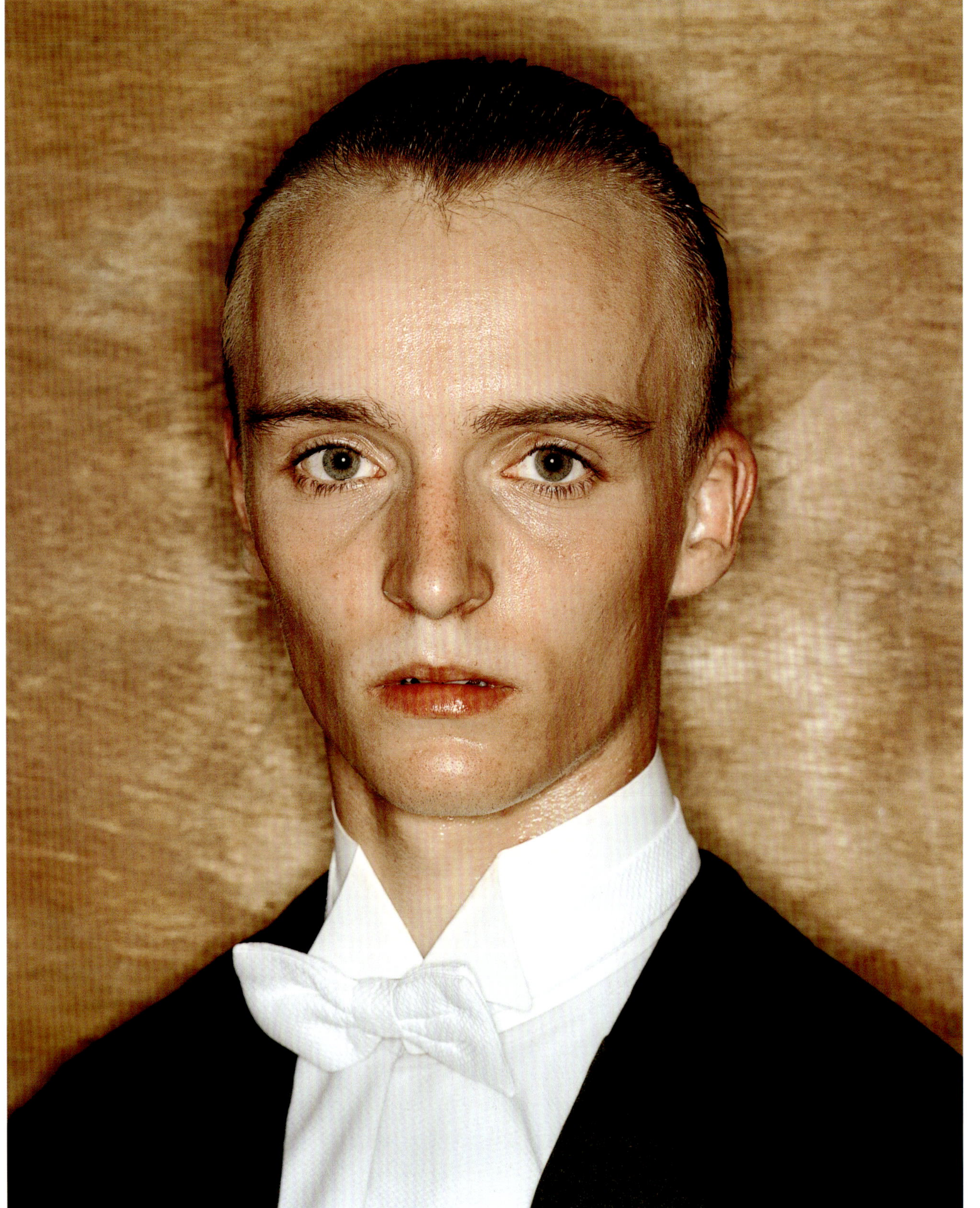

Critical Mass Morten Nilsson

Dancers

The photographs in the Dancers series fascinate and intrigue from the outset. Are these real live people, are they shop-window dummies, or wax models from Madame Tussauds?

On taking a closer look, going beyond the fixed bright stares, the beads of sweat beneath the make-up betraying movement, signs of stage nerves, you realise that these competition dancers have chosen to cocoon themselves for the occasion in the smoothest, most perfect image so that jury and audience may devote all their attention to body line, the simple colours of the clothes, and the measured and regulated steps placed amongst twirling dresses, somewhere between sensuality and gymnastics, by these icons of eternal youth.

They are in performance, photographed in situ as witnessed by certain clues, a half-opened curtain, the scratches on a wall or the ribs on a wooden panel, contrasting with the smooth artificial appearance of the faces striving for perfection.

Morten Nilsson has succeeded in going beyond appearances and has captured the fallible yet touching side of humanity, like Diane Arbus previously: a clumsy movement, an evasive worried look, a rather direct flash shot, a misbehaving hairdo or make-up in need of repair.

Morten Nilsson plunges us into the bang-up-to-date world of performance and identity. Dancers becomes a sort of metaphor of the Western world, of consumerism and appearances, of conformity and private emotions.

– Xavier Canonne and Marc Vausort
Musée de la Photographie
Centre d'art contemporain de la Communauté française Wallonie-Bruxelles

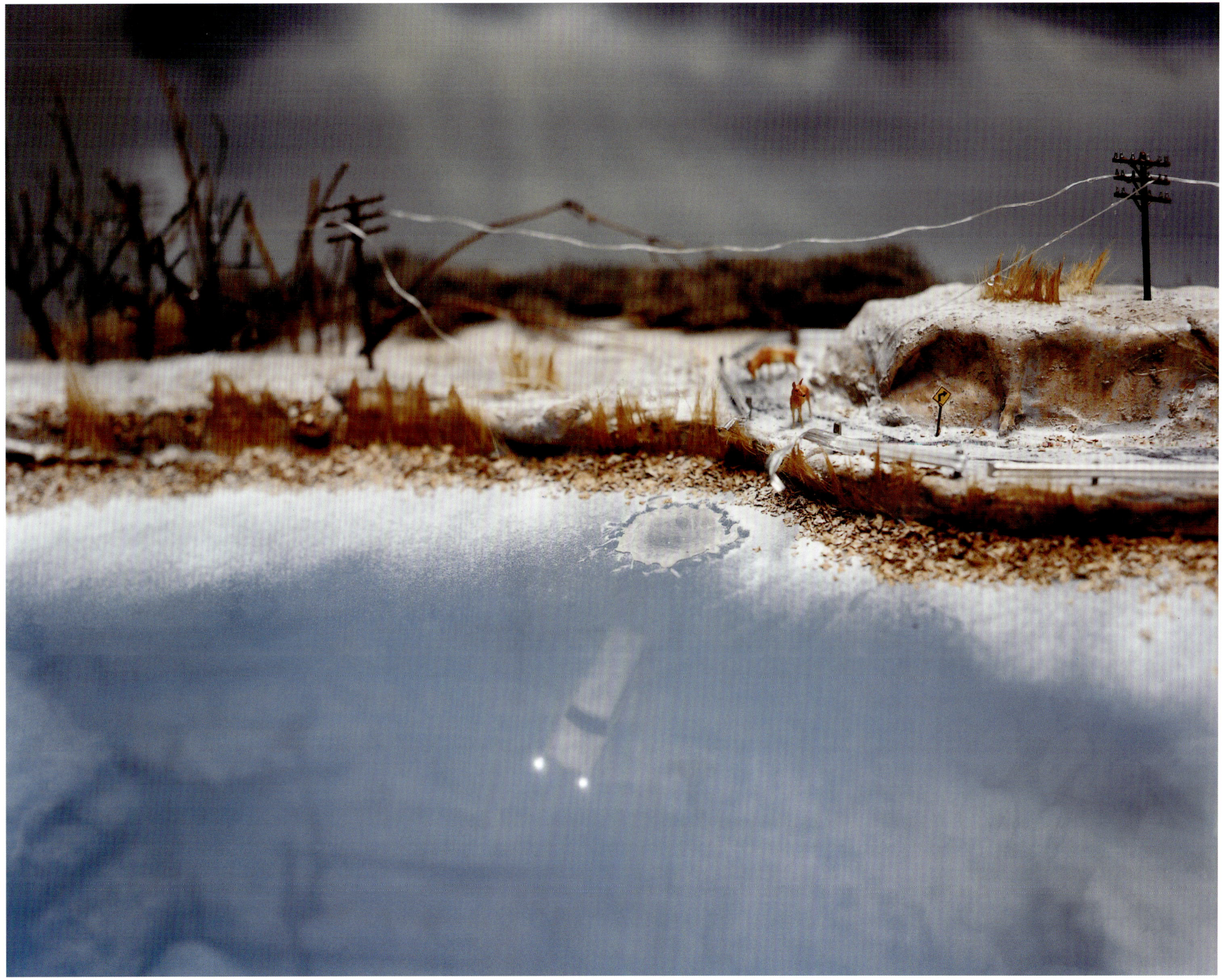

My photographs show scenes oddly familiar, yet not quite believable. Inspired by personal experiences as well as my impressions of the world around me, I construct highly detailed dioramas in which the balance of nature tips to the absurd. By focusing on the moment just before or after the story's climax, at the point of uncertainty when time seems to slow down, I invite the viewer to use their own experiences to complete the narrative.

Critical Mass

Lori Nix

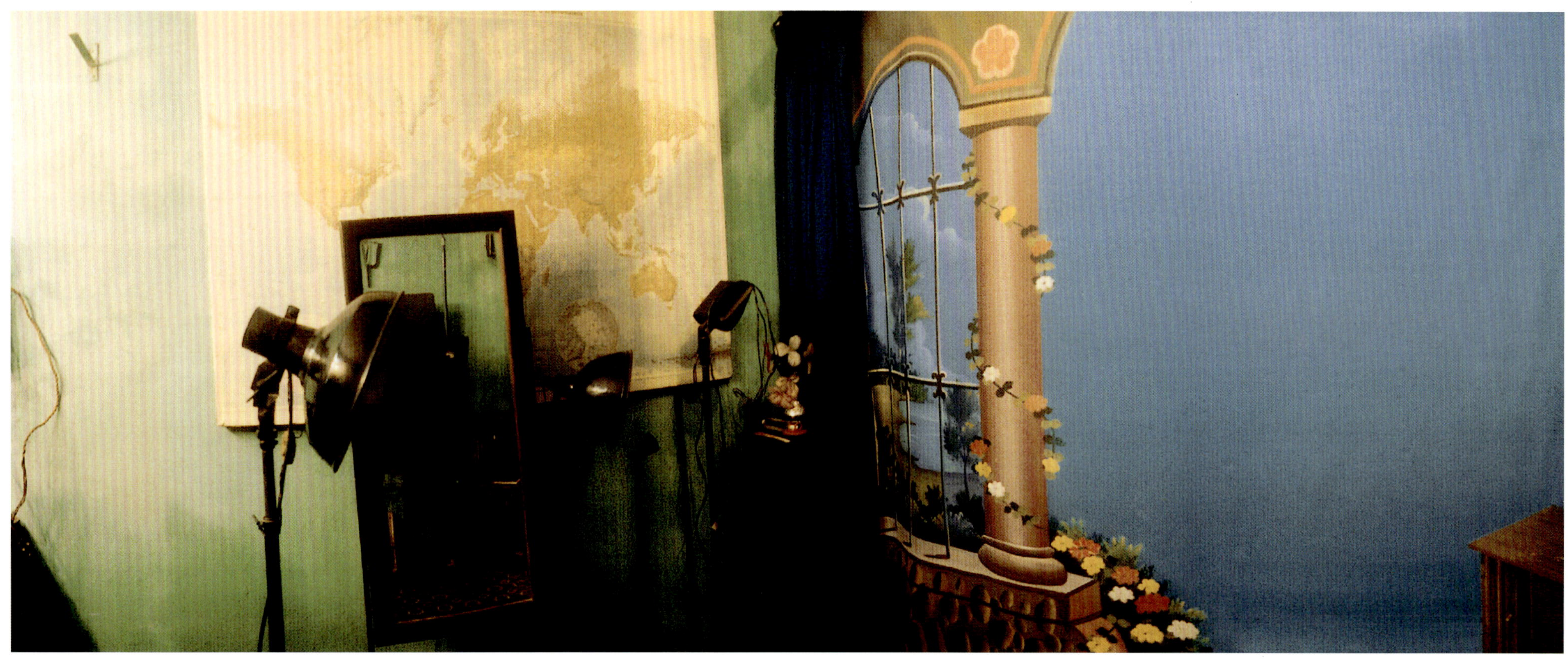

In Camera

....these images spring from a representational strategy that is concerned not with categorization and the closure of identity but with the manipulation of a repertoire of signs signifying possible states of being. Just as in architecture king-building involves the accumulation of different national styles and rooms associated with different places and epochs, so these photographic images suggest a person-building in which different performances are acquired. In both domains, the person or thing represented is merely a starting point for a much wider confabulation. In this respect architecture and photography operate as parallel technologies of augmentation, both working to leave substantive traces of what otherwise would be mere dreams.

– Christopher Pinney – *Camera Indica: The Social Life of Indian Photographs*

The images in the In Camera series are of photographic studios in Sri Lanka, Pakistan, India, and Vietnam. Old photo studios provide environments where the past, the present, the traditional and the contemporary collide and where painted backgrounds and props give clues into notions of class, taste and aspiration.

The series builds on premises of traditional documentary photography but mixed with painterly and cinematic (implied narrative) additions. The panorama camera is perfect for this work in the way it compacts the world, widens it like Cinemascope yet flattens it to be read like a page of literature.

The backdrops, dealing with representations of the natural and man-made world, are, in their fashion, idealized versions of both. The pastoral, always a subject of painting, is here utilized to both ground the sitter (posing, of course, indoors) in the great, though tamed, outdoors and to enhance his stature in the world at large. The indoor scenes harken back to painting too and strive to bolster, if not promote, the sitter's social status. These juxtapositions – along with that of the mundane clutter surrounding the magical painted backdrops – are full of longing, hope, ambition and irony. The lushness of the Cibachrome prints emphasizes – and attempts to duplicate – the vibrancy and liveliness that the studio owners infuse into their own work.

Abby Robinson

For more than 7 years now I have been using a flatbed scanner instead of a traditional camera to record and interpret the objects I collect. I frequent flea markets, searching for old tintypes and toys that seem to have a story to tell. Then in my studio I make small pastel drawings as backgrounds and scan each element into my computer separately. Using Photoshop I am able to arrange and play with these layers in much the same way that I worked with objects in my studio for a still life photograph. I work very spontaneously and intuitively, trying to come up with images that have a resonance and a somewhat mysterious narrative content. There is no one meaning for any of the images, rather they exist as a kind of visual riddle or open-ended poem, meant to be both playful and provocative.

The predecessors to these images were my color photographs, made in my back yard over a period of ten years from 1986 until 1996. I used natural light and found objects to create and photograph enigmatic, loosely narrative scenes, often involving old toys and other representations of the human figure. Although I became aware of the possibility of using a computer to manipulate photographic imagery in 1992, it was not until 1996 that I felt the output available was of sufficient quality to attract me to this technique. After some initial experimentation, I found a way to scan and collage which enabled me to create something visually unique—not a photograph and not a painting, but an original digital image.

My final prints are made on an inkjet printer on a paper that gives the texture and look of a print or watercolor. Although they are not traditional photographs, I definitely think of my scanner as a light-sensitive recording device. And there is a camera involved in making many of the images (those containing tintypes)...it just happens that the camera was used over 100 years ago by a photographer who remains anonymous.

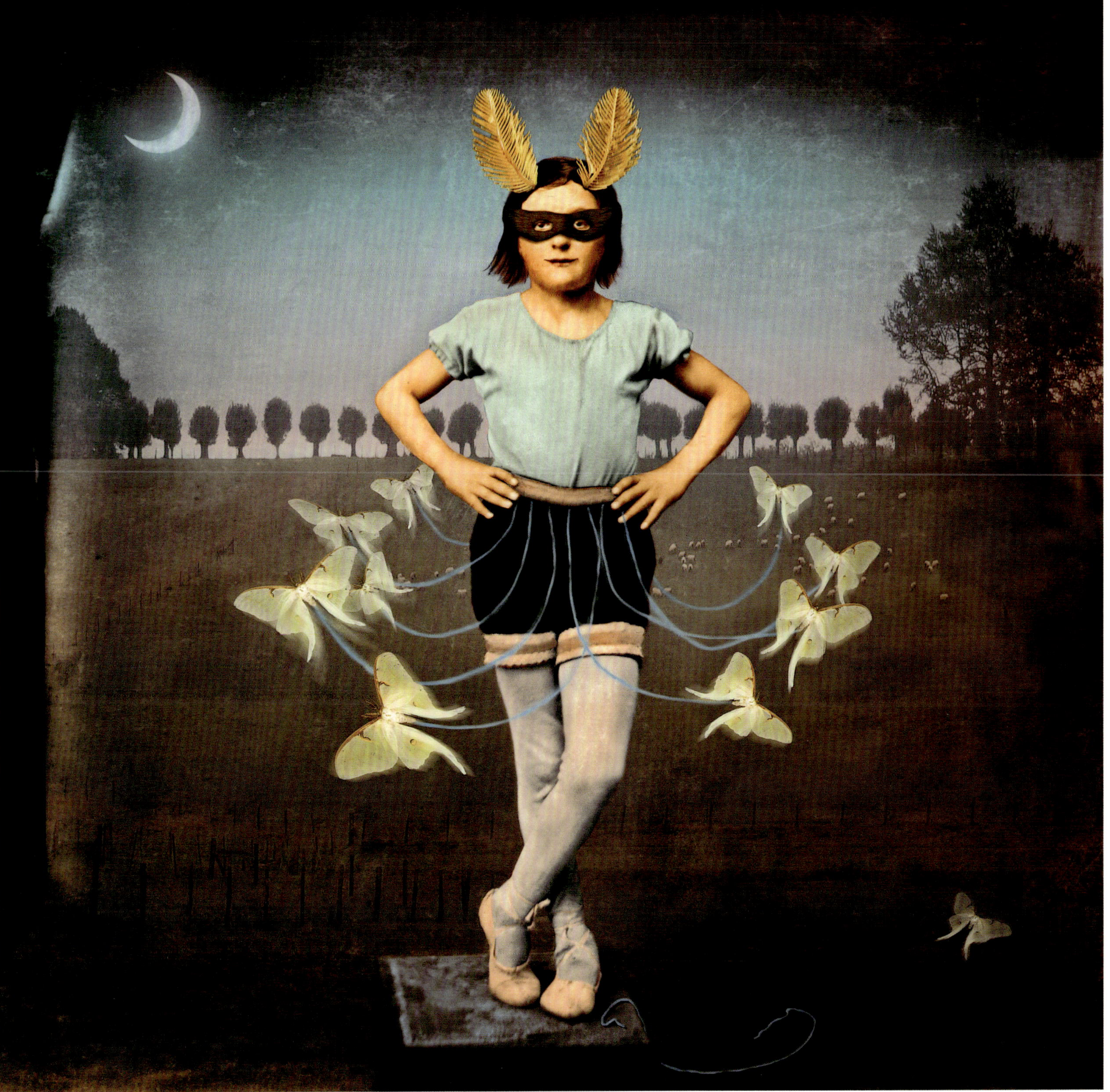

Critical Mass Maggie Taylor

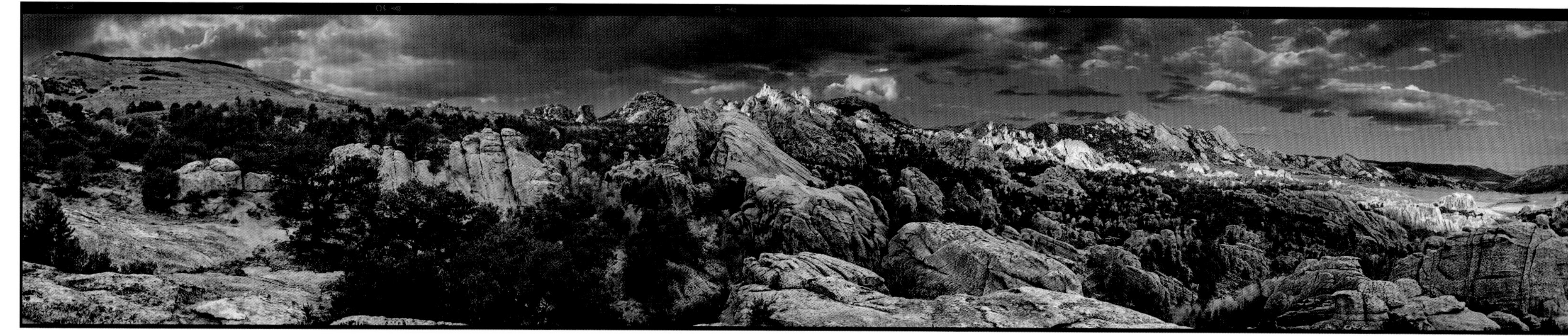

City of Rocks

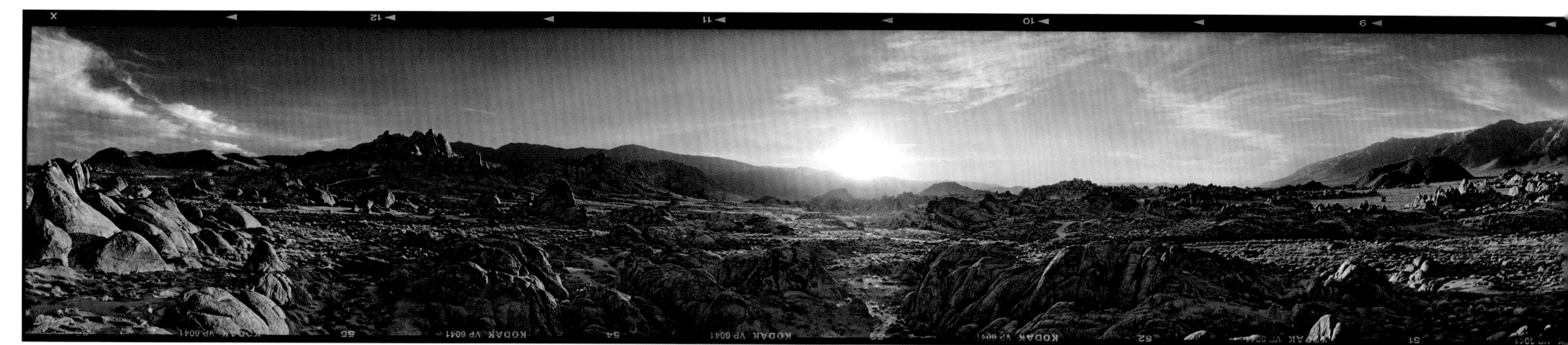

Alabama Hills

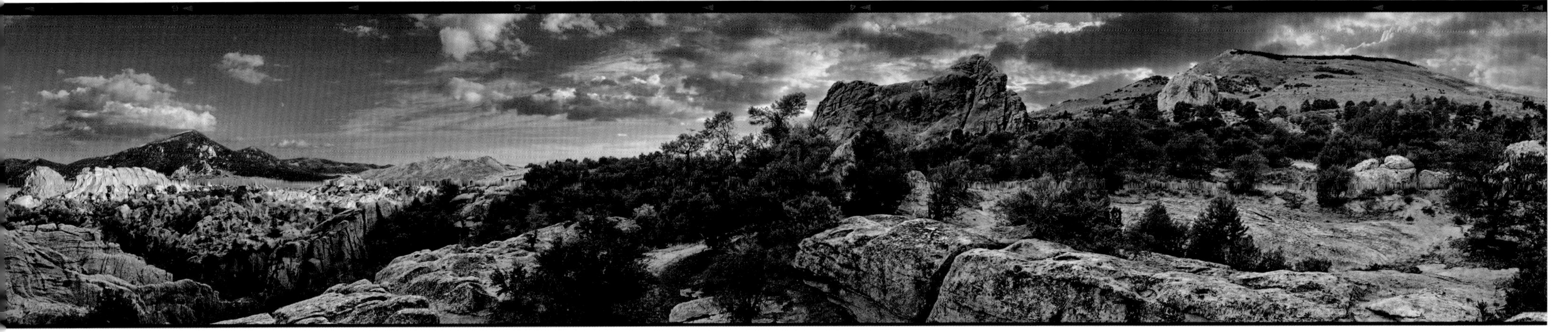

Gregory Gorfkle

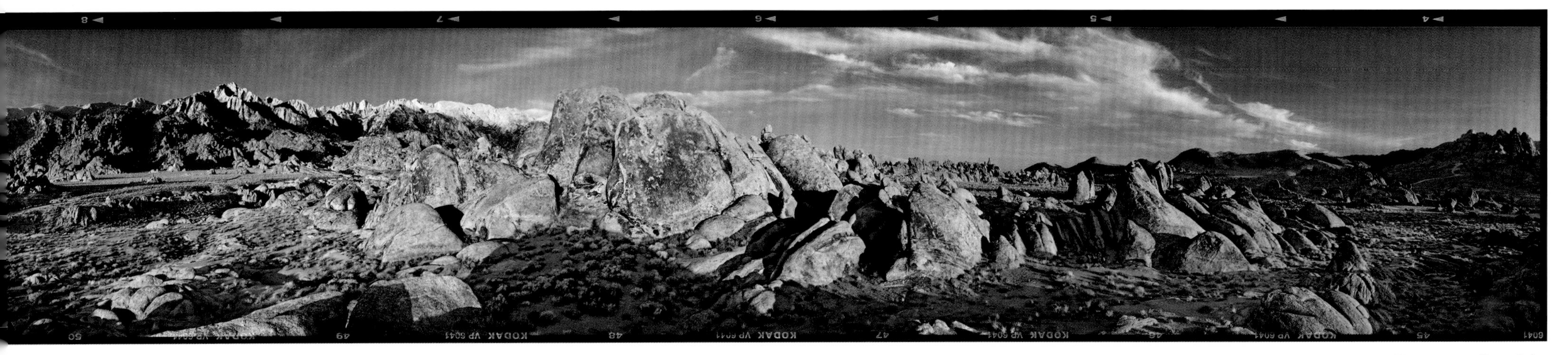

Gregory Gorfkle

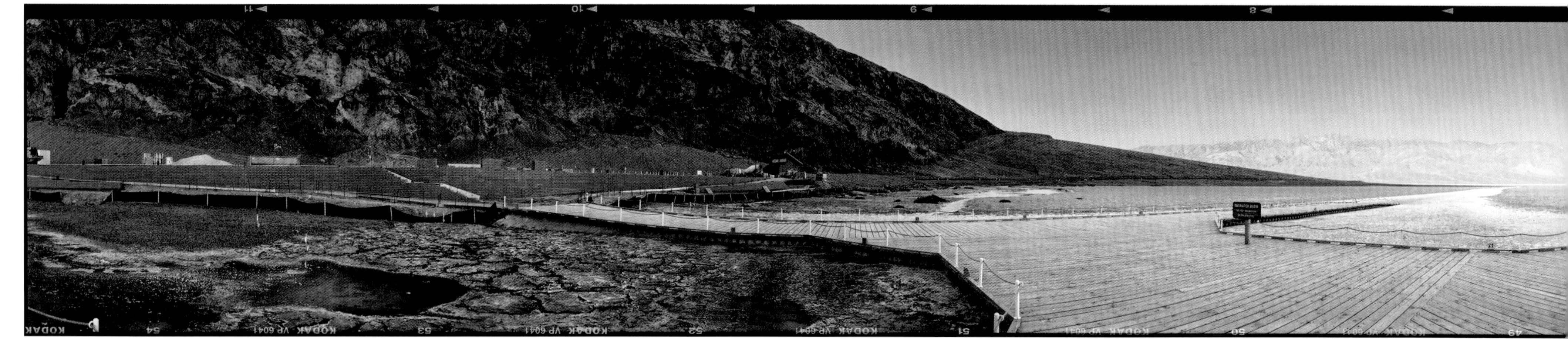

Badwater Basin, Death Valley

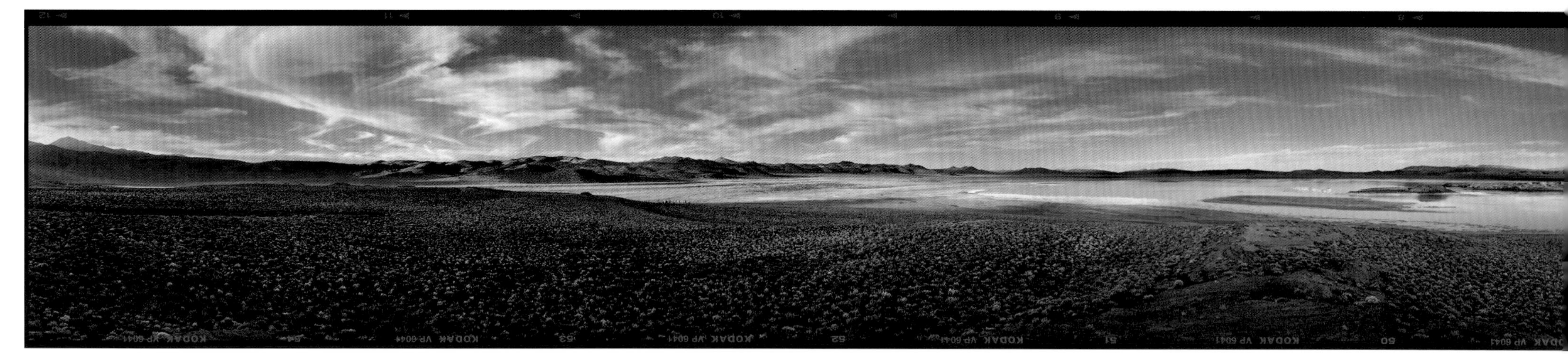

Mono Lake Basin

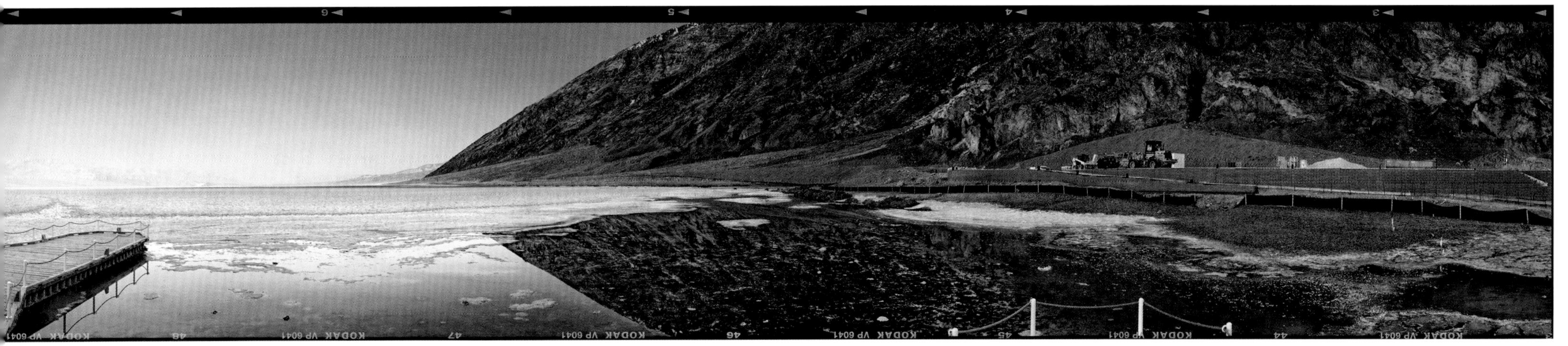

Gregory Gorfkle

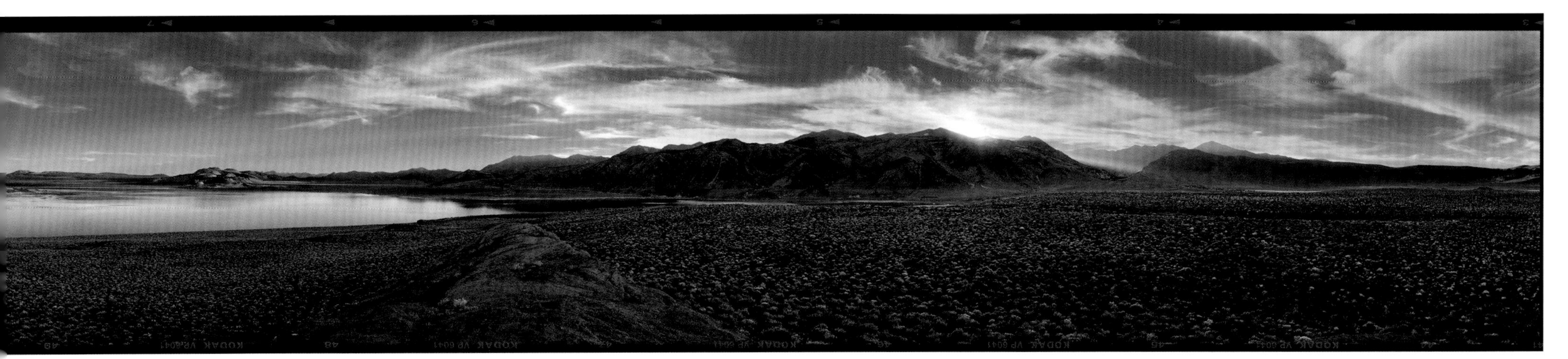

Gregory Gorfkle

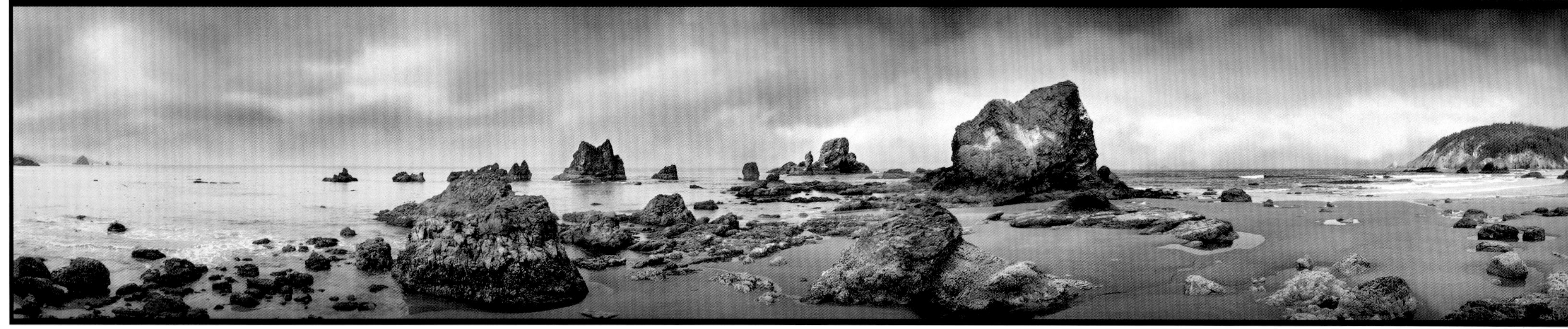

Ecola Point

My fascination with the 360-degree photograph is its unique circumstance to display all the information surrounding a single position and one's capacity to hold this point of view in a single glance. Each scene takes on new meaning in this way. Each landscape held in context to its surroundings reveals an integrity and veracity that doesn't exist with standard modes of photography. The photographs are contemporaneous views of the American West from a perspective rarely noticed.

I use an unusual camera system with conventional lenses and film. Using eyesight alone, without a mechanical viewing system the scene is positioned onto the film plane. In a single exposure the camera rotates around a circle while film passes behind an opened shutter to record the scene. The print presents a complete view, prompting one to imagine that world in a single glance, as it otherwise would wrap around them.

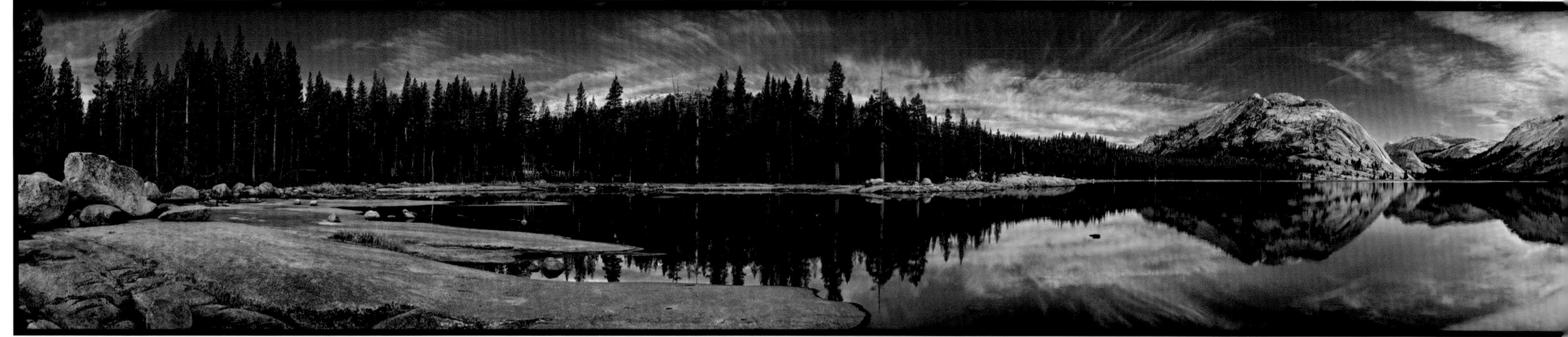

LakeTenaya

The prerequisite I've imposed on this work is to include the entire 360 degrees, even the "uninteresting parts," in the photographs. The totality of the landscape is essential to each composition. I'm intrigued by the spatial quality of 360-degree photography and even more by the field work itself. There are no insignificant parts of a scene.

I exist in a world that surrounds me, yet I'm predisposed to limitations that cognitively suggest otherwise. I've been trained from the earliest age to notice what is directly in front of me, to accentuate the meritorious and make extraneous the rest, to mentally construe a world bound by left and right like a viewing screen and from day to day I consider the world from this vantage point. So I'm compelled to consider an image less than 360-degrees as if it were the entire world and the 360-degree image that wraps entirely around a point a view as if it were bounded by a perspective of left and right and confined by that dimension.

When I come to photograph a place my inclination is to regard the greater part a scene as insignificant and

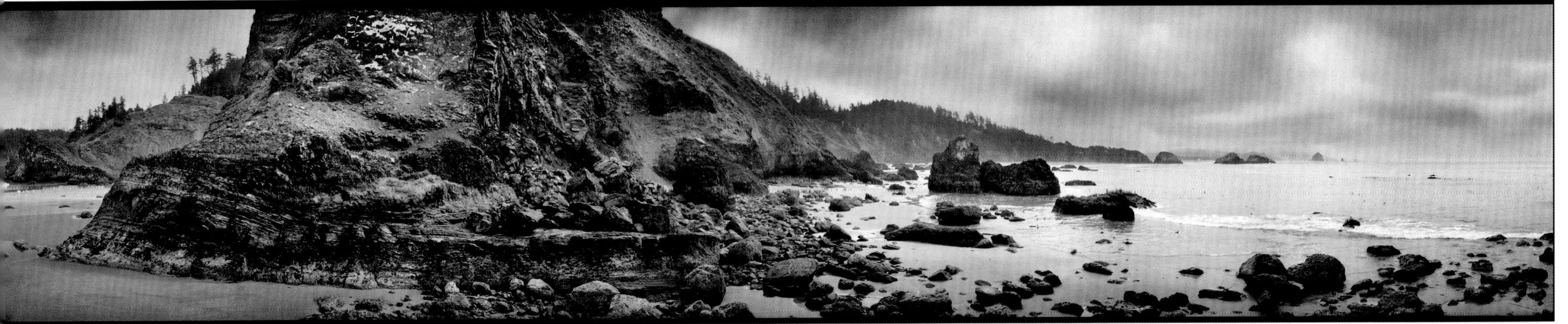

Gregory Gorfkle

accentuate only a few of its aspects. My basic visual training and physical structure draw me away from considering the 360-degree view, to focus on less expansive and arguably more interesting features. However, through this approach my perception serves more perhaps to obscure a scene's significance than present it. And caught up with detail, I hold in my mind something quite different than what plainly lies before me. Between what exists and what I'm practiced to perceive lies a gap where the reality of each scene may well be left behind.

Sensing some futility in this approach I've learned to resist my inclinations. I became disposed to natural patterns the environment creates and resides in and conscious of my relationships therein. At first I found it difficult to hold and consider a scene in its entirety, as it extends beyond my peripheral vision. Initially I came to understand the elements involved in conceptualizing space around me as linear and fragmented. I learned to

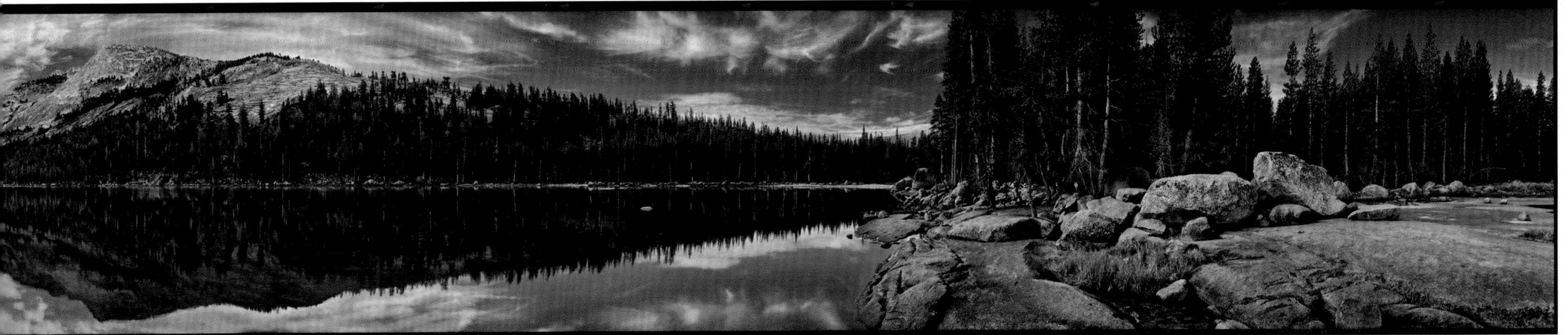

Gregory Gorfkle

disrupt that approach, to perceive my position relative to patterns that wrap around me and as they exist contiguously. Scenes take on new meaning in this way. I move in relation to these patterns, through and among objects with considerations to view and a perspective that regards an entire field. I'm neither on one side nor another, nor between two or more, but move from center to center to become aware of a much greater vision at work with a cognitive sense of sight rather than by eyesight alone.

The 360-degree photograph allows me to step out and away from behind a linear framework to experience my interaction with the landscape, the relationships that bind it around me and me to it.

The complete panorama presents a vision that is challenging. It expands the breadth of visual literacy. It adds dimension and context to what I perceive and what I envision.

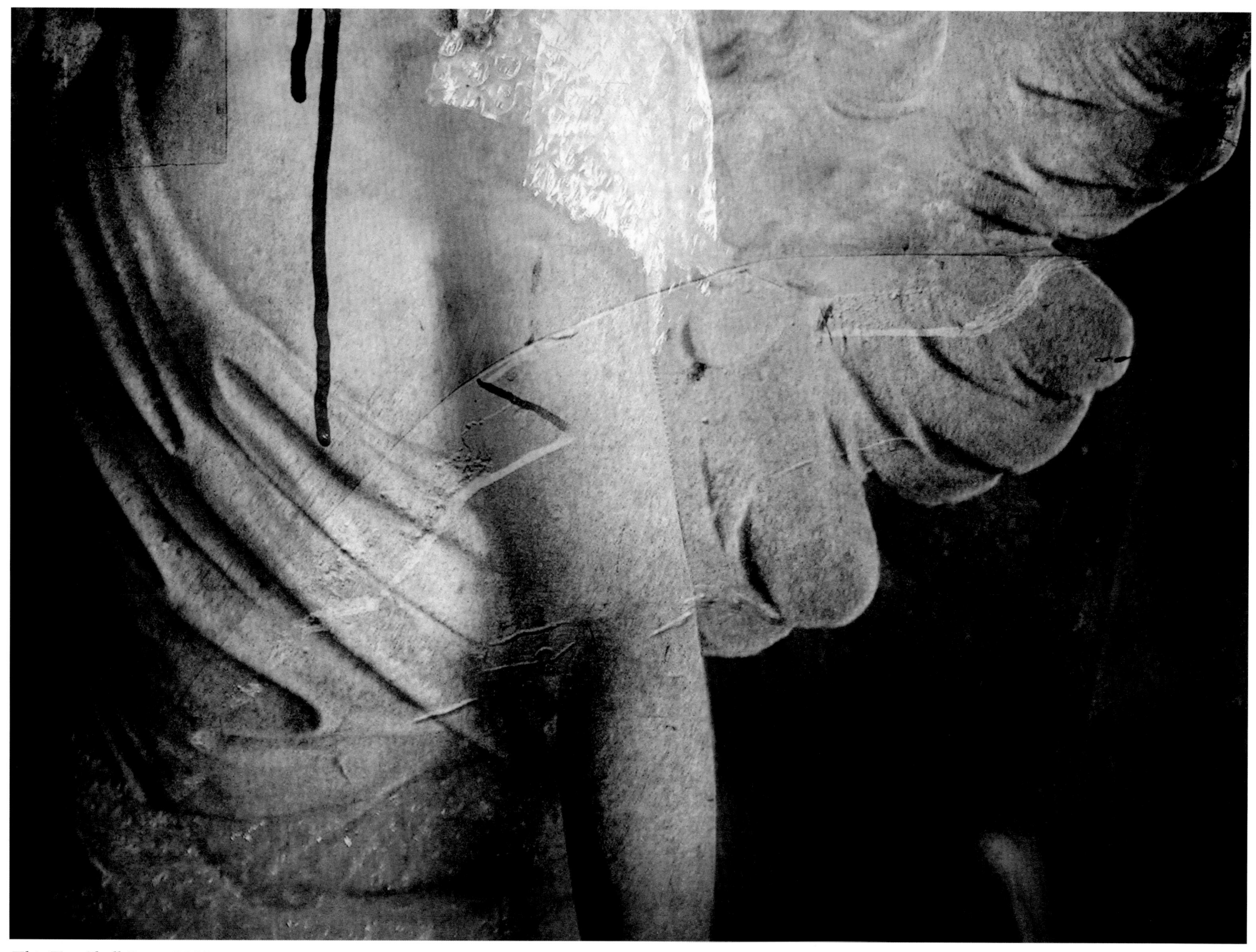

This Too Shall Pass, 2002

Germán Herrera

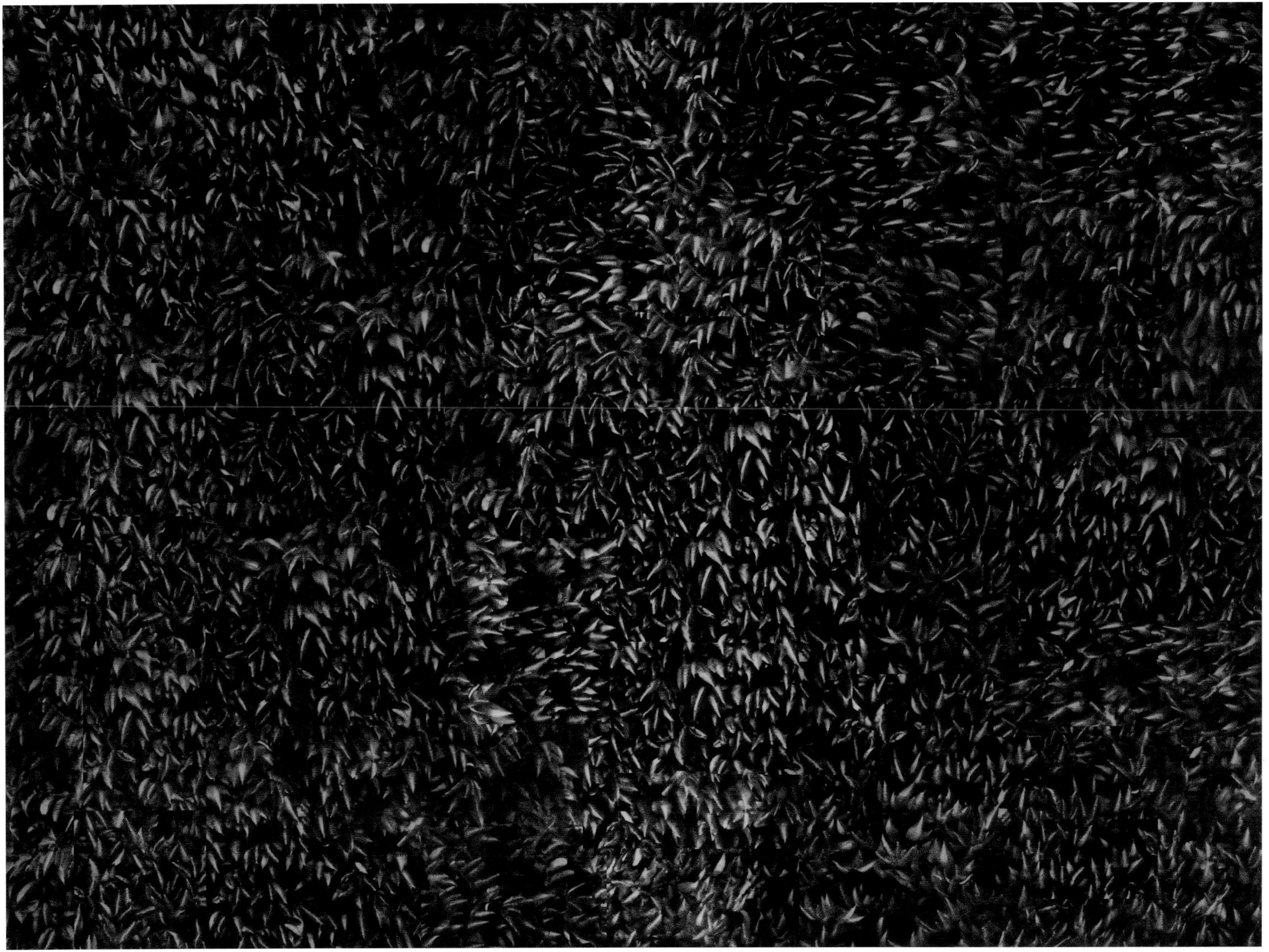

Emergence, 2003

Germán Herrera

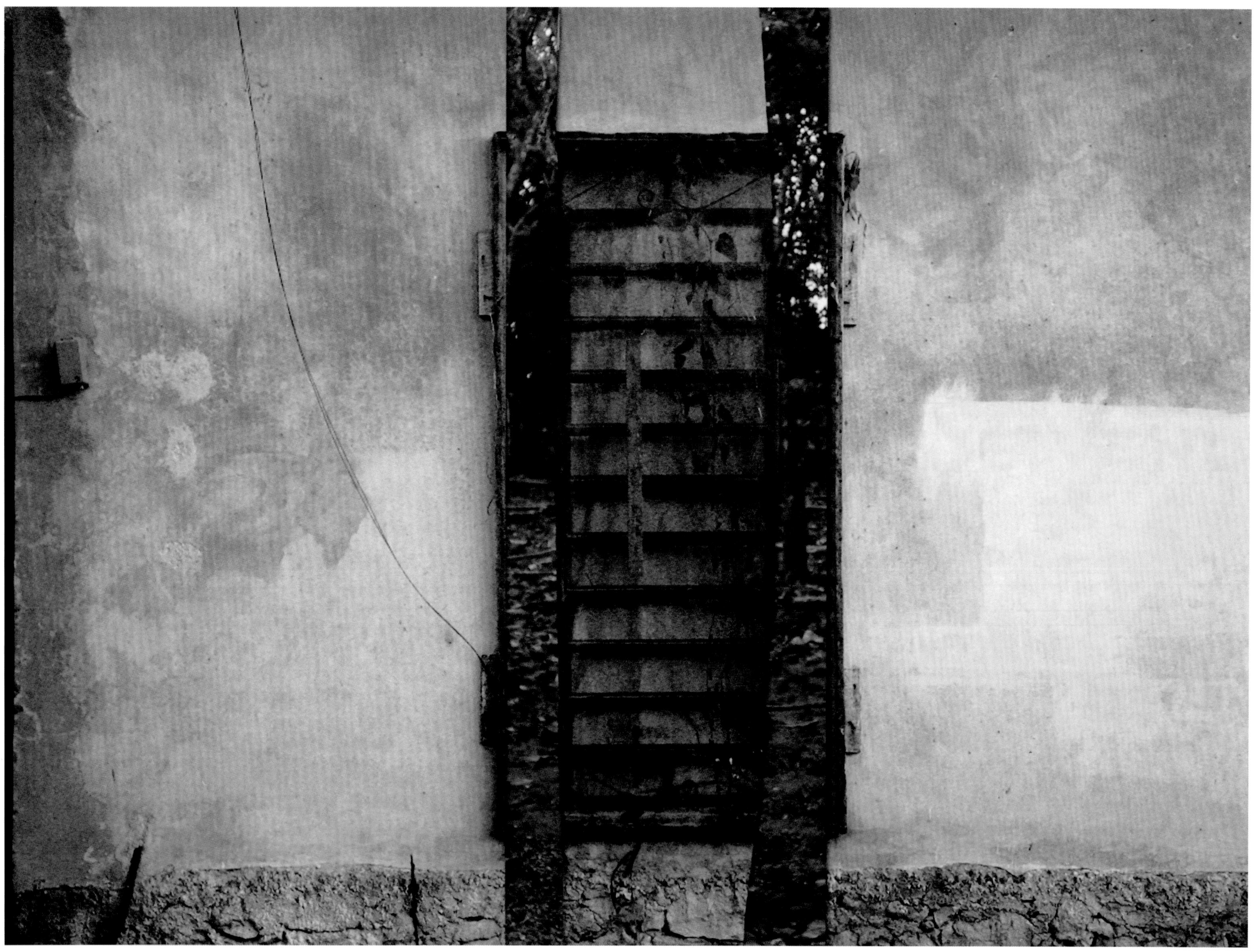

Another Door, 2004

Germán Herrera

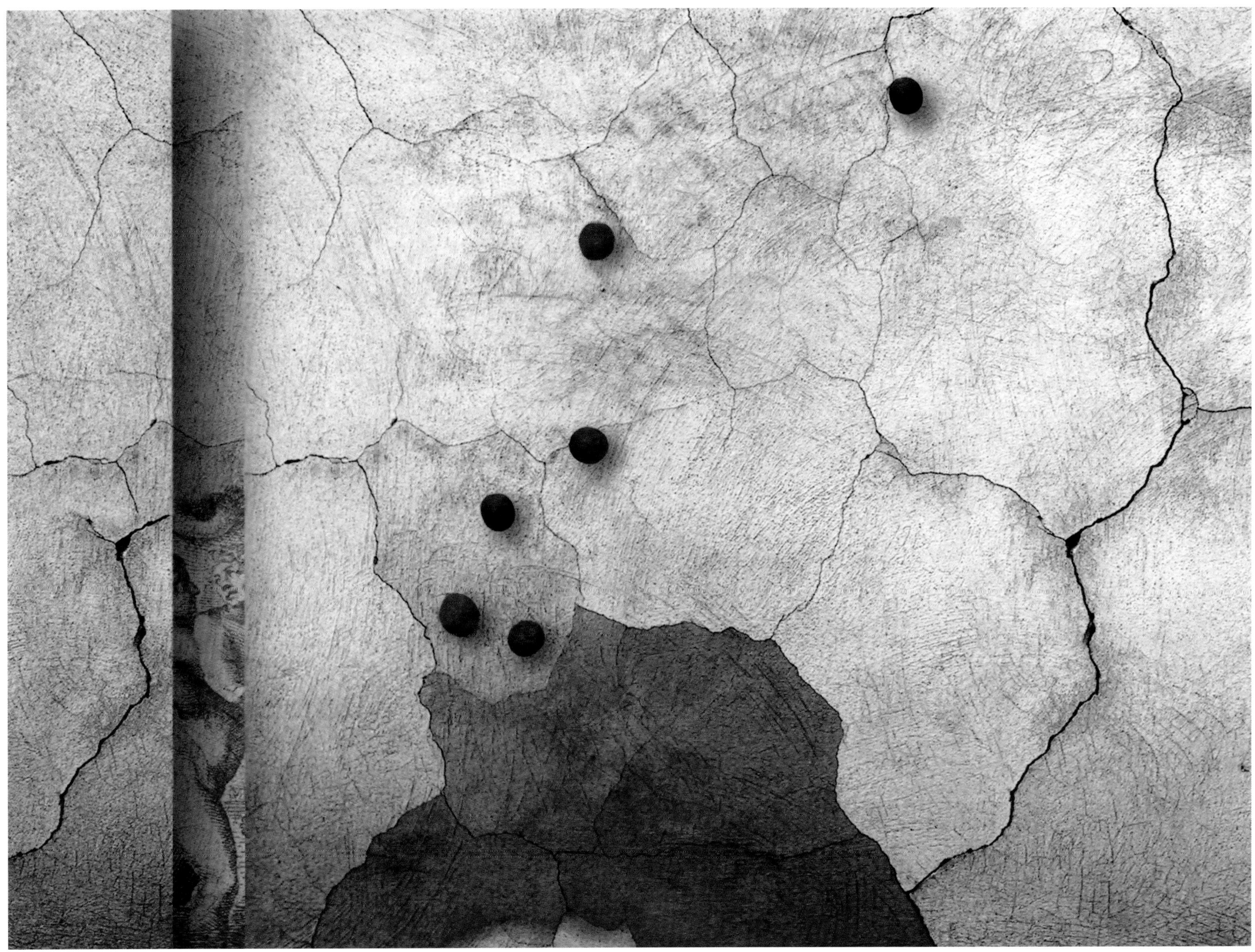

Cantor, 2004

Germán Herrera

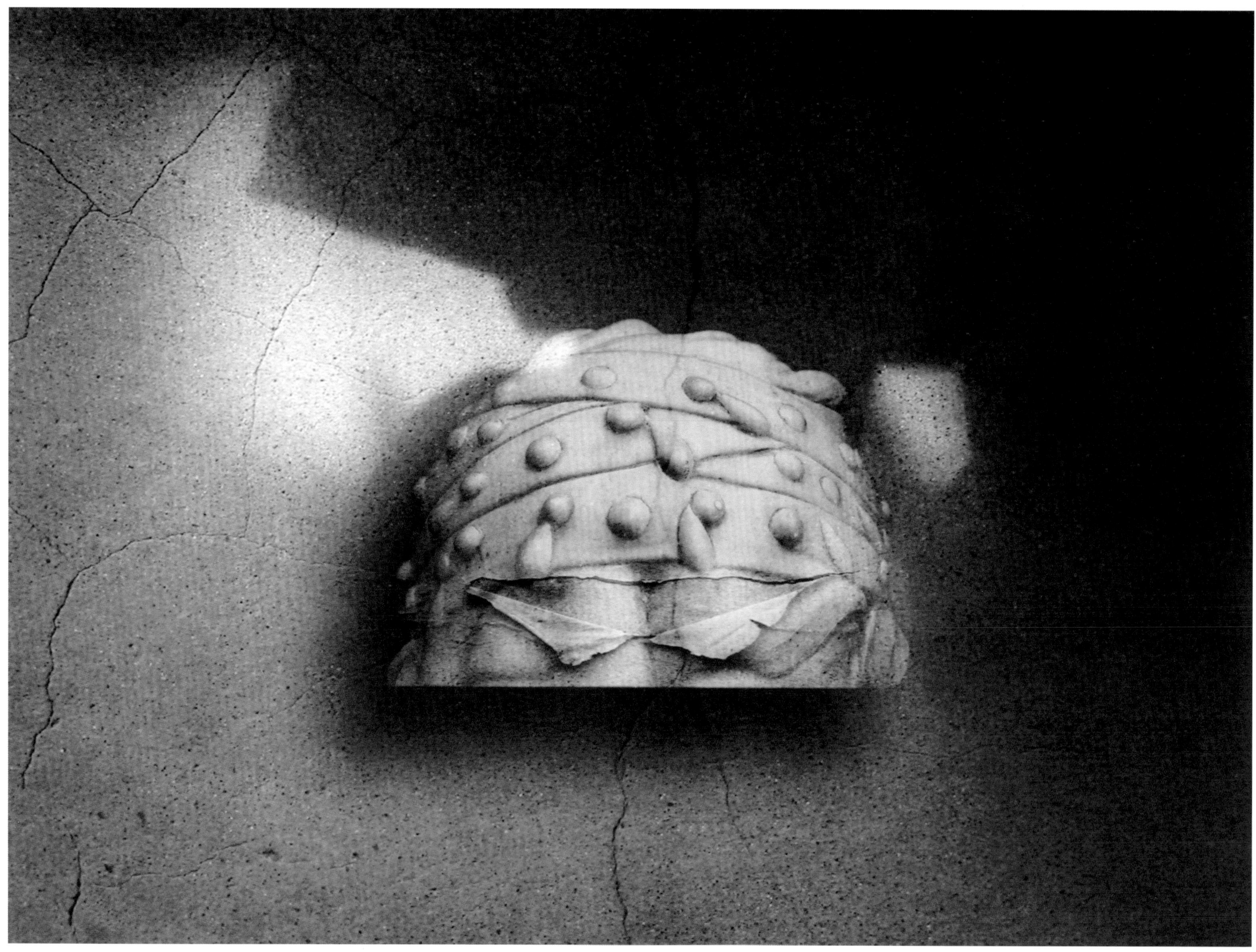

Maria Magdalena, 2003

Germán Herrera

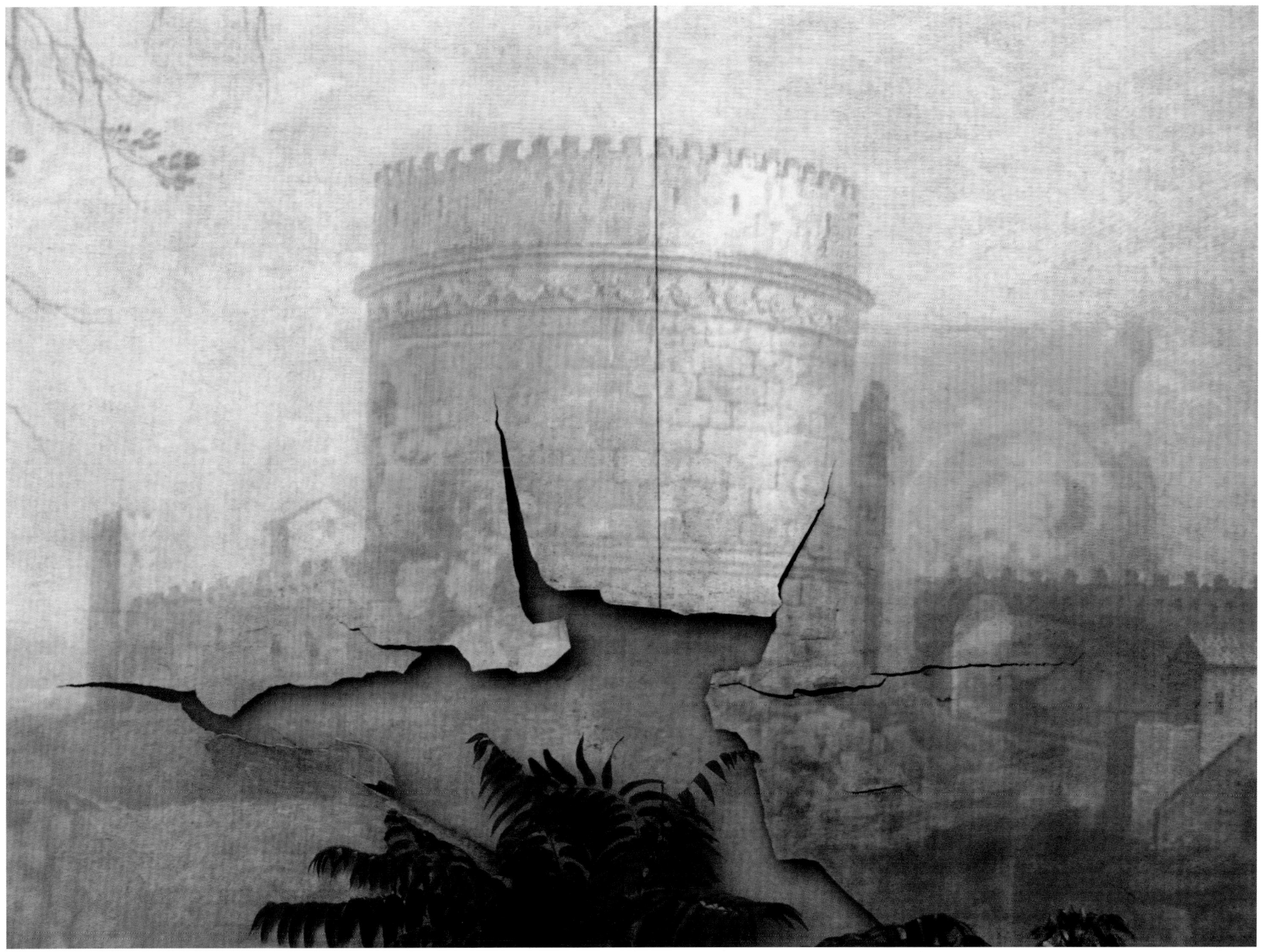

Towers Tend To Crack, 2004

Germán Herrera

A Book of Mirrors

A flock of *feelings*,
disguised as images.

We also create ideas, all of which,
move on to become reality.

Then you look...
What am I creating?

...a Book of Self.

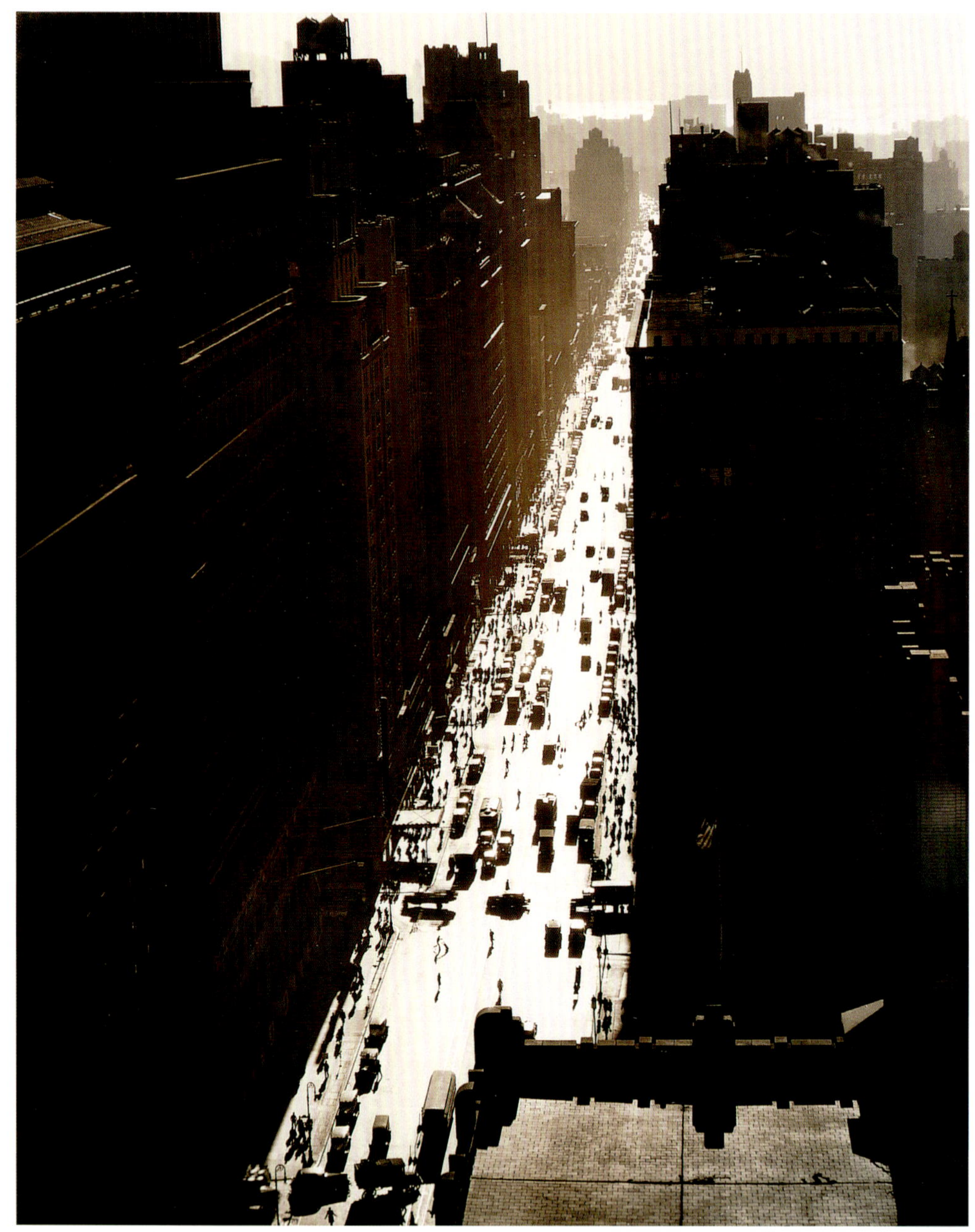

Seventh Avenue Looking South from 35th Street, 1935 Berenice Abbott

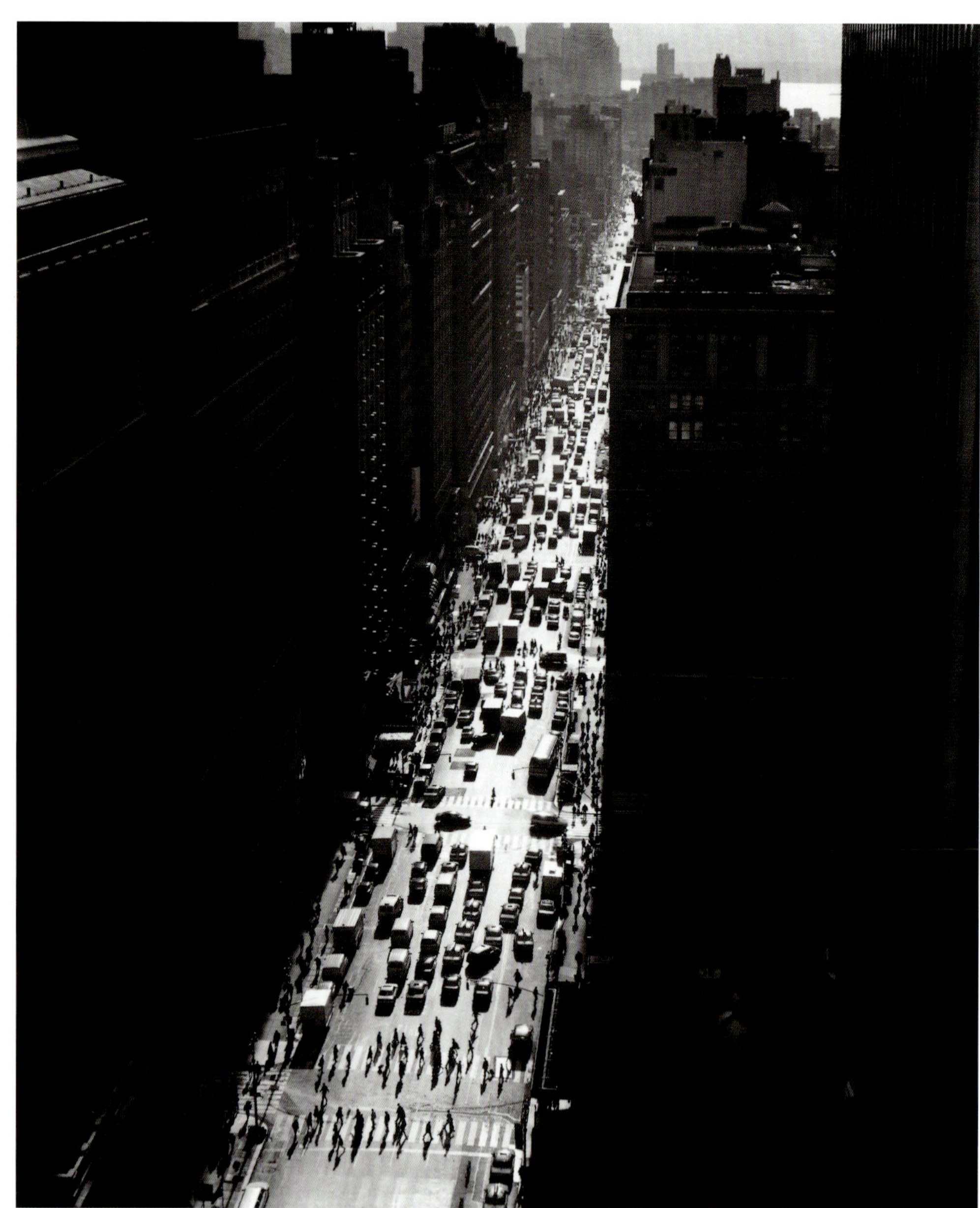

Seventh Avenue Looking South from 35th Street, 2001 Douglas Levere

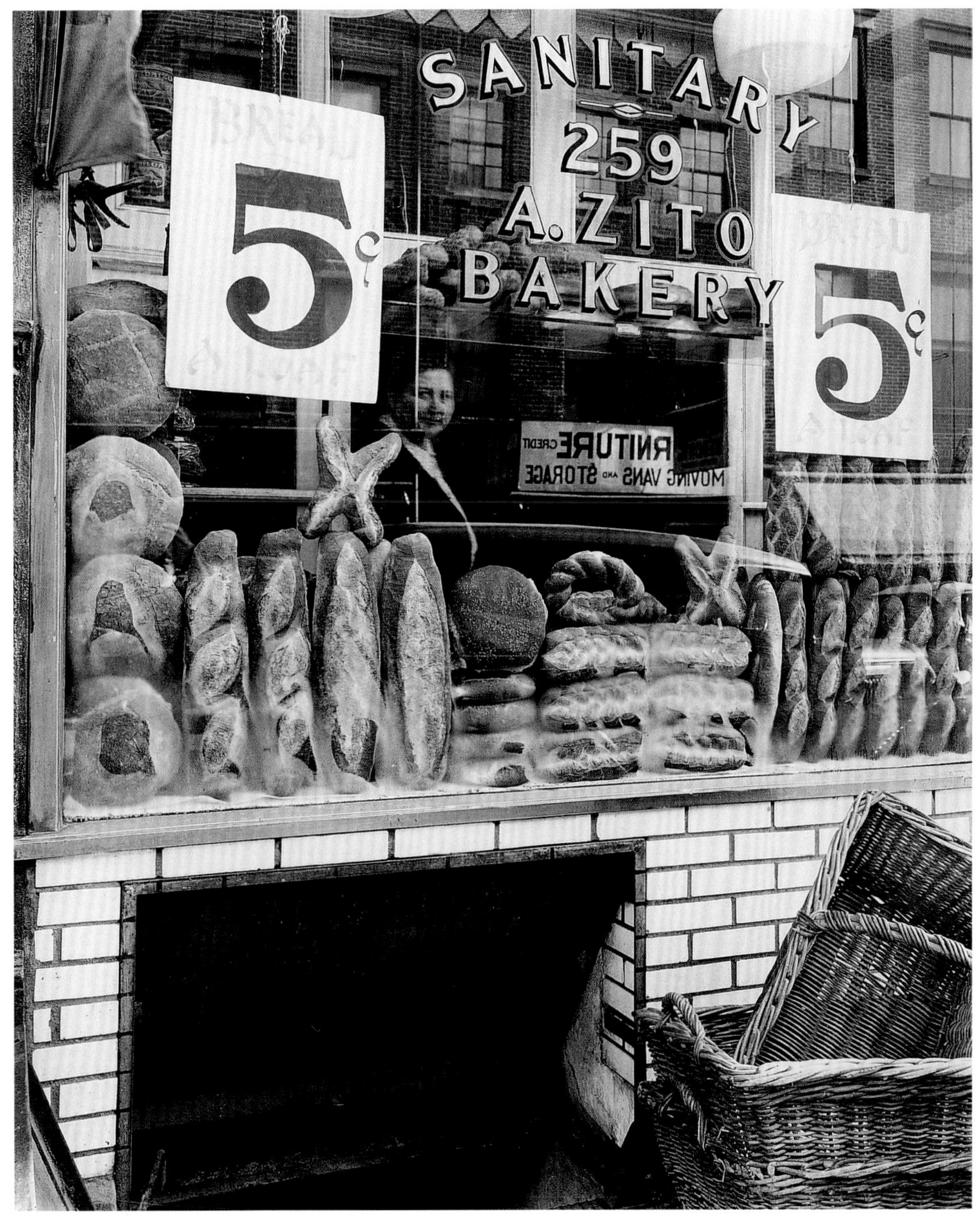

Bread Store, 259 Bleeker Street, 1937 Berenice Abbott

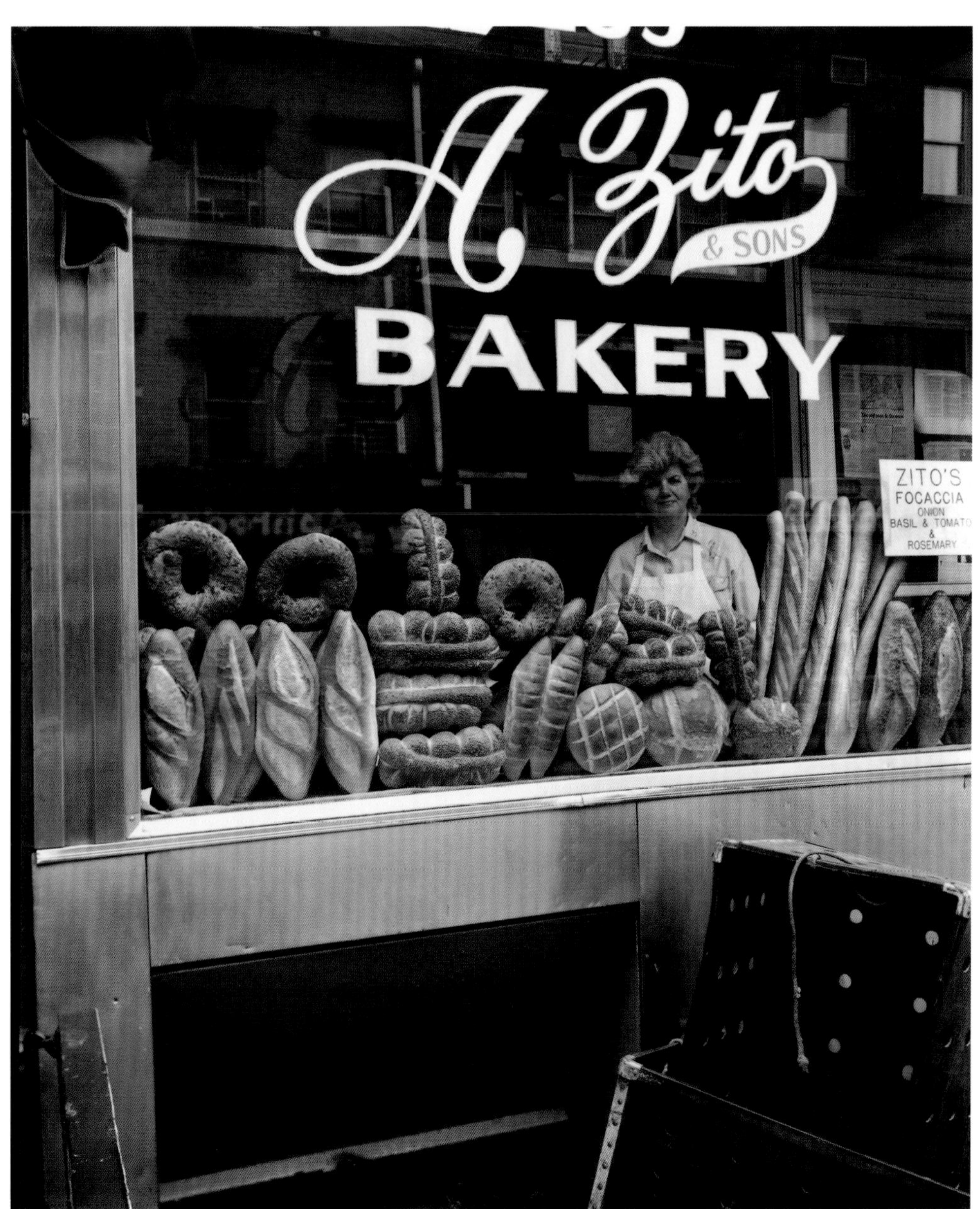

Bread Store, 259 Bleeker Street, 1998 Douglas Levere

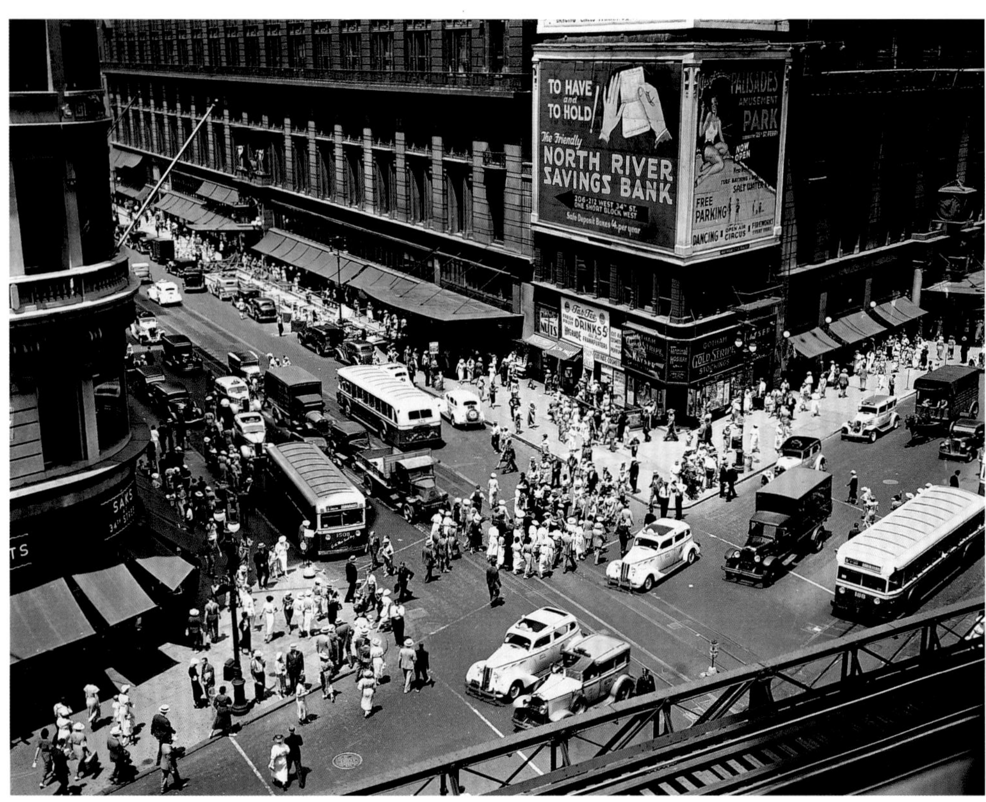

Herald Square, West 34th Street & Broadway, 1936

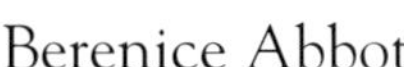

Berenice Abbott

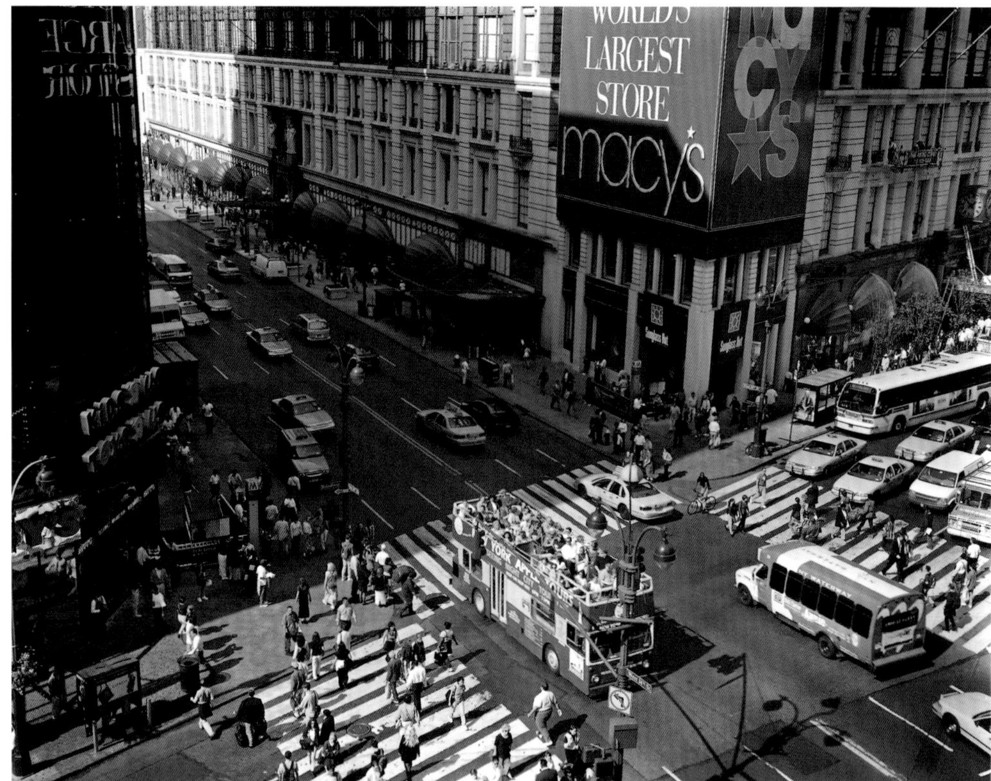

Herald Square, West 34th Street & Broadway, 1997

Douglas Levere

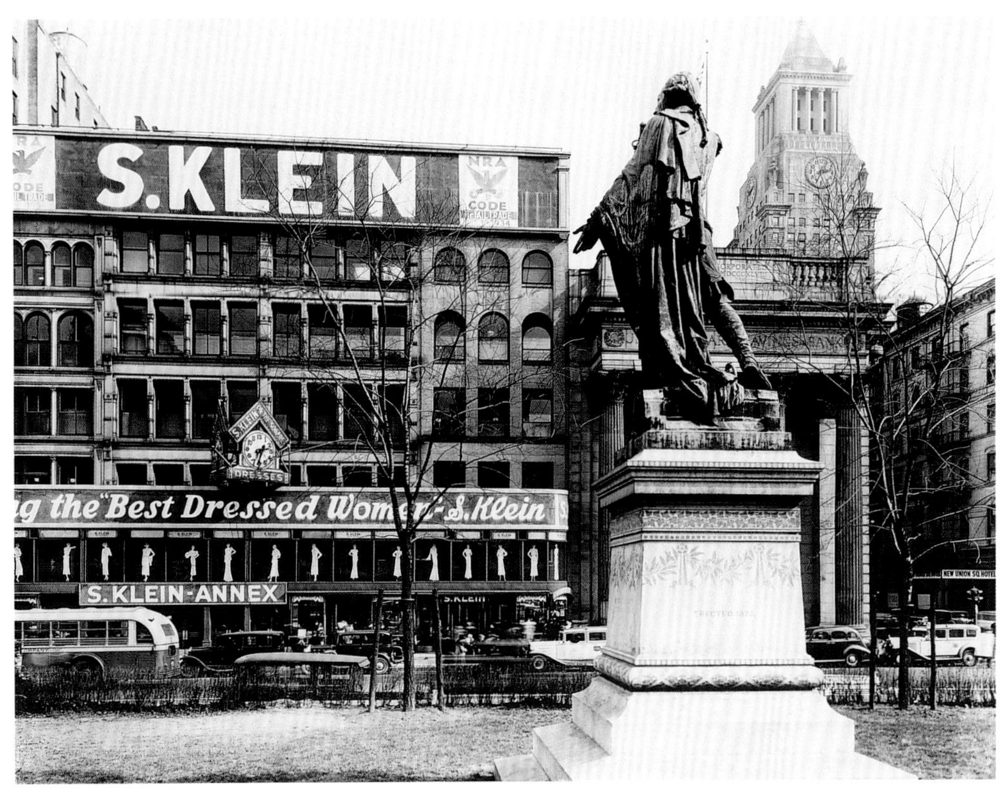

Union Square, 4th Avenue between East 15th & 16th Streets, 1936

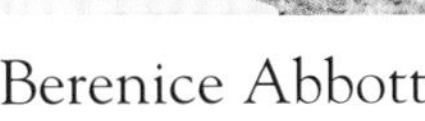
Berenice Abbott

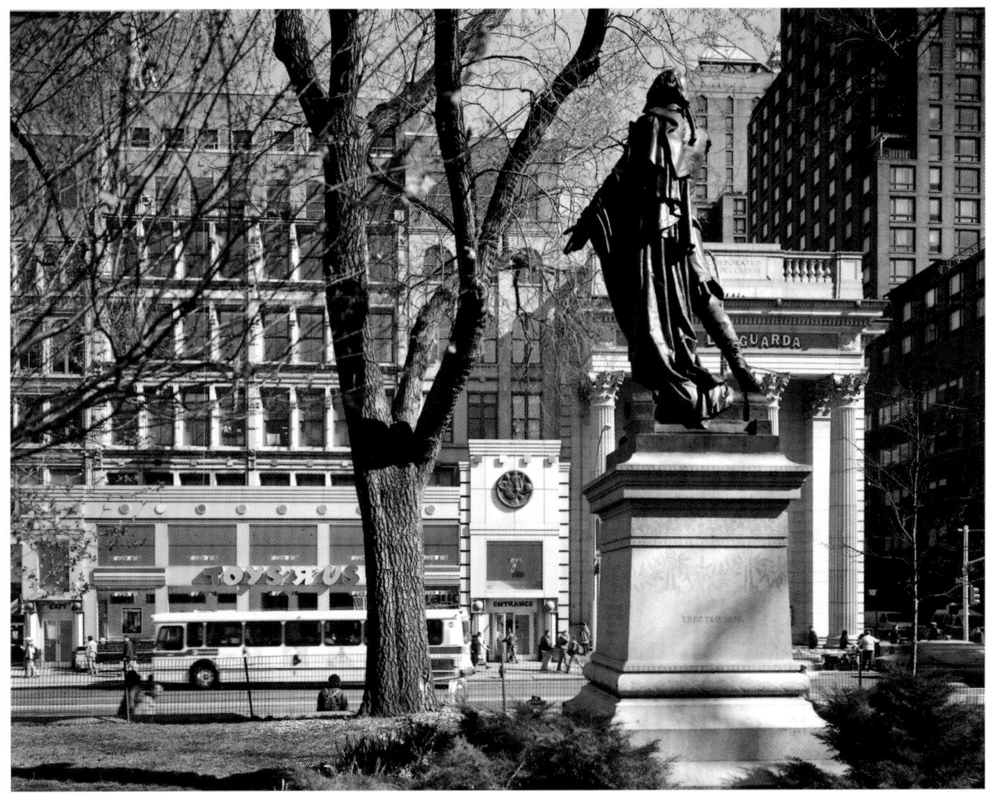

Union Square, 4th Avenue between East 15th & 16th Streets, 2002

Douglas Levere

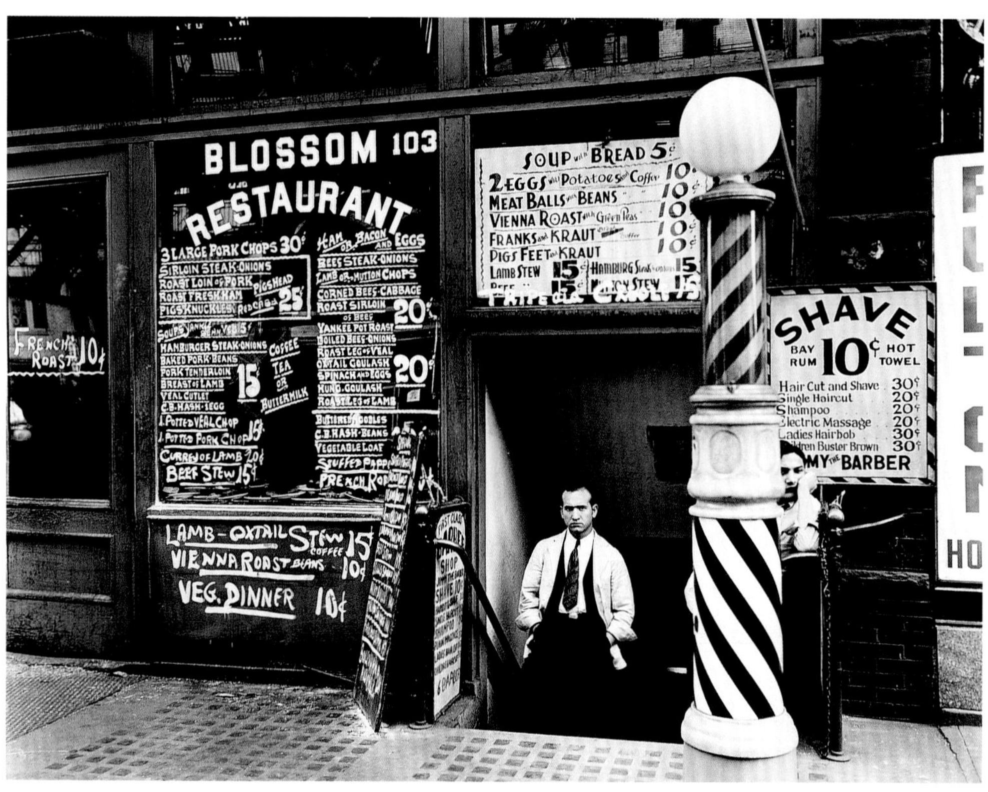

Blossom Restaurant, 103 Bowery, 1935

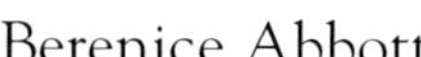
Berenice Abbott

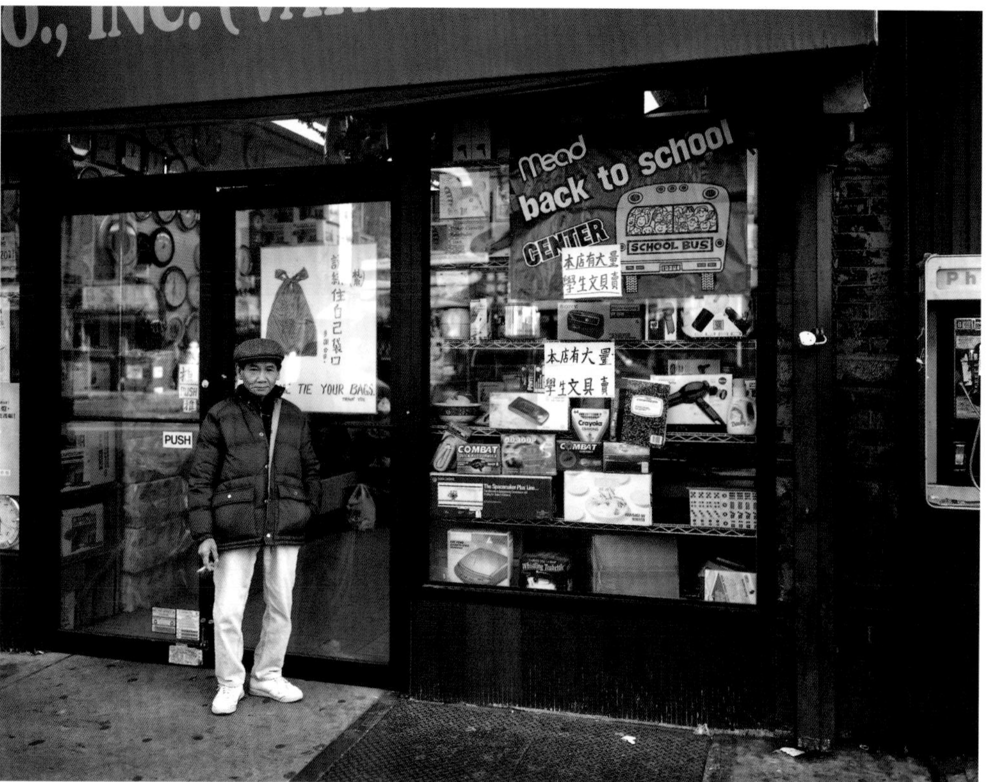

Blossom Restaurant, 103 Bowery, 1998

Douglas Levere

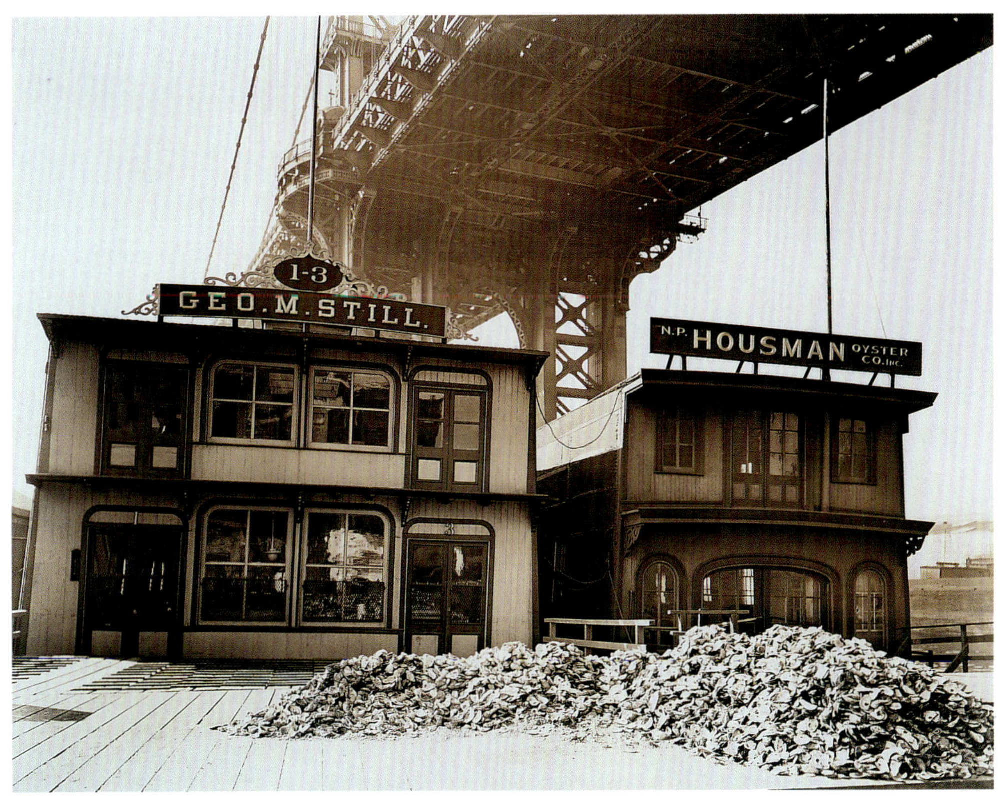

Oyster Houses, South Street & Pike Slip, 1937 Berenice Abbott

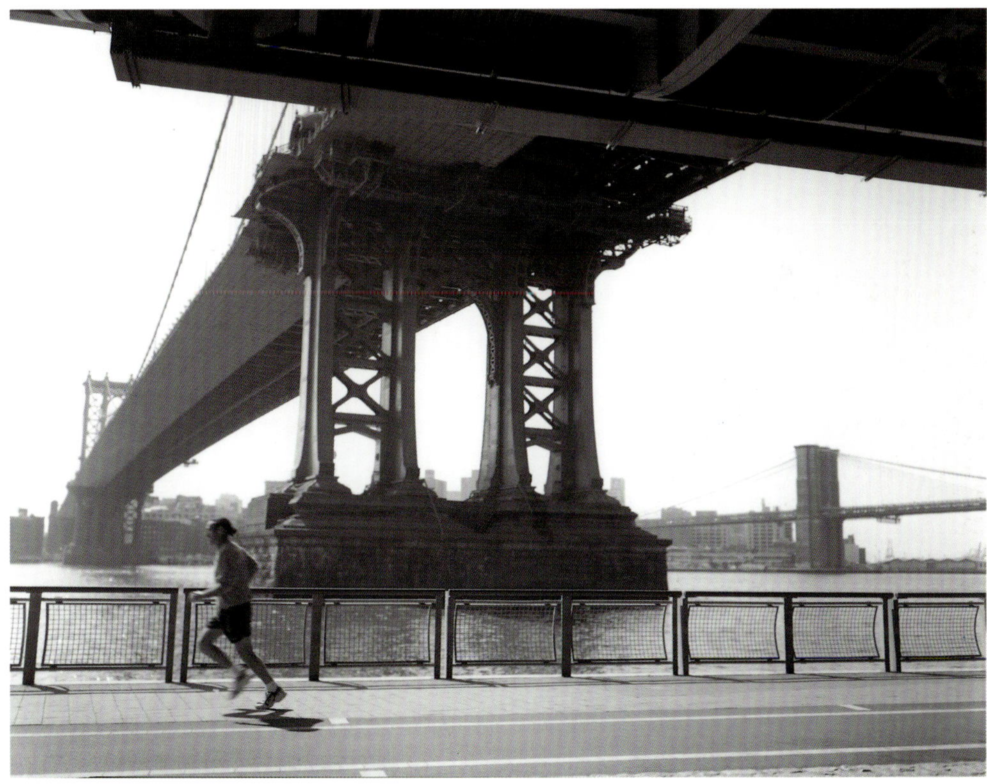

Oyster Houses, South Street & Pike Slip, 2002 Douglas Levere

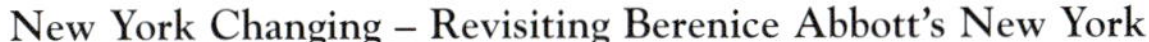

New York Changing – Revisiting Berenice Abbott's New York

Berenice Abbott's Changing New York project captured a modern vision of Manhattan and its surrounding boroughs in the 1930s. From 1997 to 2003, Levere returned to the original sites with the identical 8x10 Century Universal camera that Abbott used, at the same time of day and year Abbott's photographs were taken, revealing New York Changing over sixty years.

A chance glimpse at Abbott's "Broadway near Broome Street" in Manhattan launched Levere's project. As it happened, the location of the photograph was the doorstep of Levere's SoHo loft. "It was the view I see walking out of my door every day," Levere said. "I was mesmerized." In an instant, the contrast between Abbott's photograph and the image in his mind spoke volumes about the history of his neighborhood, and the generations who had made their lives in New York City.

The paired images produce a remarkable commentary on the evolution of New York City over several decades and encourage the viewer to consider the rate and meaning of progress. This juxtaposition of the past and present comes with obvious changes: the brownstone becomes a housing project, the neighborhood store becomes a skyscraper. Often, however, the encounter results in a more subtle reflection of the changing tides of our culture.

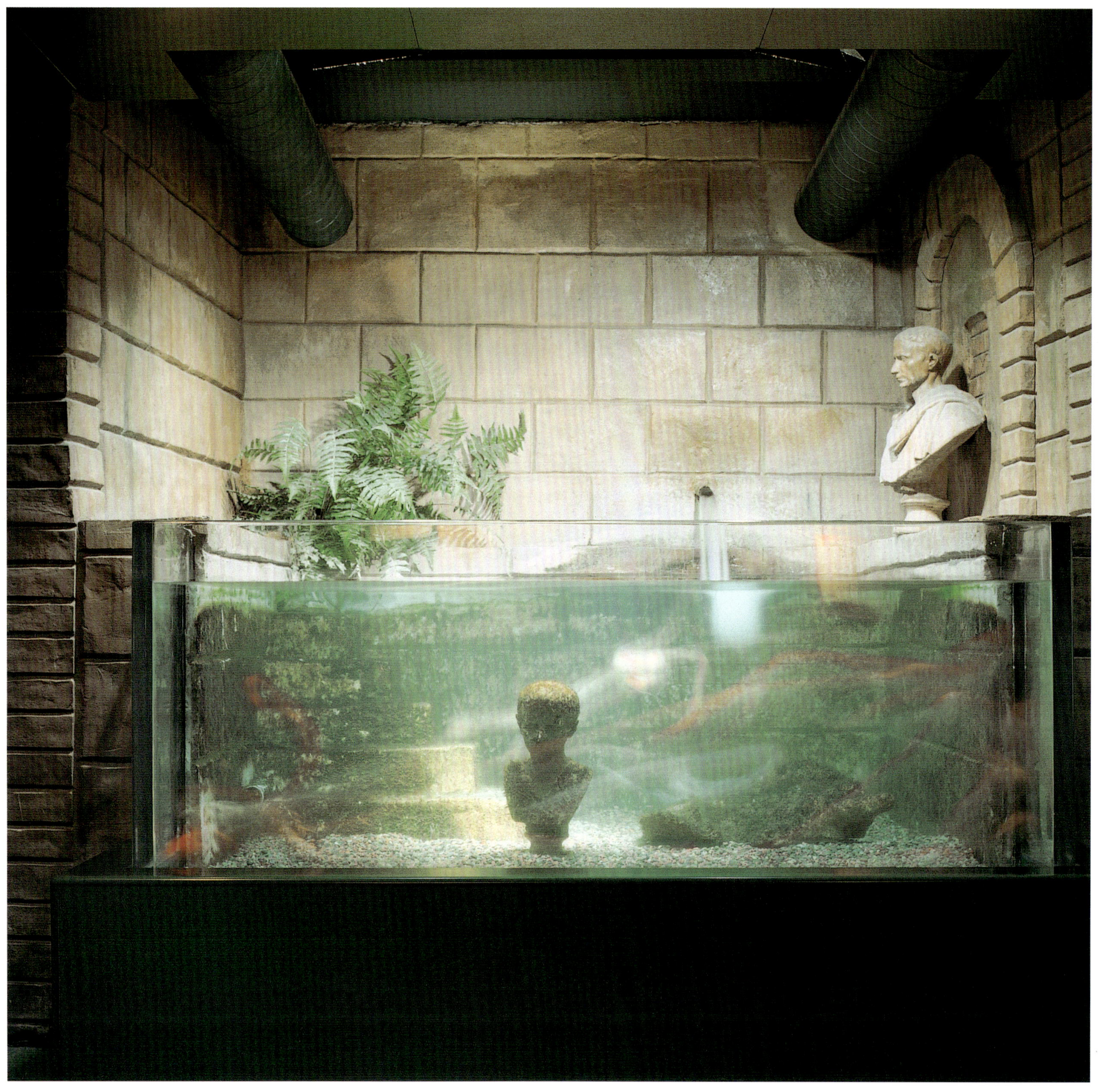

Encyclopedia – "Aquarium" Allen Maertz

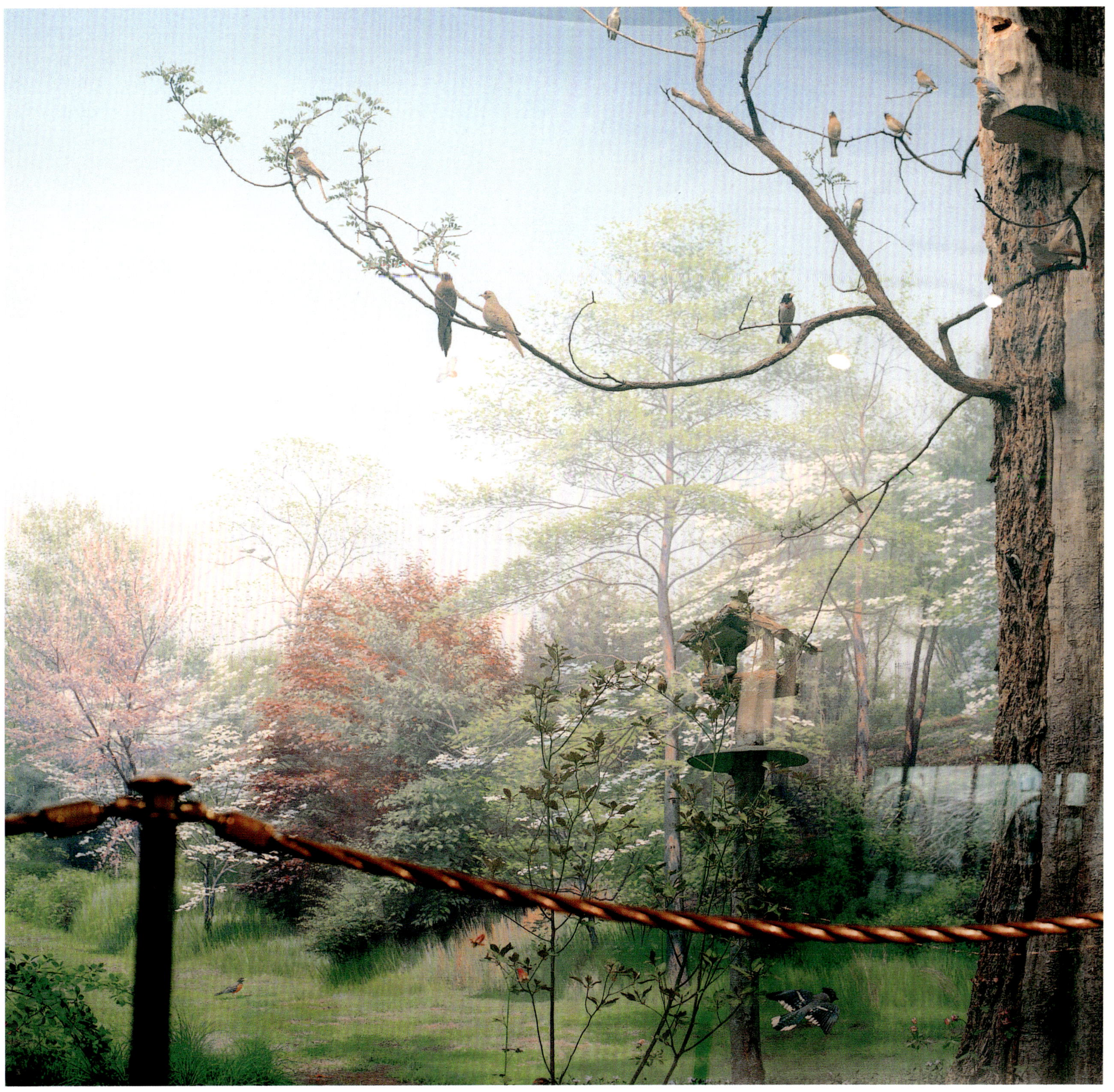

Encyclopedia – "Birds" Allen Maertz

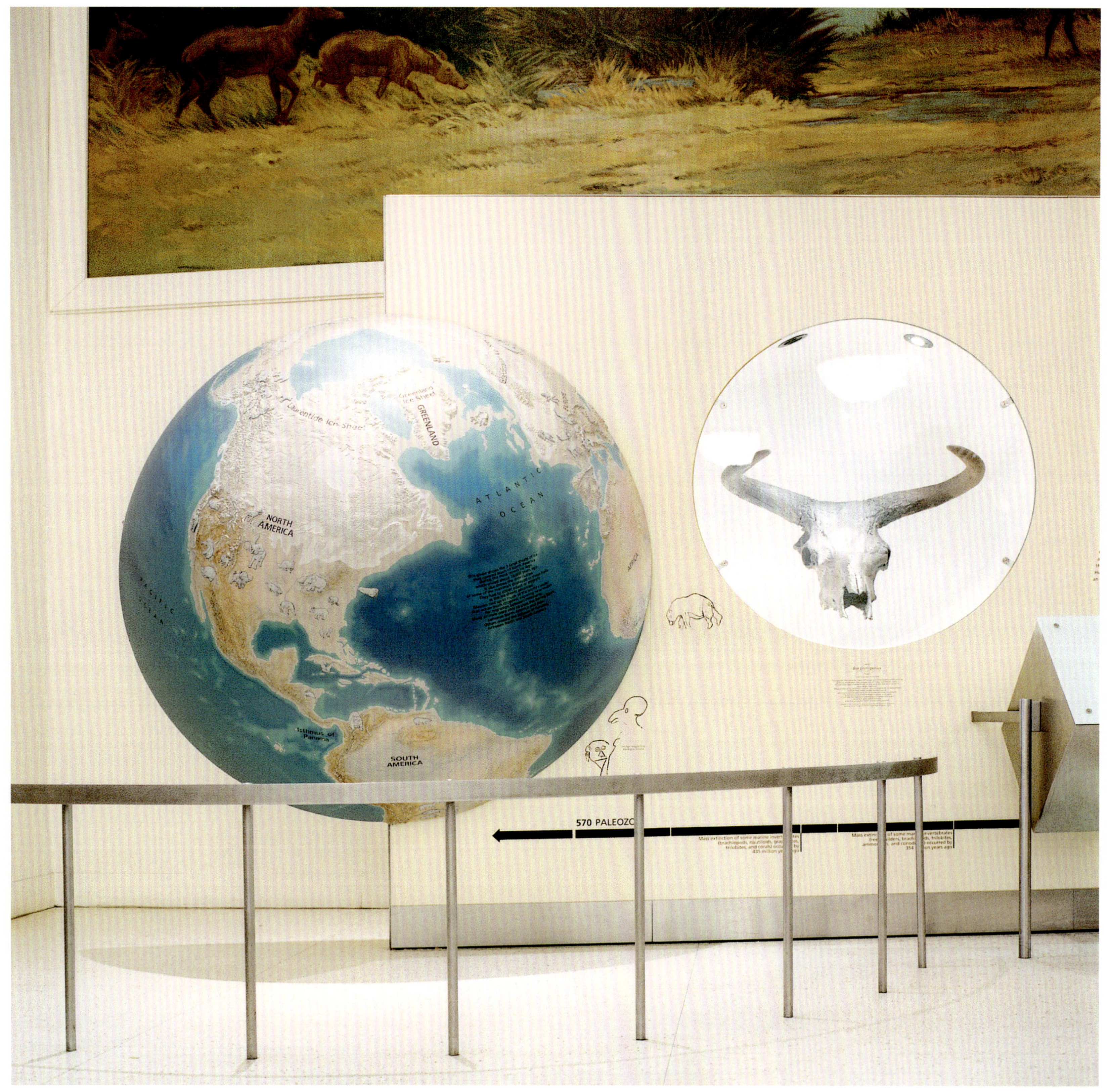

Encyclopedia – "Ice Age" Allen Maertz

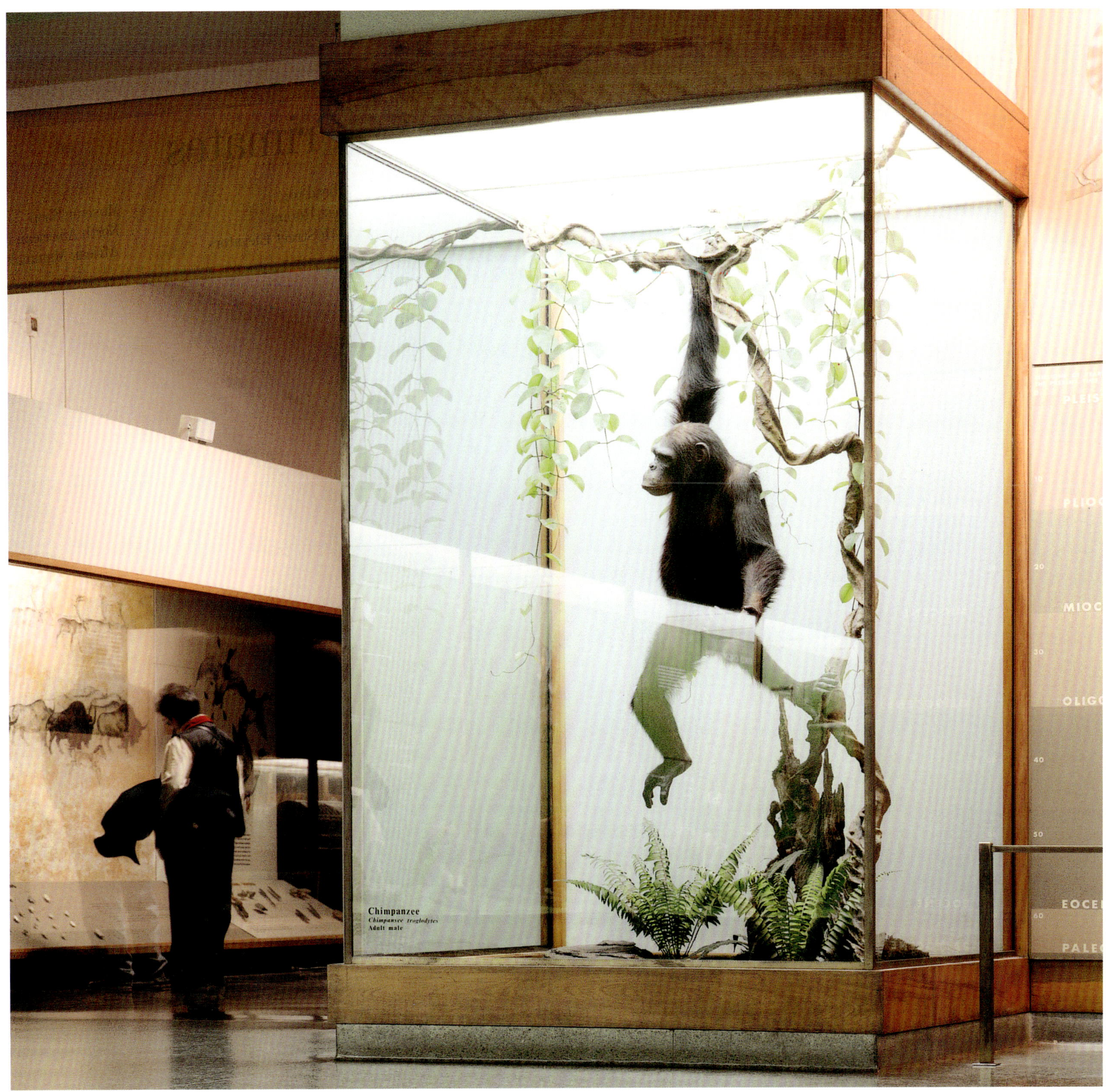

Encyclopedia – "Chimpanzee"

Allen Maertz

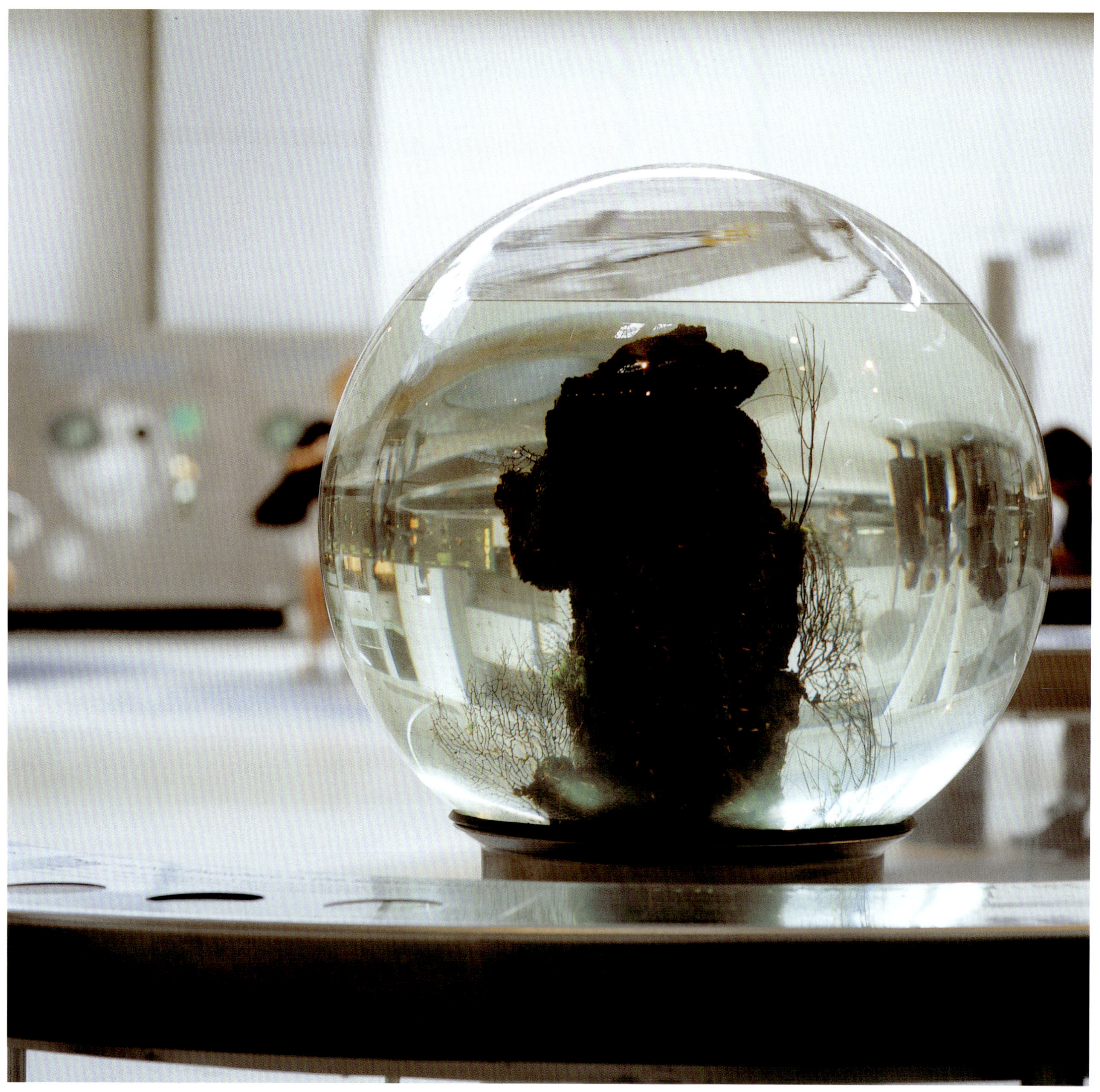

Encyclopedia – "Biosphere" Allen Maertz

Using the literal meaning of an encyclopedia (a systematically arranged work containing exhaustive and factual information on a branch of knowledge or art) as a starting point, I focus both globally and locally on the political and cultural influences that construct modern perceptions of knowledge. Encyclopedia encompasses the mythologies of history, science and art in their corresponding public institutions and how these concepts and ideas are mediated for consumption in the public sphere.

However, Encyclopedia is more than an exploration of hegemonic visuality (the assumption that all displays/presentations are complicit in serving the political/ethical systems of any authority). It is also a treatise on photological knowledge (the framing of multiple narratives that comprise the historical, political, cultural, scientific and ethical tropes of a nation through physical and constructed visual images and displays which are used along with all its myths, symbols and memories).

In the course of my re-presentation of this public culture of knowledge and art, questions of objectivity and of purpose reemerge, ironically duplicating the same problems inherent in creating public culture. Selection, style, chance, the personal and the political all compete in the process of its compilation.

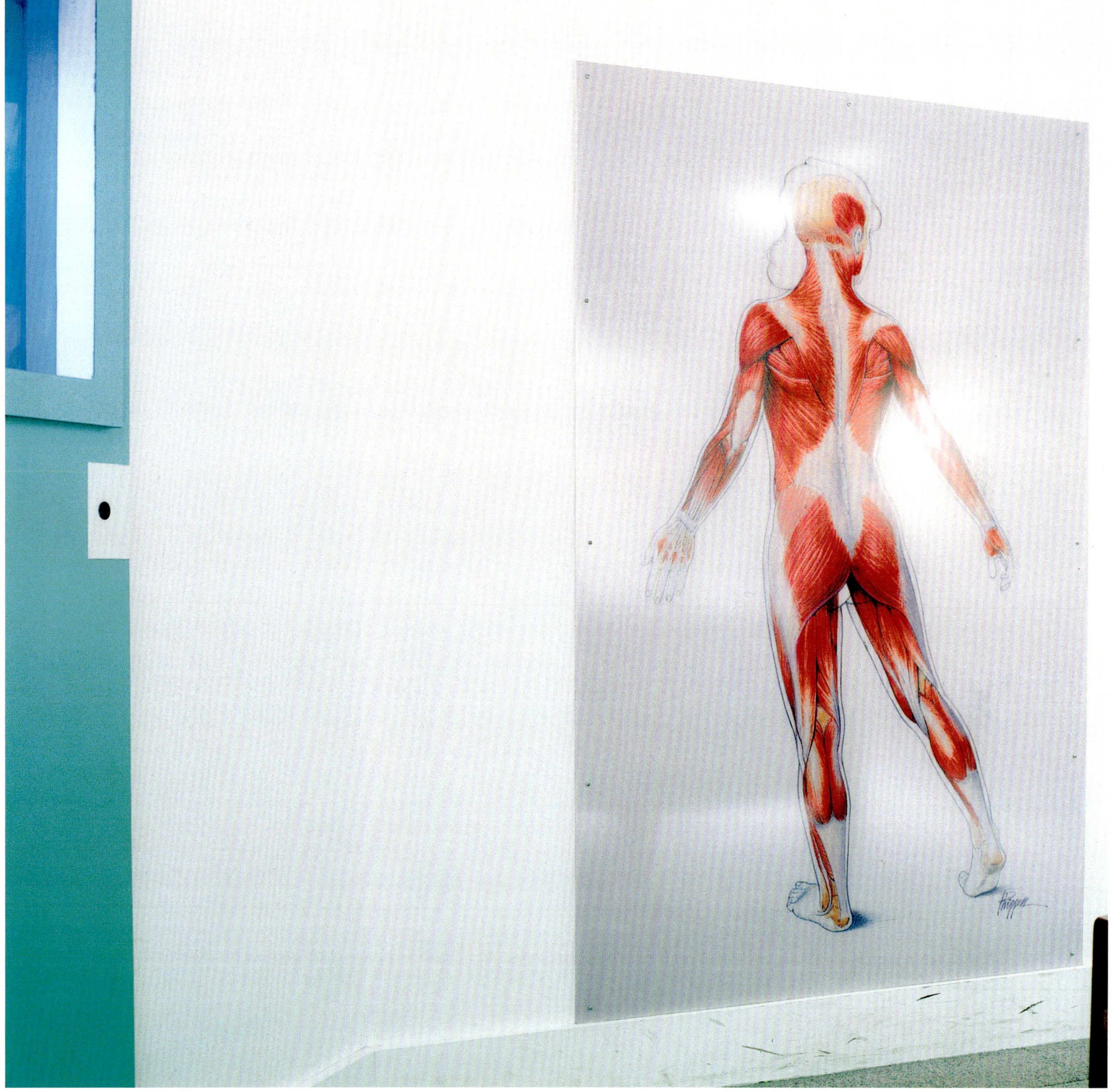

Encyclopedia – "Muscles" Allen Maertz

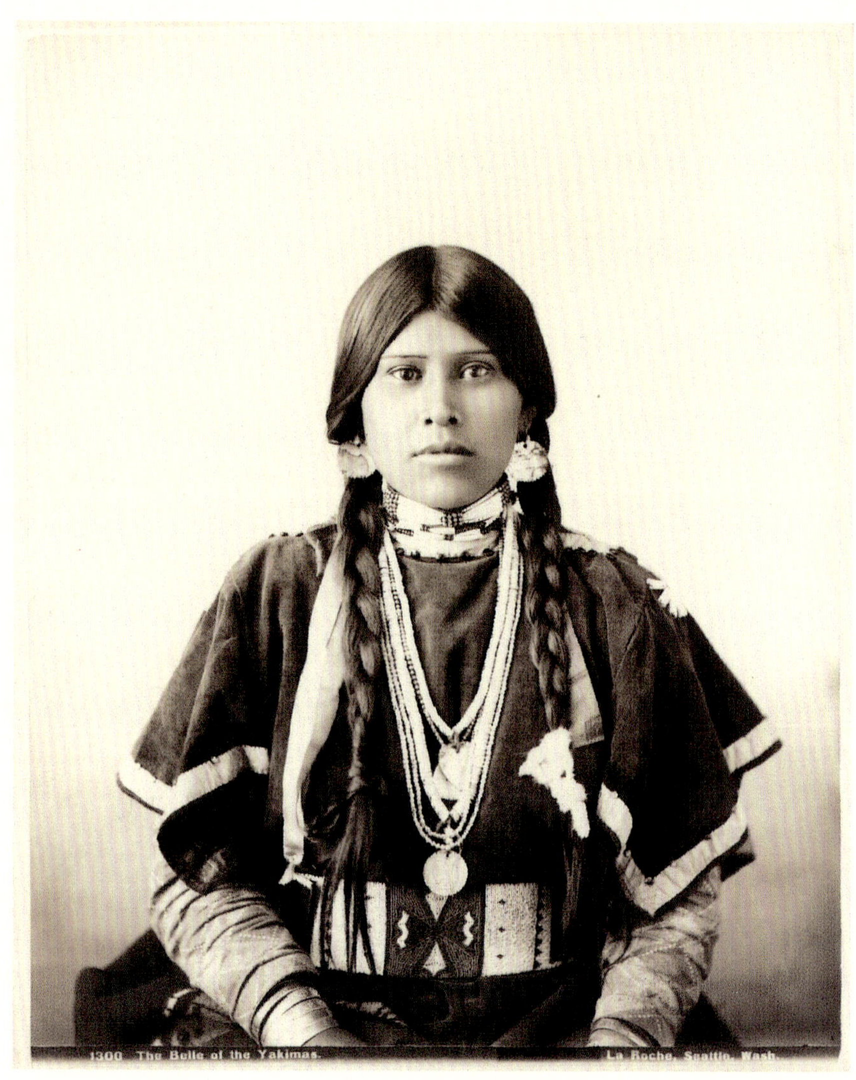

THE BELLE OF THE YAKIMAS

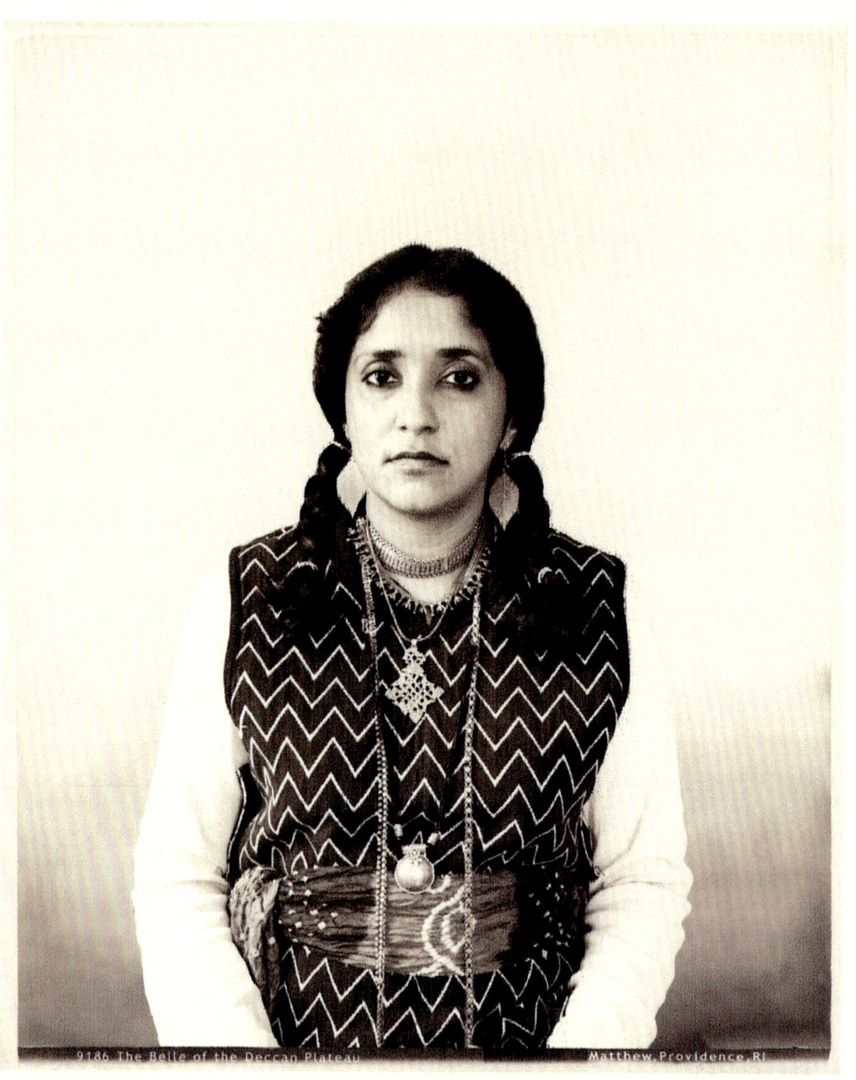

THE BELLE OF THE DECCAN PLATEAU

Annu Palakunnathu Matthew

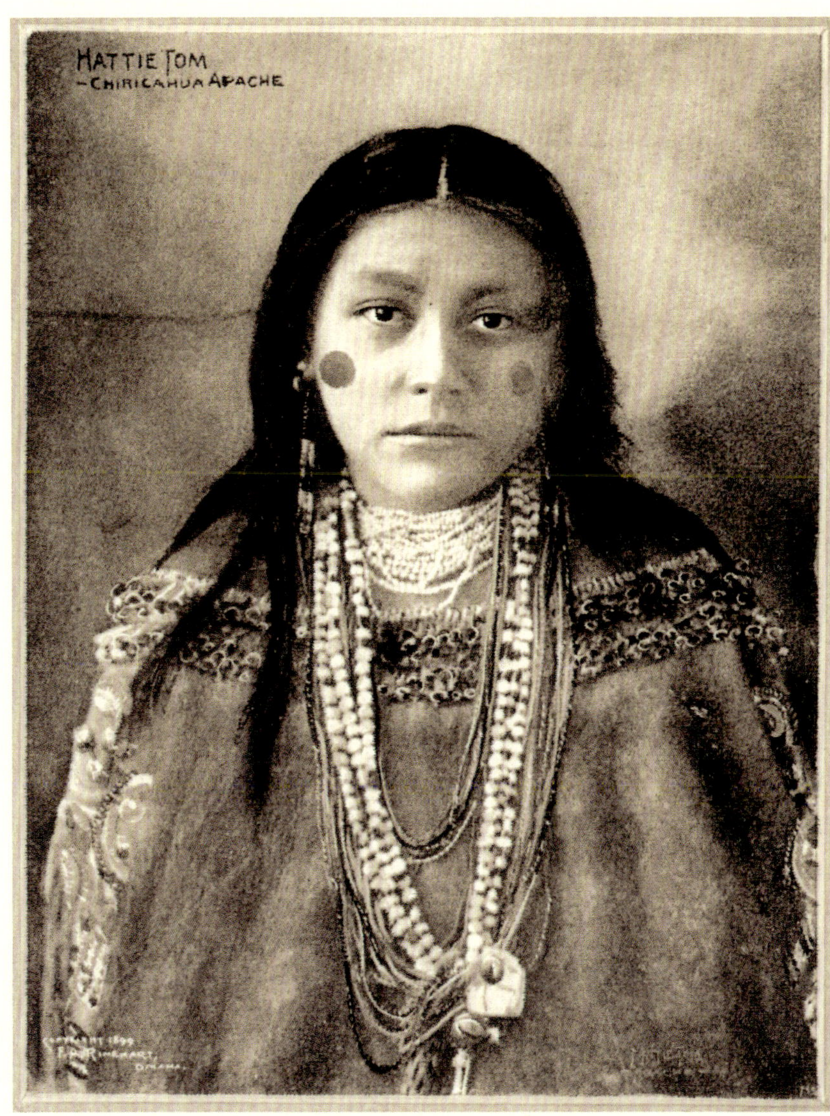

AMERICAN INDIAN WITH DOT ON FACE

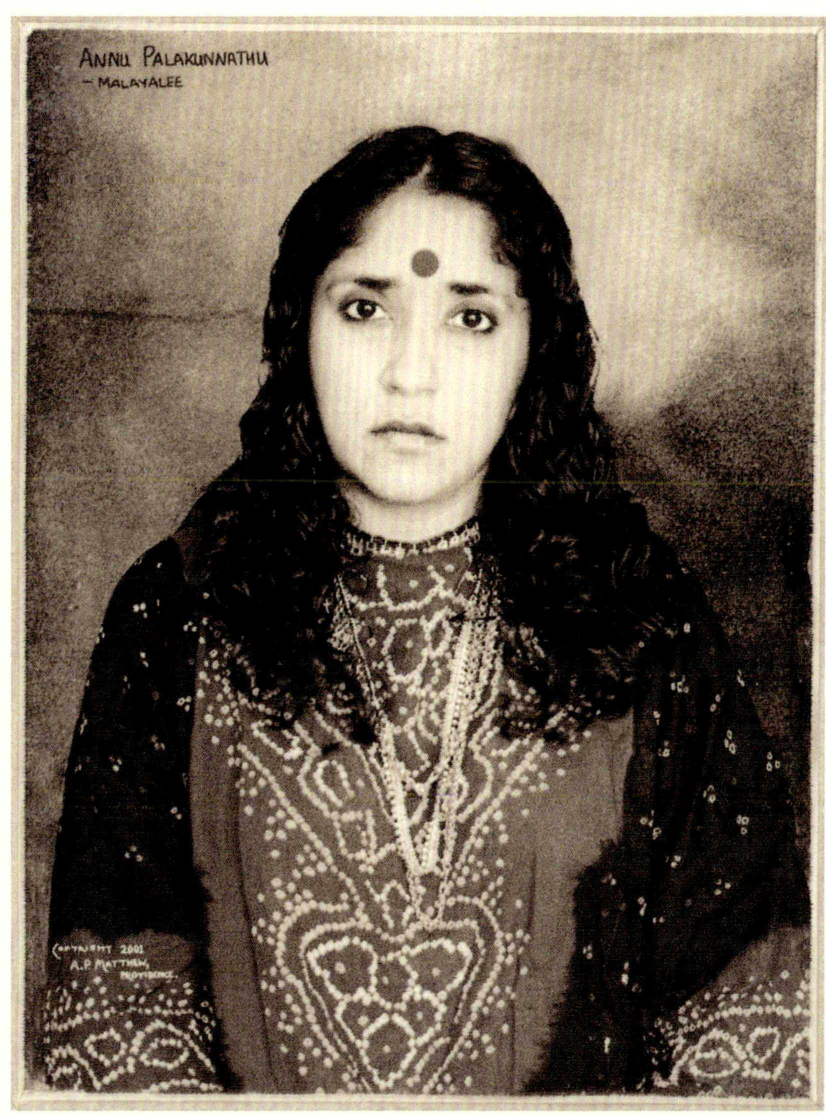

INDIAN AMERICAN WITH DOT ON FACE

Annu Palakunnathu Matthew

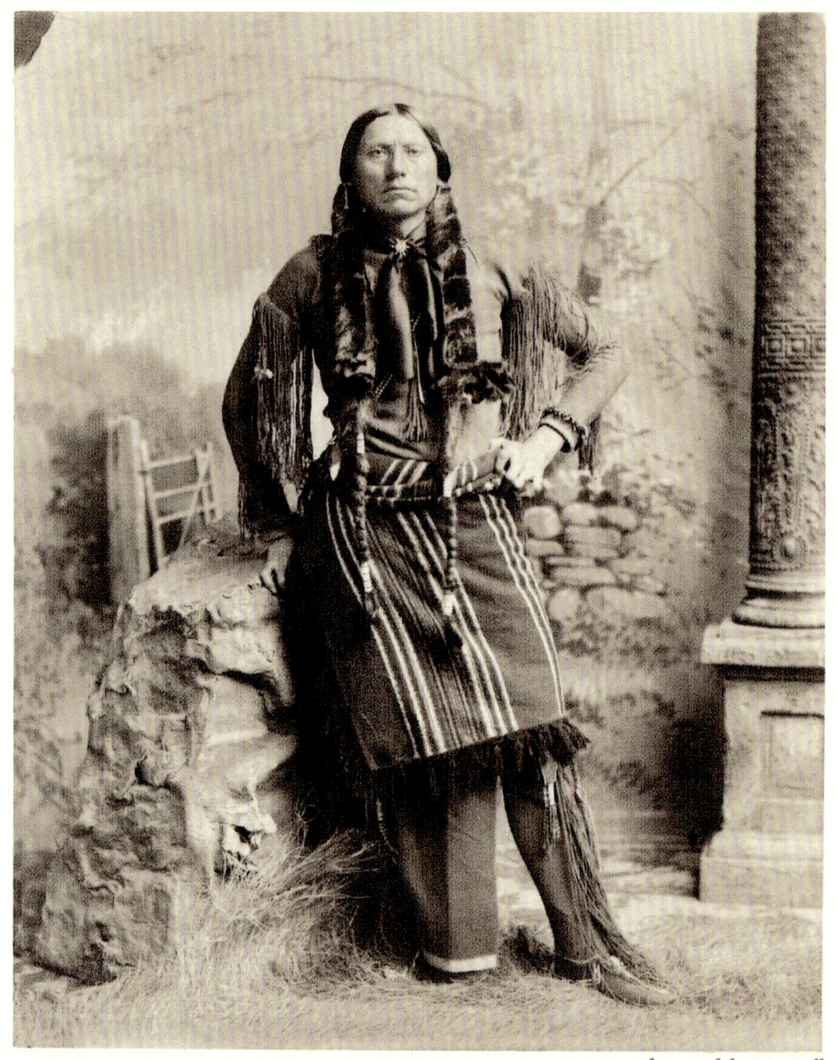
Photograph by C.M. Bell

Quanah Parker. Washington D.C., 1880s

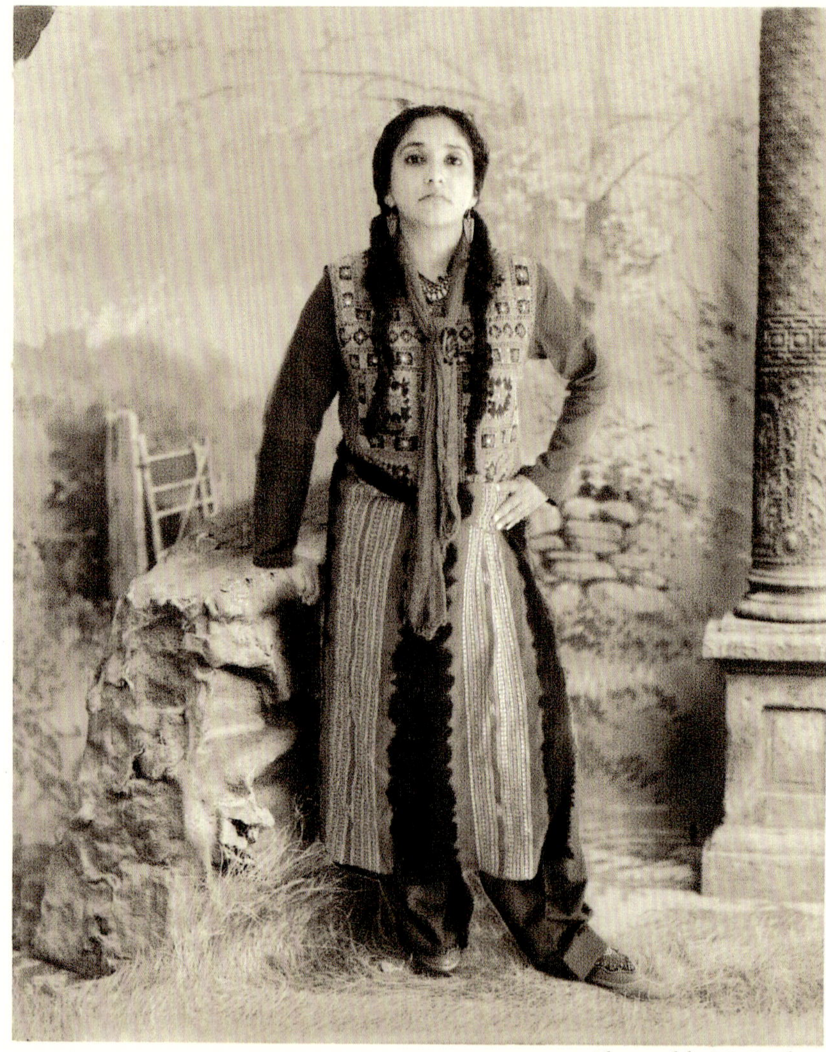
Photograph by A.P. Matthew

Annu Palakunnathu Matthew. Providence R.I., 2000s

Annu Palakunnathu Matthew

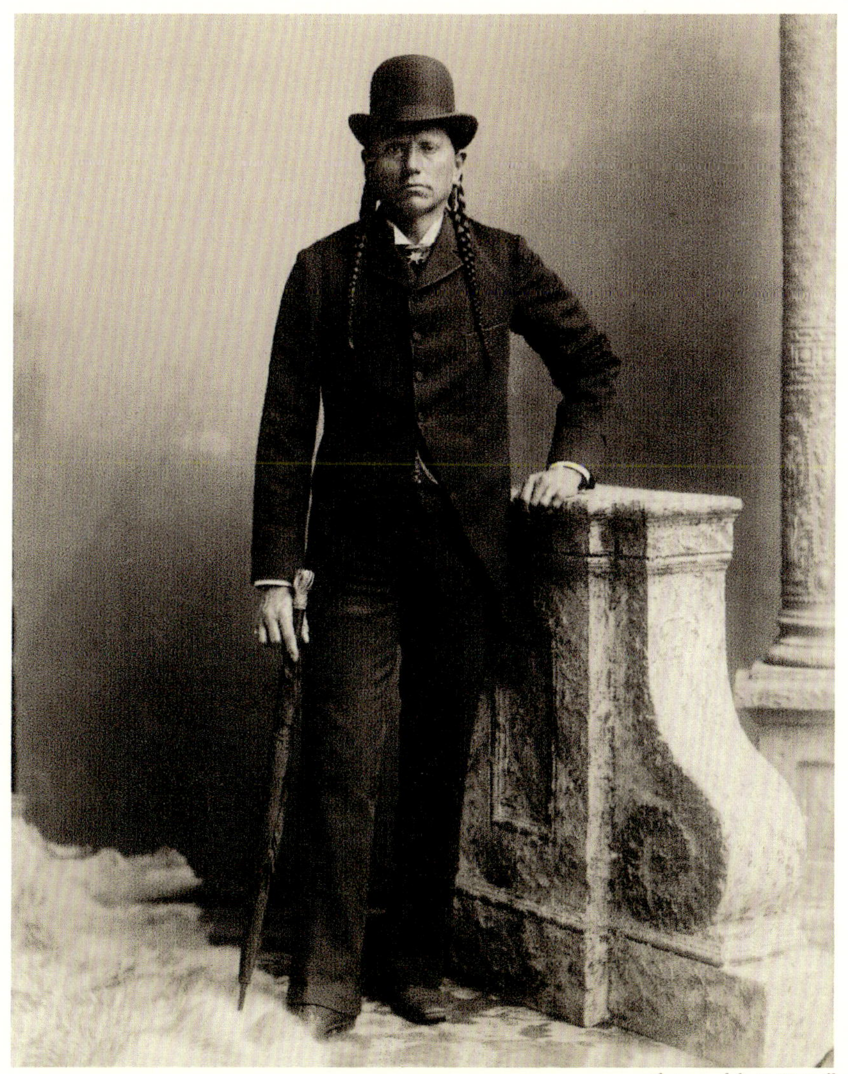

Photograph by C. M. Bell

Quanah Parker. Washington D.C., 1880s

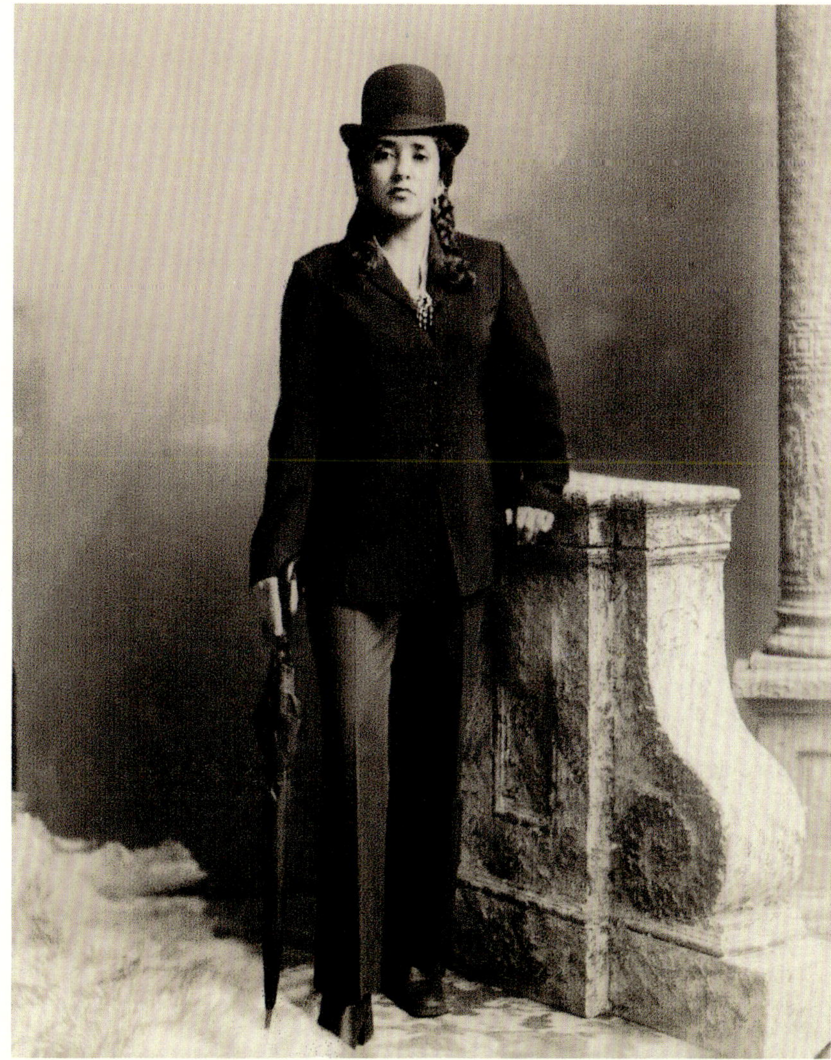

Photograph by A.P. Matthew

Annu Palakunnathu Matthew. Providence, R.I., 2000s

Annu Palakunnathu Matthew

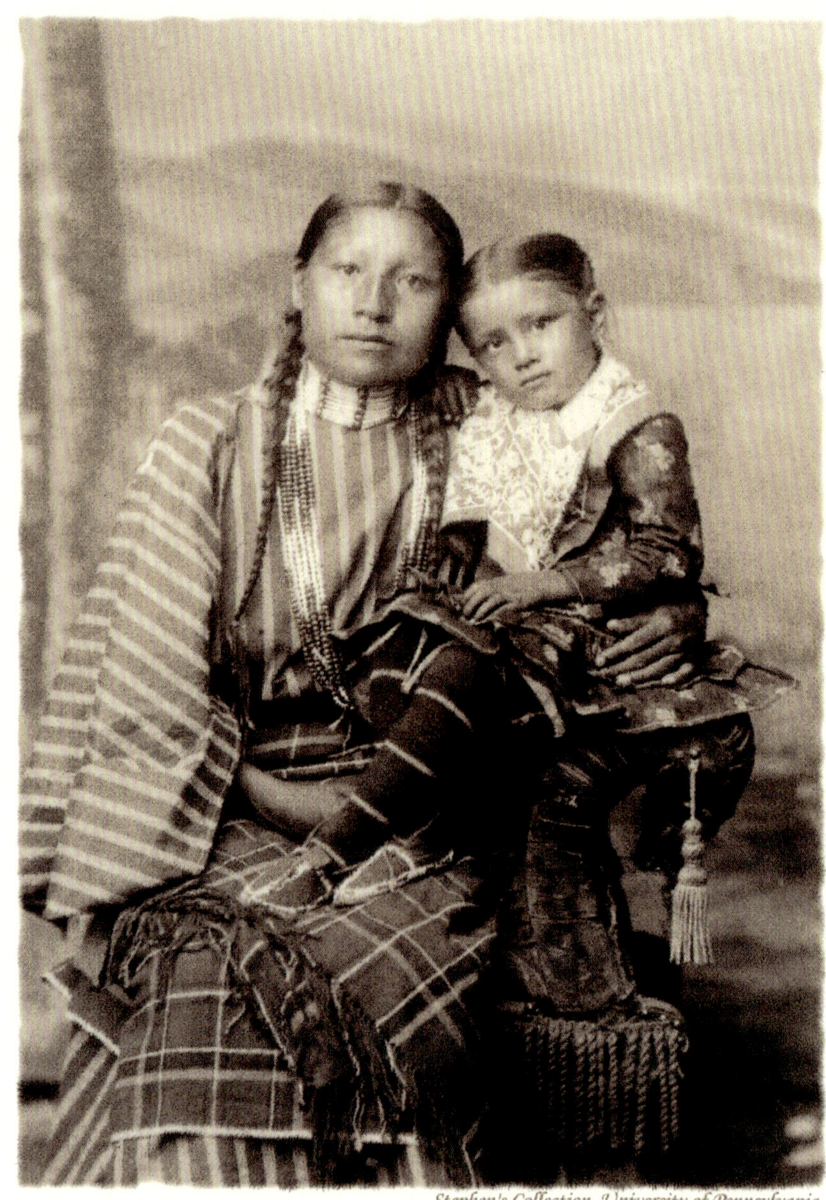

Stephen's Collection, University of Pennsylvania

TRADITIONAL AMERICAN INDIAN MOTHER AND CHILD

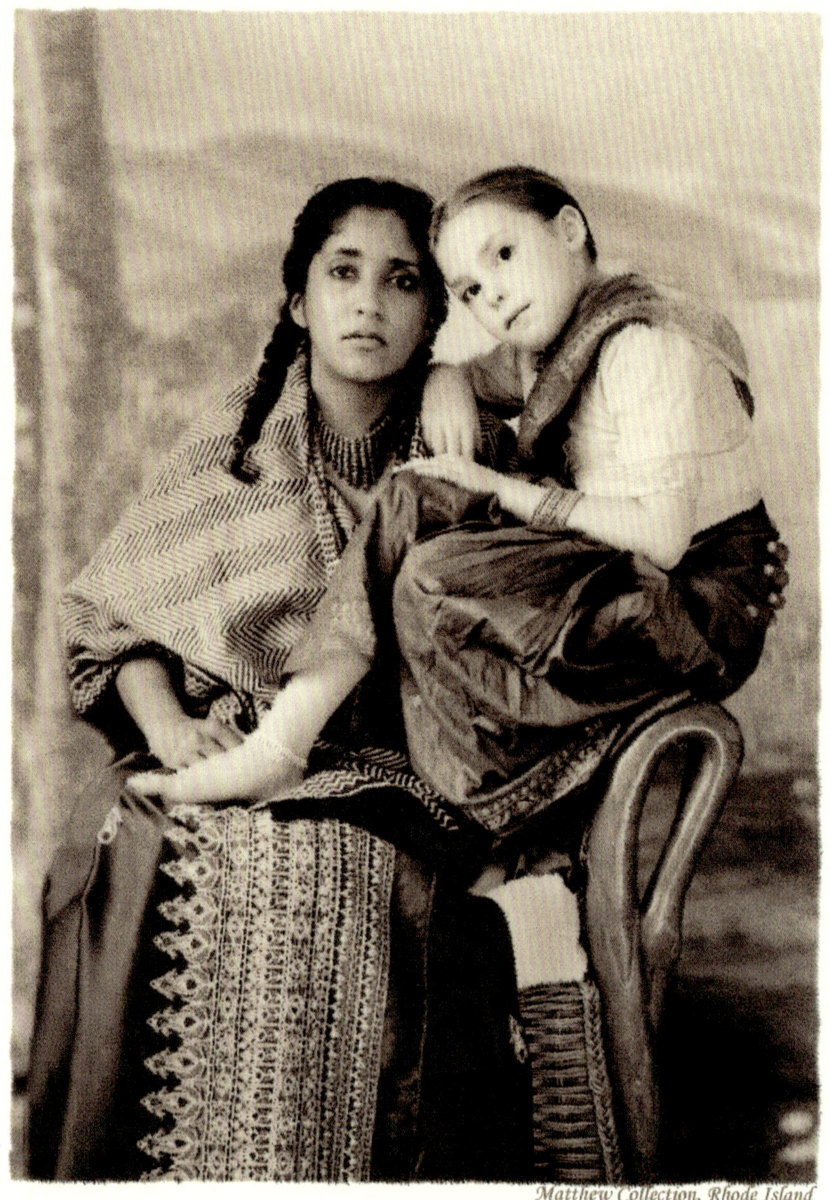

Matthew Collection, Rhode Island

CONTEMPORARY INDIAN AMERICAN MOTHER & STEPCHILD

Annu Palakunnathu Matthew

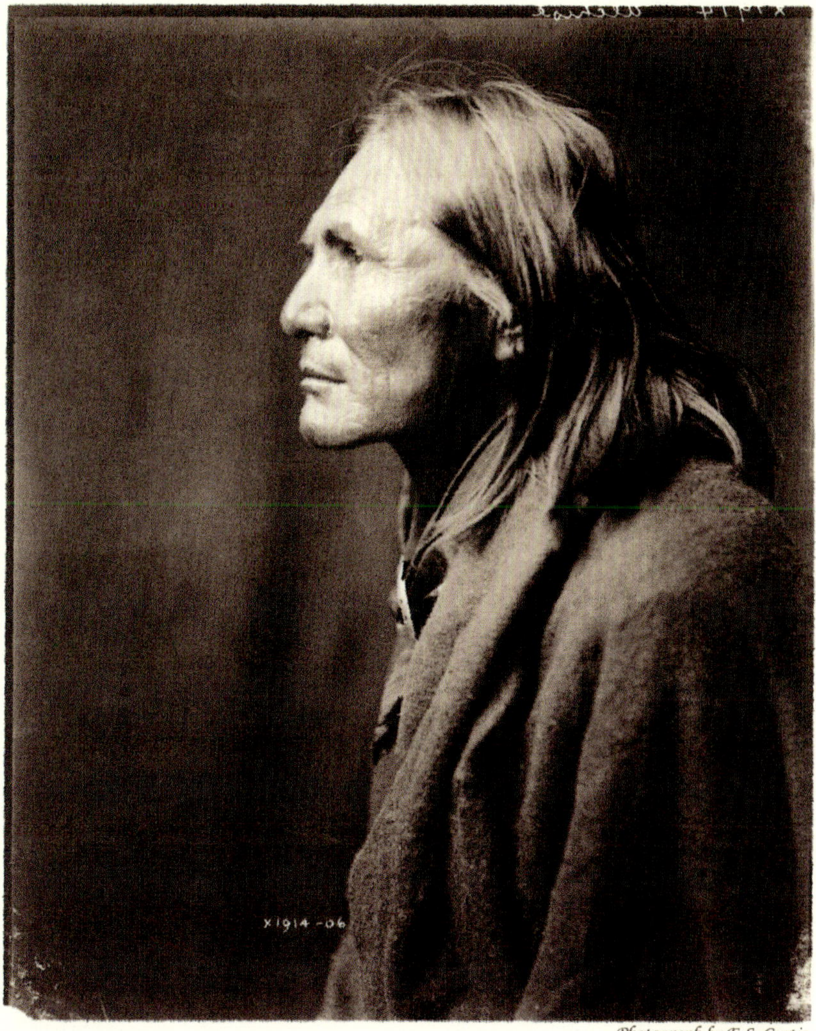

Photograph by E.S. Curtis

RED INDIAN

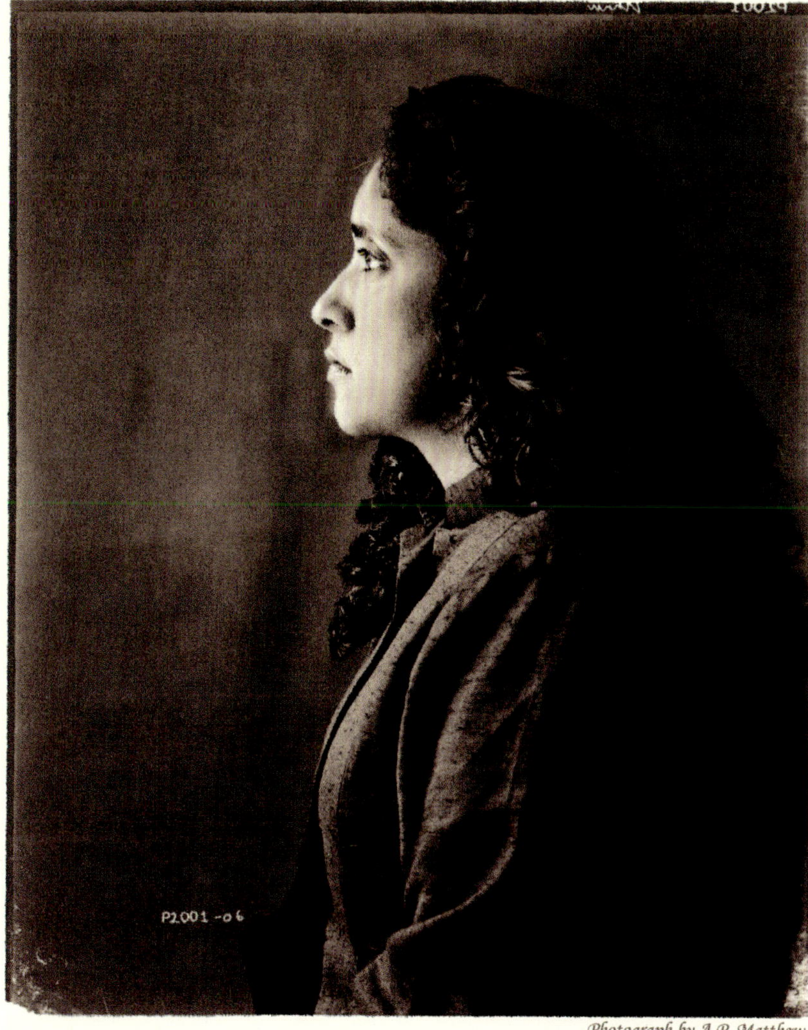

Photograph by A.P. Matthew

BROWN INDIAN

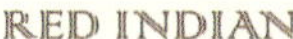

An Indian from India

As an immigrant, I am often questioned about where I am "really from." When I say that I am Indian, I often have to clarify that I am an Indian from India. It seems strange that all this confusion started because Christopher Columbus thought he had found the Indies and called the native people of America collectively as Indians.

In this portfolio, I look at the other "Indian." I play on my own "otherness," using photographs of Native Americans from the Nineteenth Century that perpetuated and reinforced stereotypes. I find similarities in how Nineteenth century photographers of Native Americans looked at what they called the primitive natives, similar to the colonial gaze of the Nineteenth century British photographers working in India. In every culture there is the "other."

The images highlight assimilation, use labels and make many assumptions. I pair these with self-portraits in clothes, poses and environments that mimic these "older" images. The clothes I wear are also "made up", similar to Edward Curtis' contrived posing and dressing up of some of his subjects into clothes of tribes other than their own. The final paired images challenge the viewers assumptions of then and now, us and them, exotic and local.

The prints are made to mimic the photogravure using contemporary digital technology and are presented in a portfolio case that copies Edward Curtis' portfolio.

Annu Palakunnathu Matthew

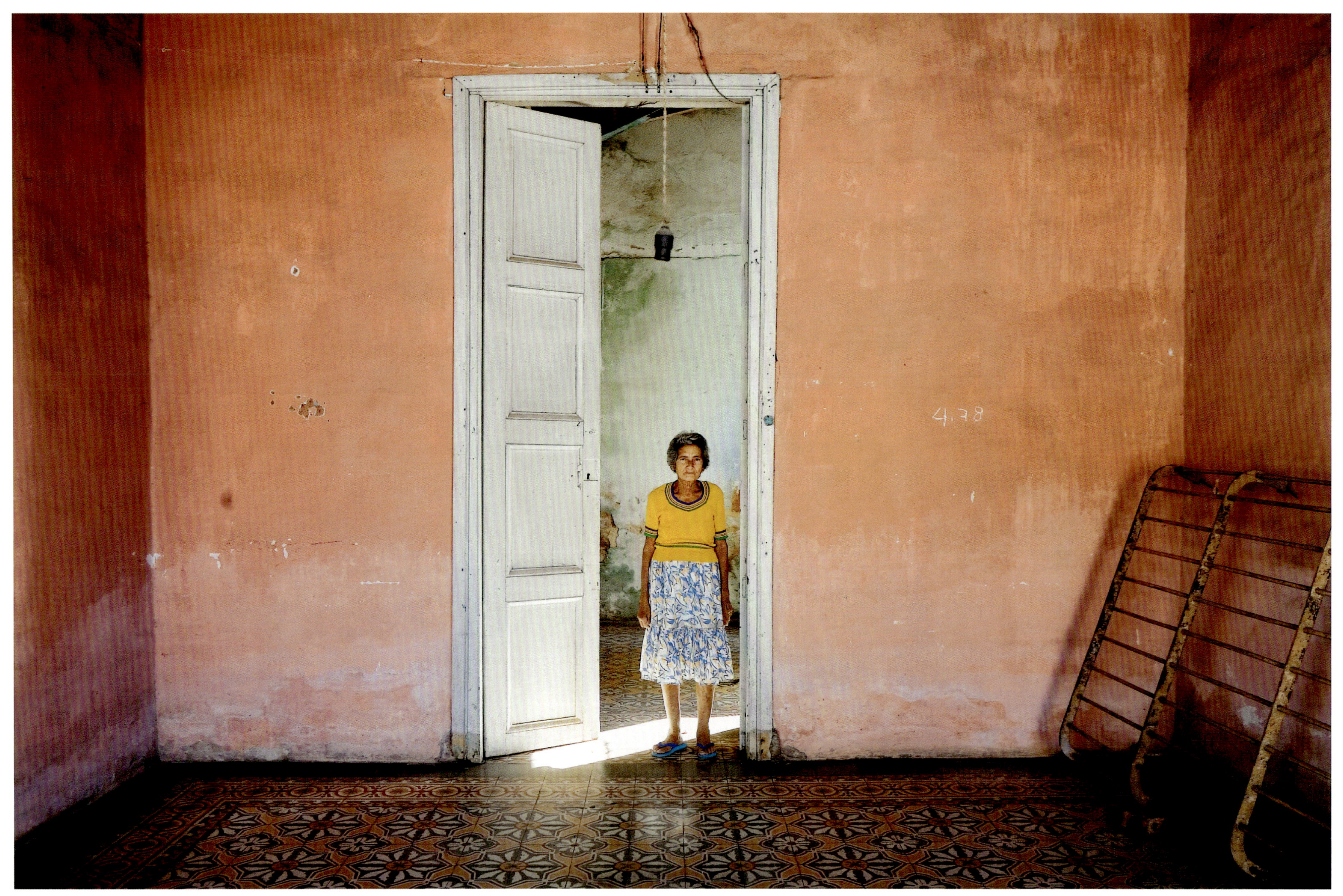

Jeffrey Milstein

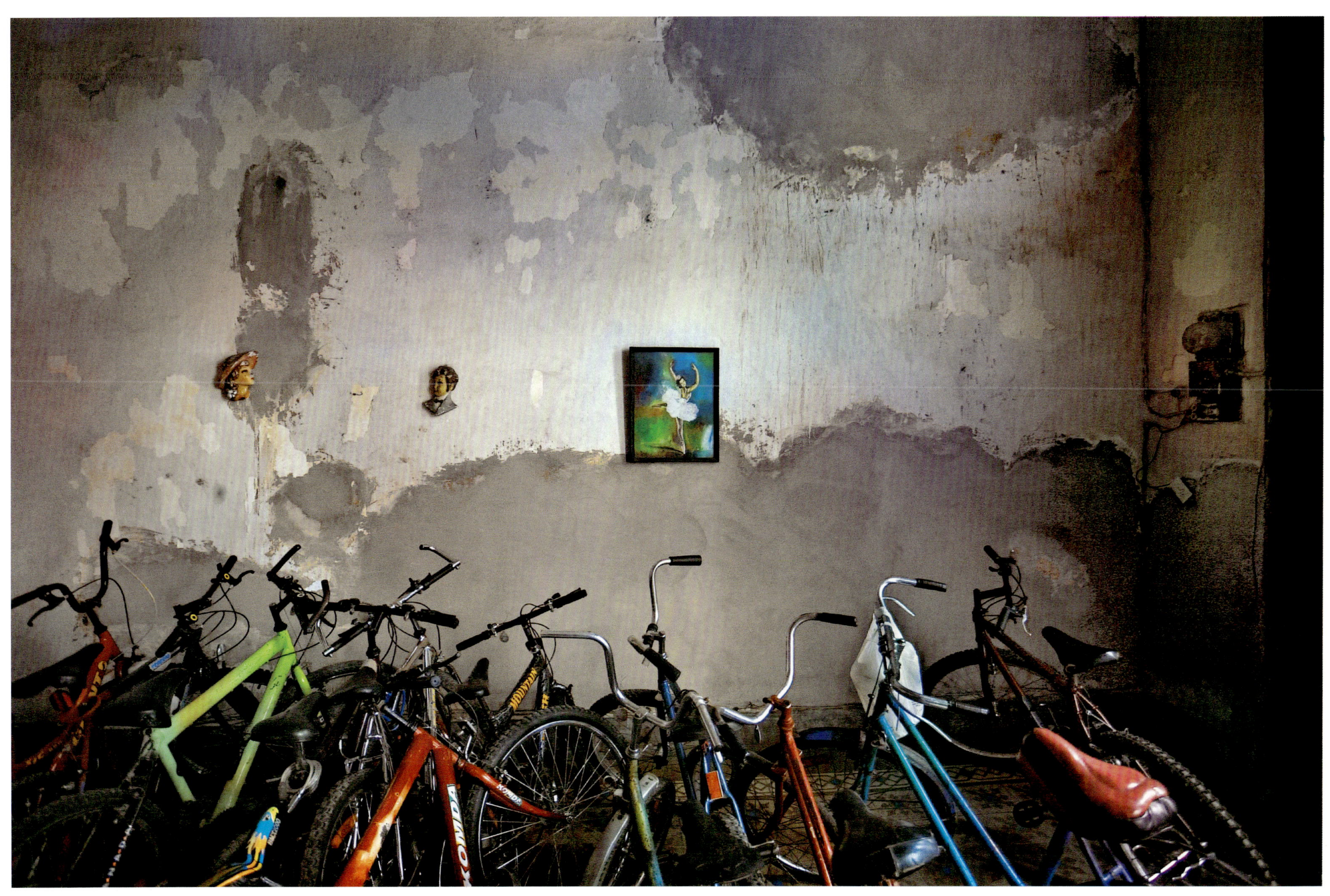

Jeffrey Milstein

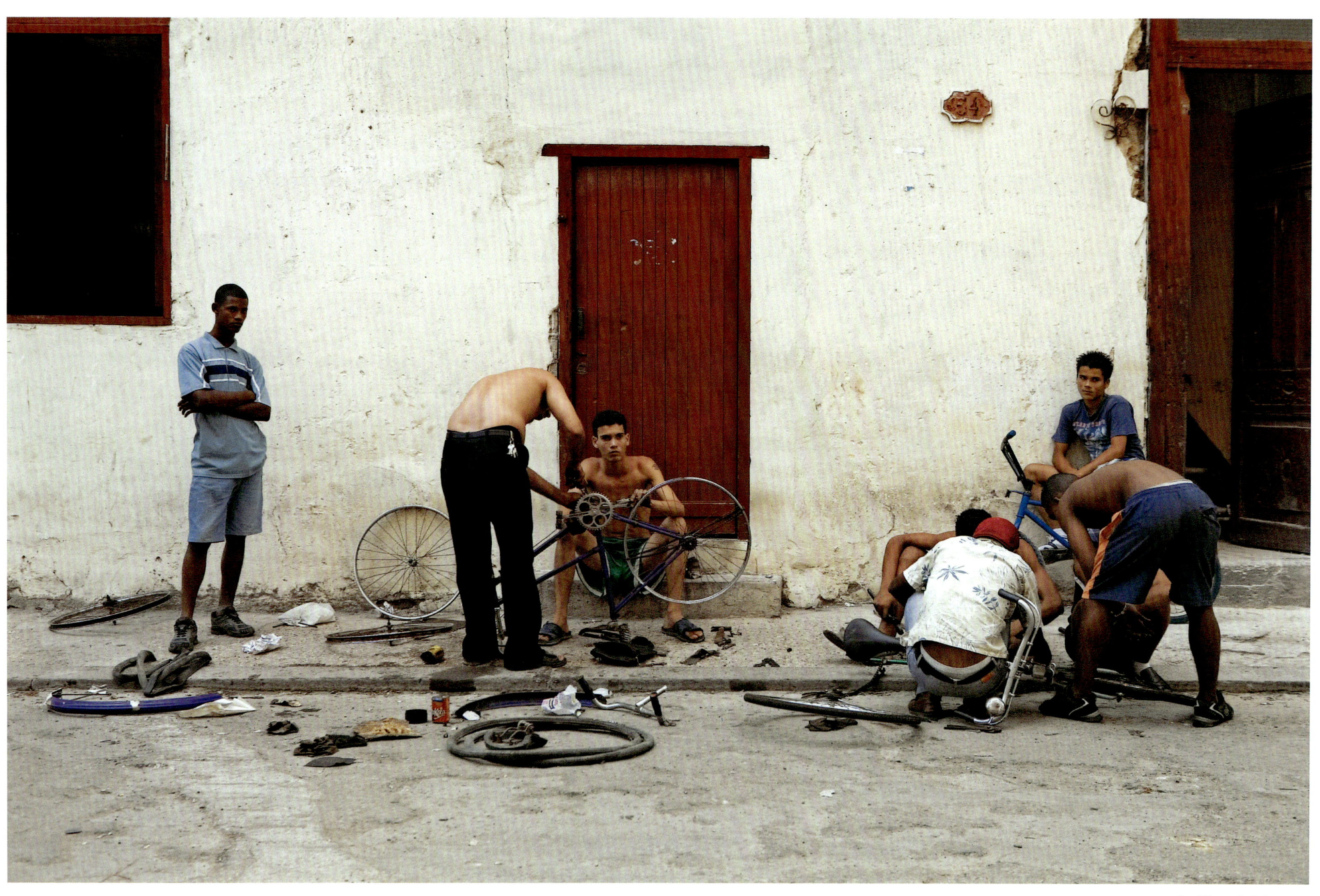

Jeffrey Milstein

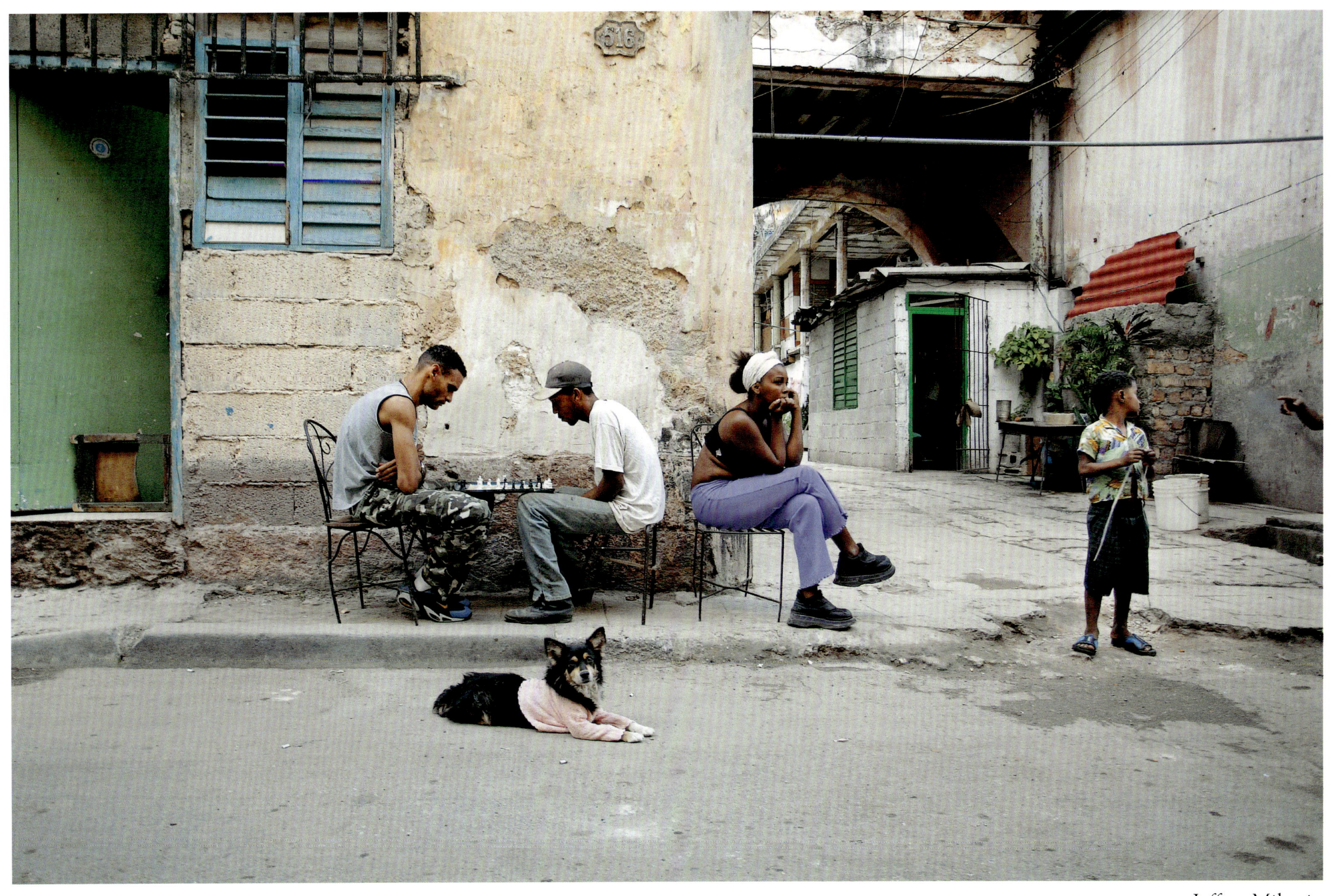

Jeffrey Milstein

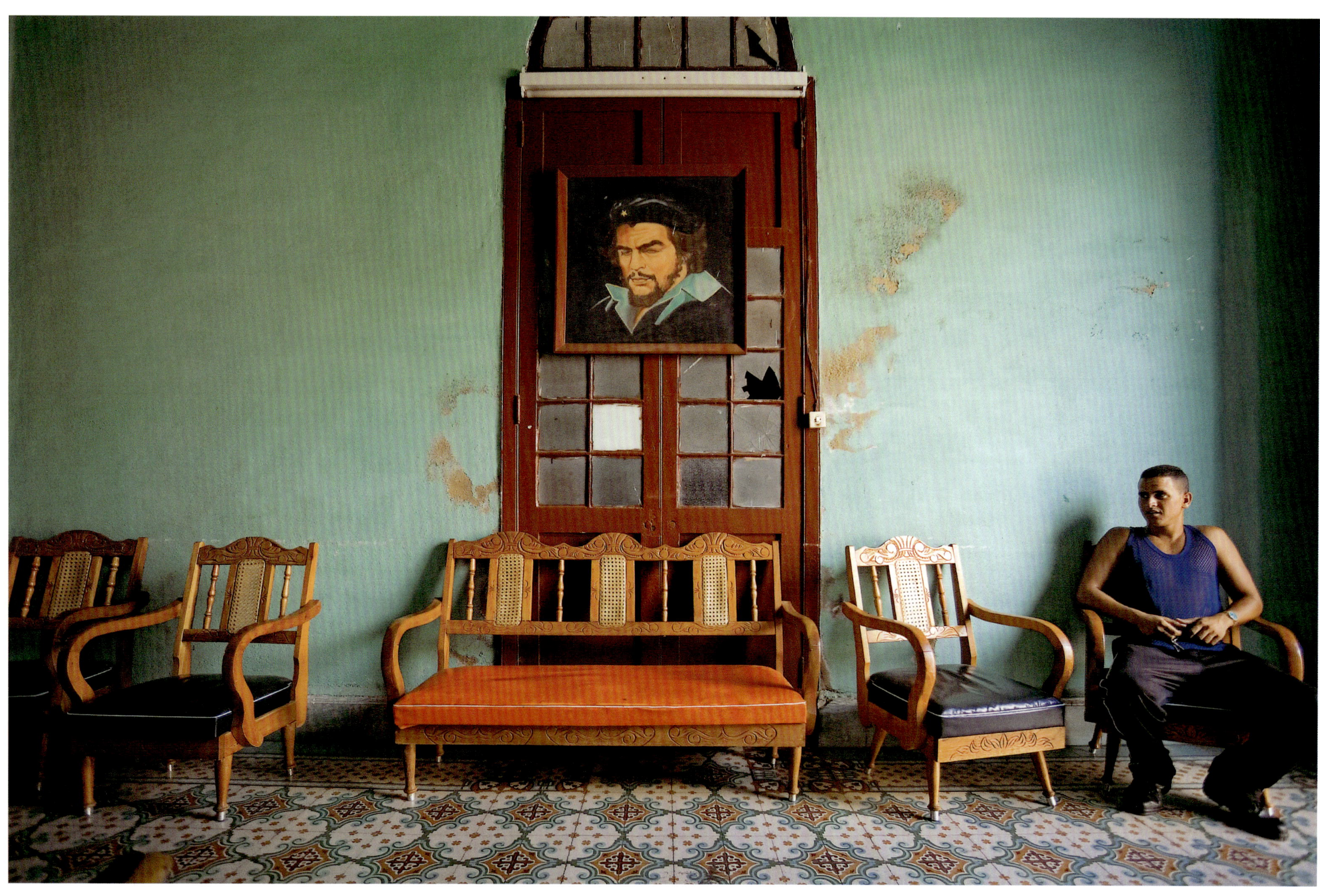

Jeffrey Milstein

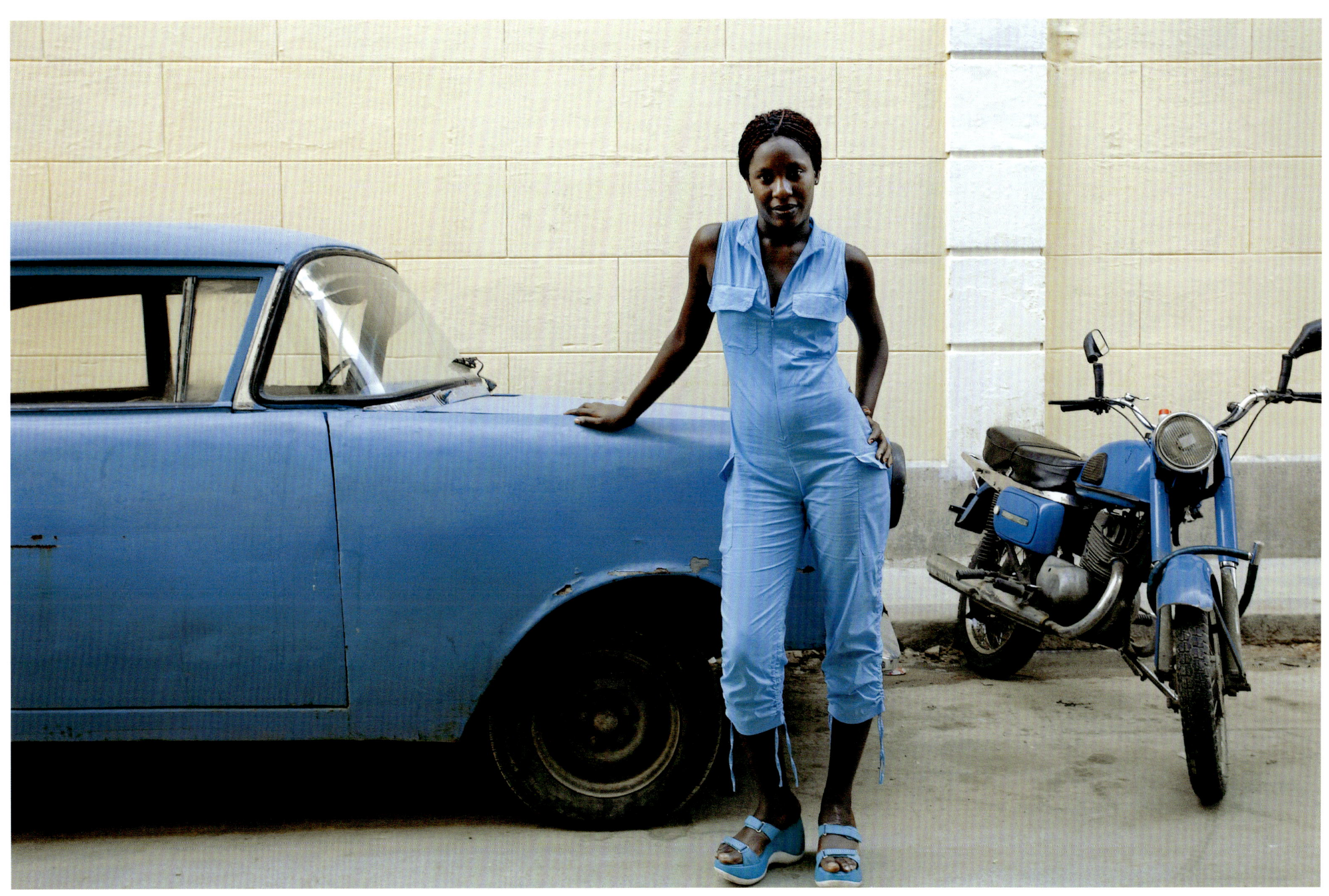

These photographs were taken during two trips to Cuba in 2004 where I visited Havana, Cienfuegos and Trinidad. Wandering alone with a hand held camera and an open mind, I found beauty and order in the chaos of the old streets. I met many warm and generous Cubans who allowed me to photograph them and invited me into their homes and places of work. I was taken with the richness and beauty of the faded architecture that was once so grand and opulent. My photography is influenced by my experience as a graphic designer and an architect. Color and strong graphic composition are important elements in my work.

Jeffrey Milstein

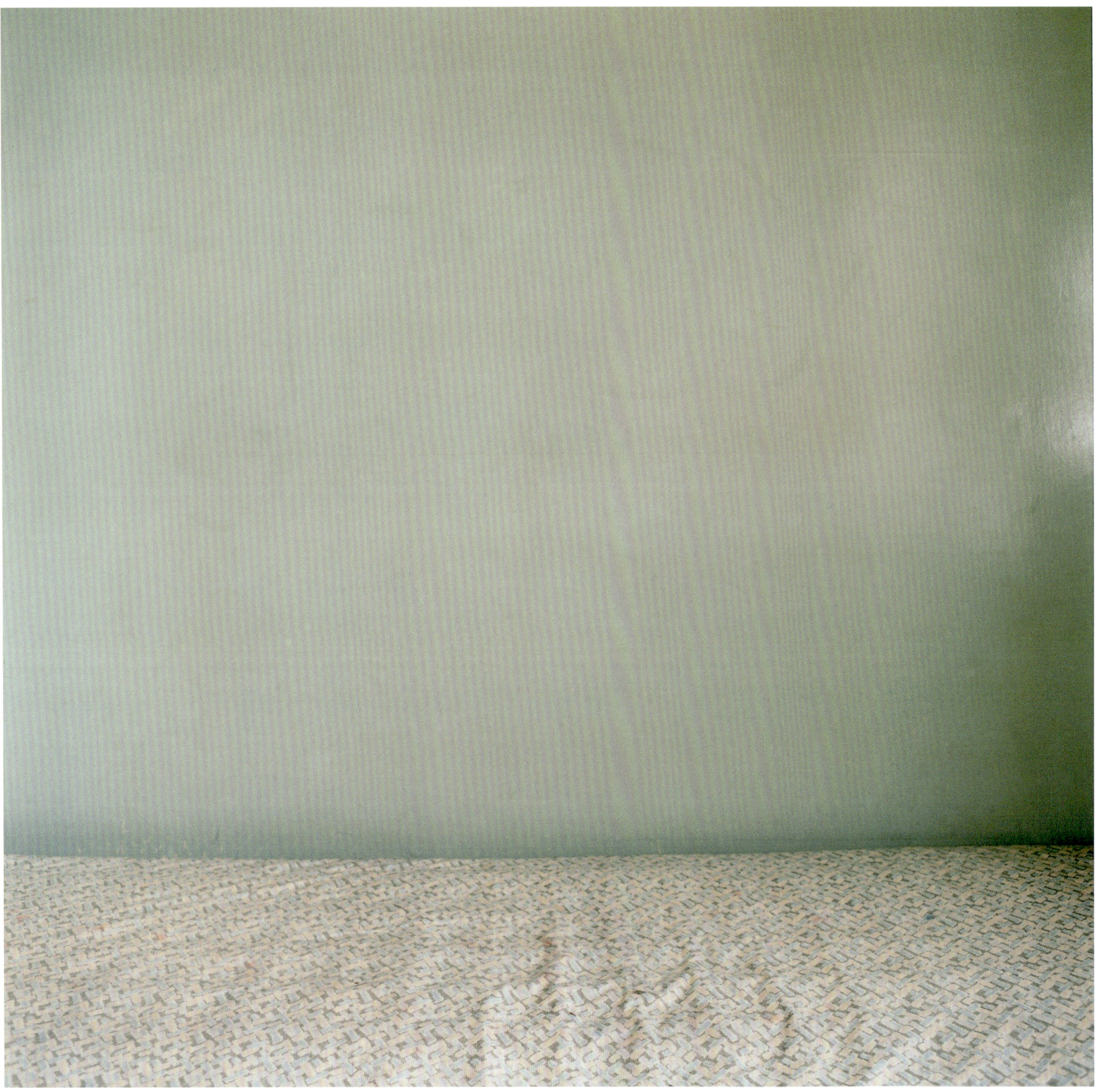

Martina Mullaney

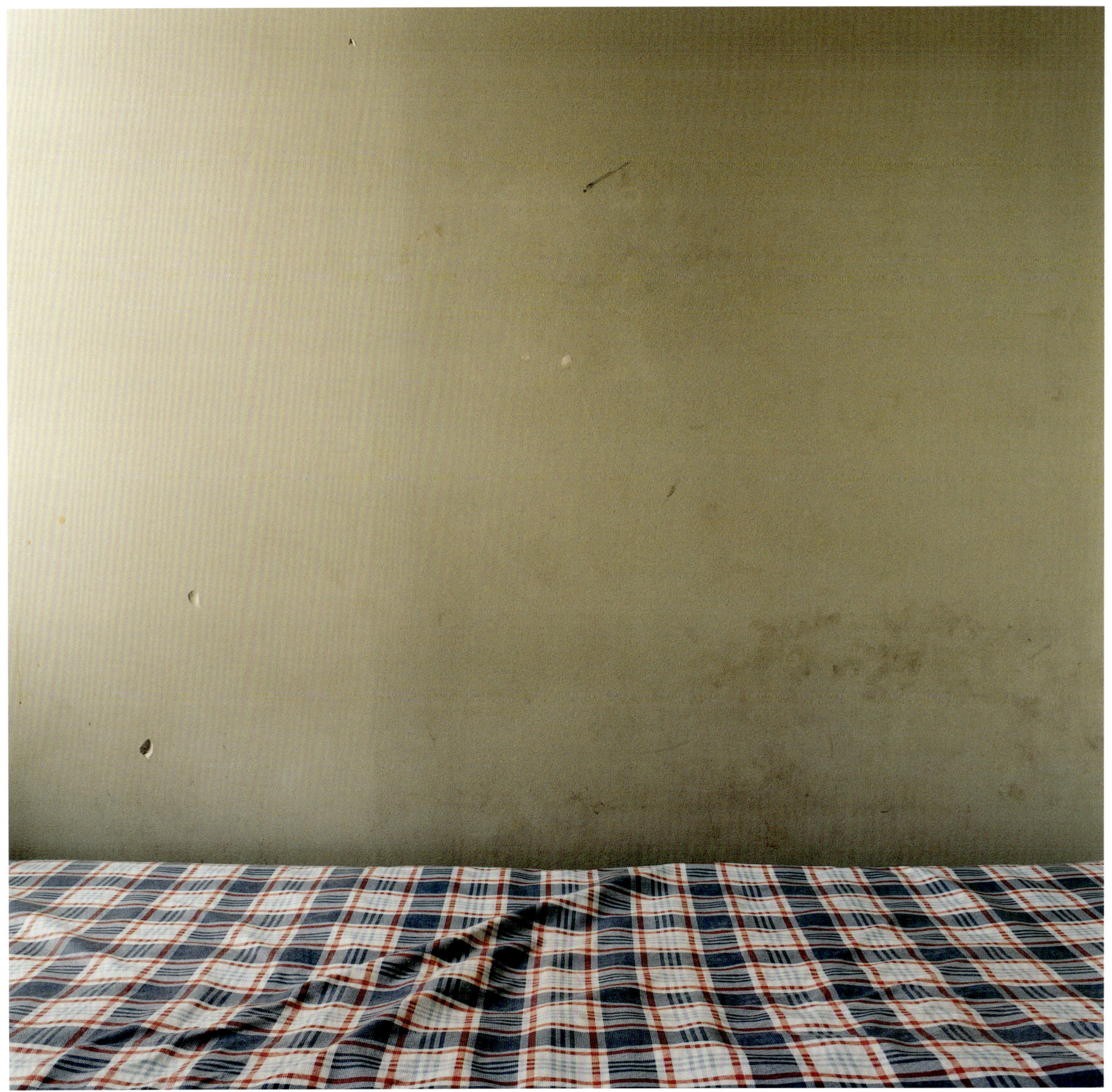

Martina Mullaney

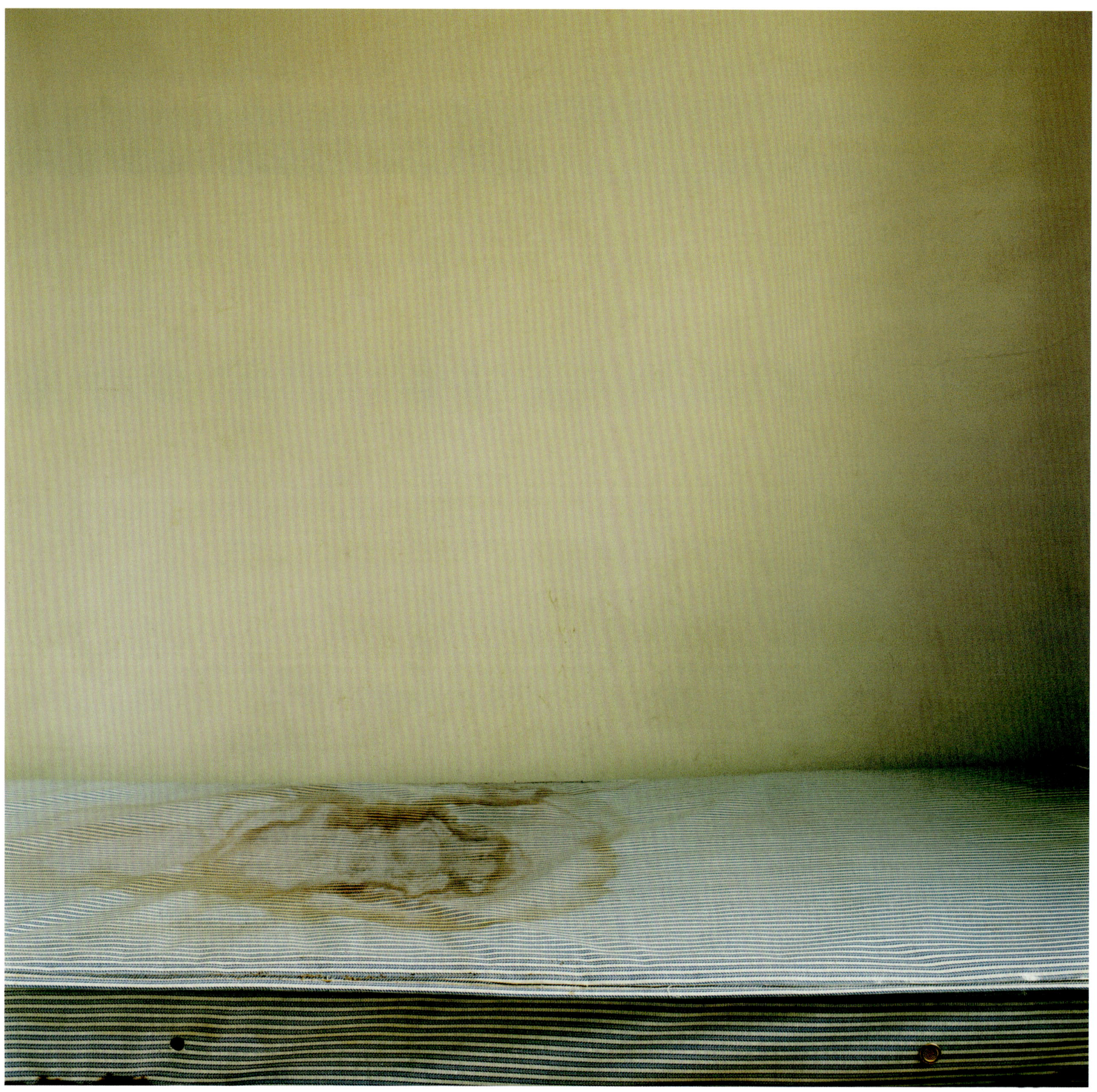

Martina Mullaney

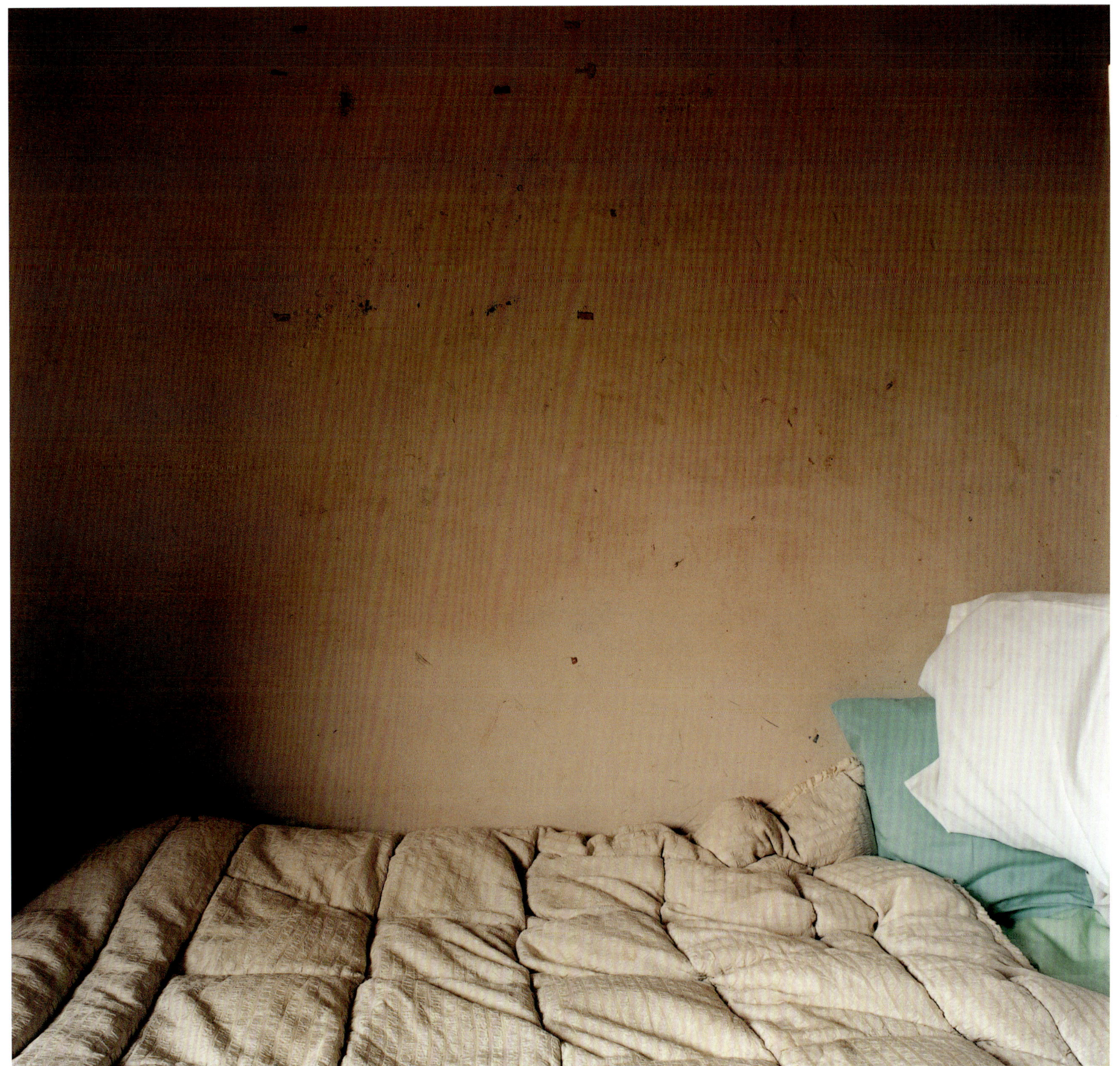

Martina Mullaney

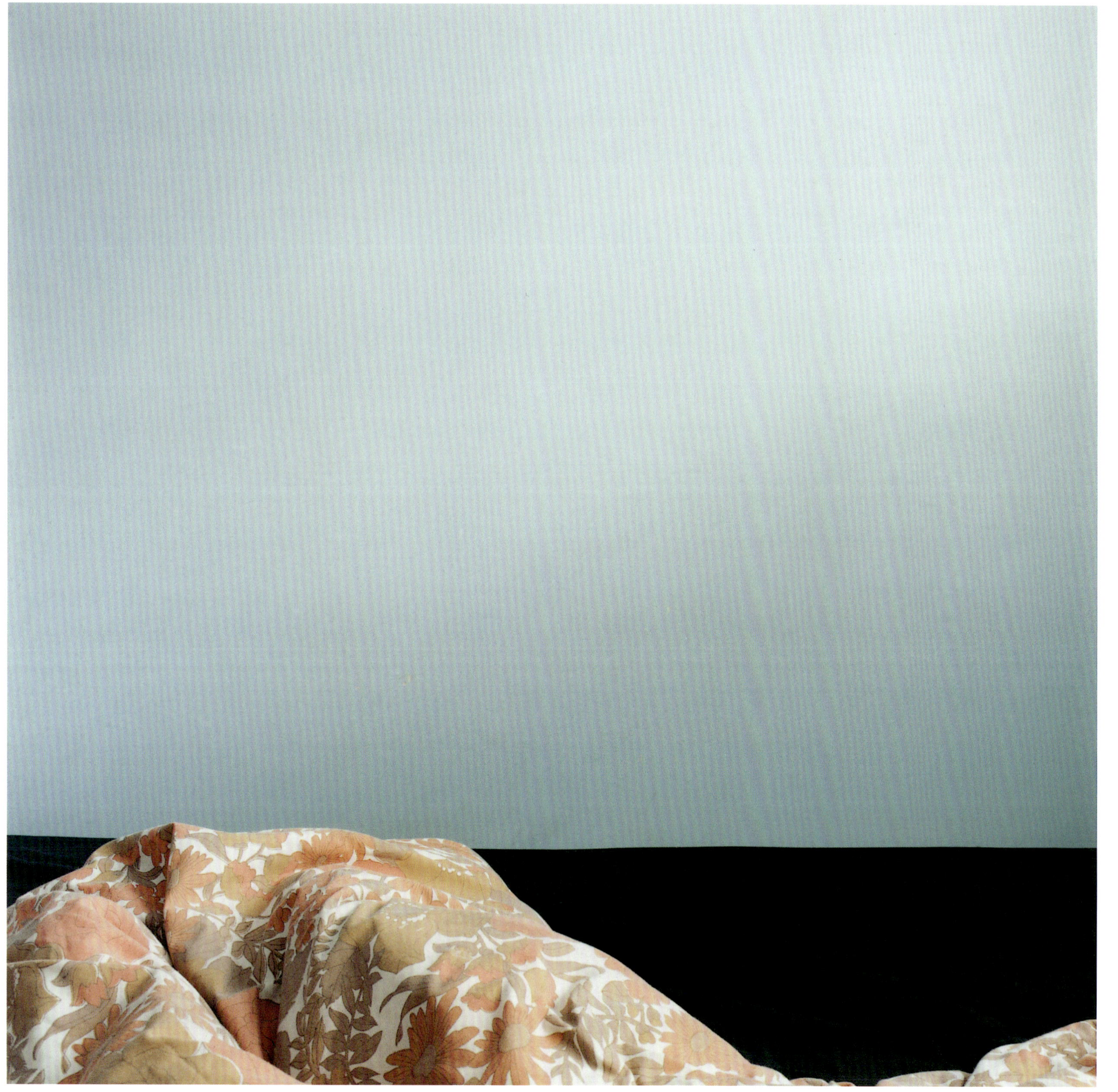

Martina Mullaney

Turn In

The following is an extract from a recent essay by Chris Townsend, I believe it describes my work much better than I am capable of.

......That concern with the everyday and the ordinary as a space where the constitution of power might be resisted or subverted - even unknowingly - is where Martina Mullaney's work enters the equation. Her photographs of beds, made in hostels for the homeless in Cardiff, South Wales, in 2002, seem to me to describe an example of Foucault's model of the heterotopia as a place of multiplicity and crossing. Through their traces of the human, they also suggest to me a model of dissent, of a kind of re-empowering of 'invisible', unacknowledged, individuals through their claim to an ownership of space. Mullaney's photographs are at once formally engaging - we might even say 'beautiful', though I don't want to venture into that particular aesthetic minefield - and repellent. They are "marked": by the stain (of human sweat and urine), by the trace (directly, of human excrement, or indirectly through crumpled sheets, sagging mattresses and pillows) of lives that are "excremental", abjected by and from a pathologically convulsed culture. We see those marks in a few pathetic belongings (a machine for making roll-up cigarettes, a box of tissues) or in signs of displacement: we see where the subject has been, never witness corporeality. Across each photograph there is a horizon between this abject space of the bed and a field of colour, however marked or disturbed with dents, scratches and crude writing. What each of Mullaney's images opens out here is a question of ownership of space. This is, I think, a central motif that permeates her work –

not just these hostel pictures, but her photographs of meals for one in solitary spaces and her collaborative projects with the homeless in different towns and cities. Few other artists are as capable of evoking that aching sense of separation which you feel on going back into a space you once lived in, that sense of encountering your own ghost, of walking on your own grave. (I'd suggest that Rachel Whiteread is another equally adept at this: both Mullaney and Whiteread are artists who, in significantly different ways, are bringing to attention the unseen histories of bounded, mundane objects and spaces and relating them to the historical discourses that frame us as subjects. Albeit that one is a sculptor and the other a photographer, both are concerned with indices, with archives if you like, of lives rendered invisible by the effects of power.) The bed has, of course, been a fit subject for art for centuries: whether in the crumpled pillows sketched by Dürer, perhaps on the eve of his marriage [3]; Delacroix's Un lit defait, or as both surface of representation and representation of itself, Robert Rauschenberg's Bed (1955). Mainly in the tradition of Delacroix, we have more recently come to see the bed as signifier of romantic passion coupled to aching loss. This is exemplified in Nan Goldin's seemingly endless recycling of bohemian tropes, but we see a similar project enacted in Tracey Emin's reworking of romanticism and expressionism through the materials of conceptual and installation art. [4] There is a separate tradition of depicting the deathbed (one also exploited by both Goldin and Felix Gonzalez-Torres), but for most modern and contemporary artists the bed is a place of erotic fulfillment and anxiety.......

Martina Mullaney

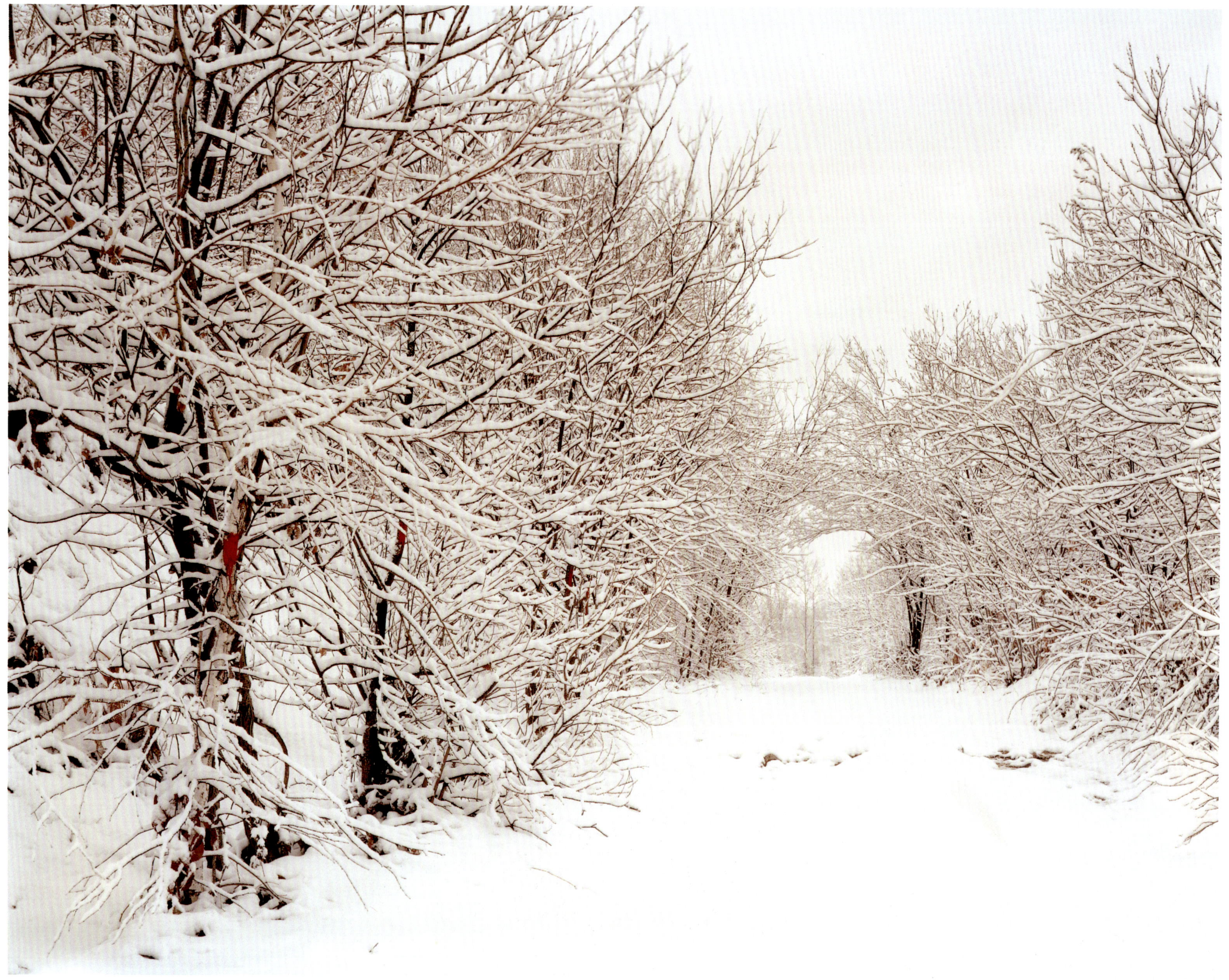

Simon Norfolk

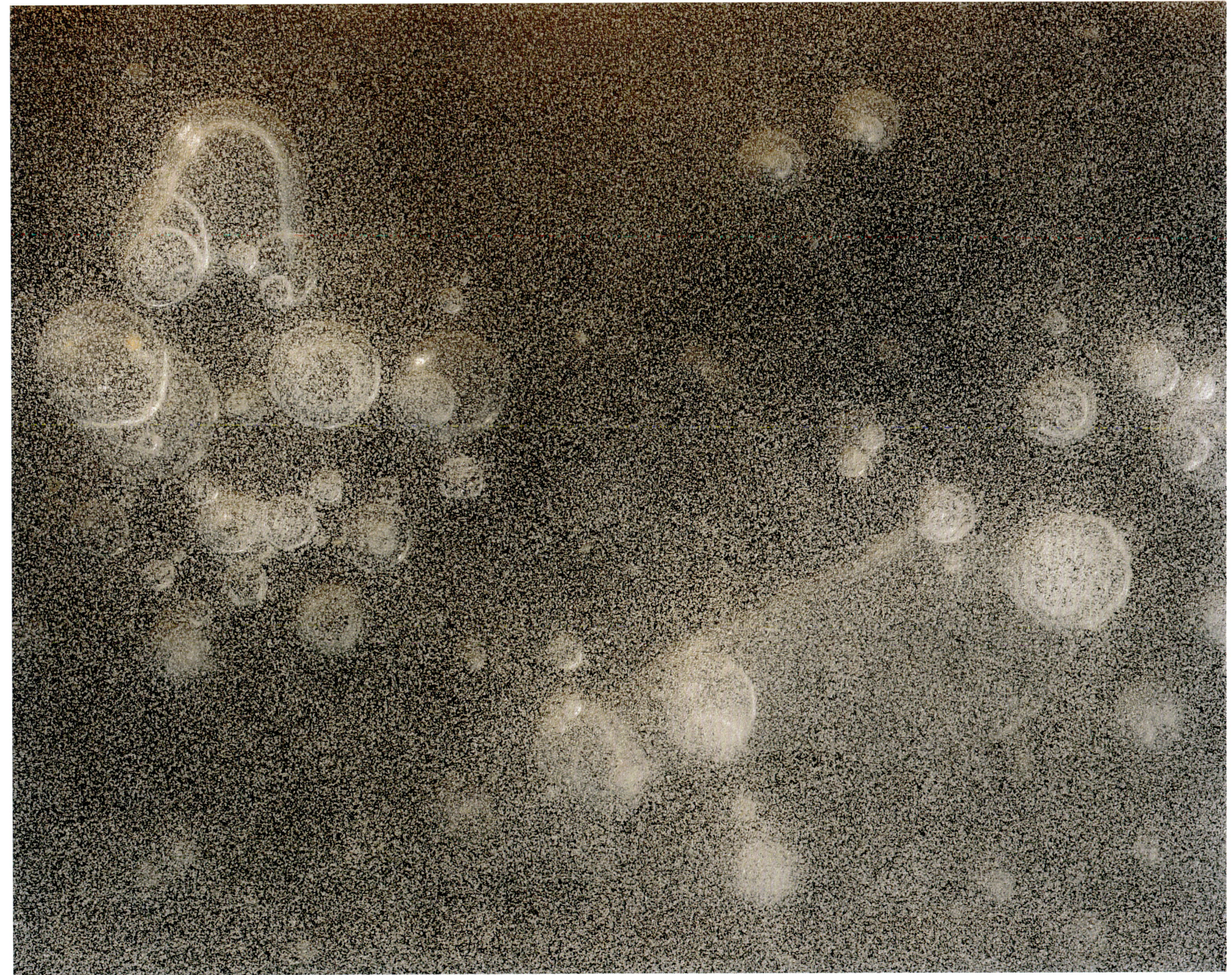

Simon Norfolk

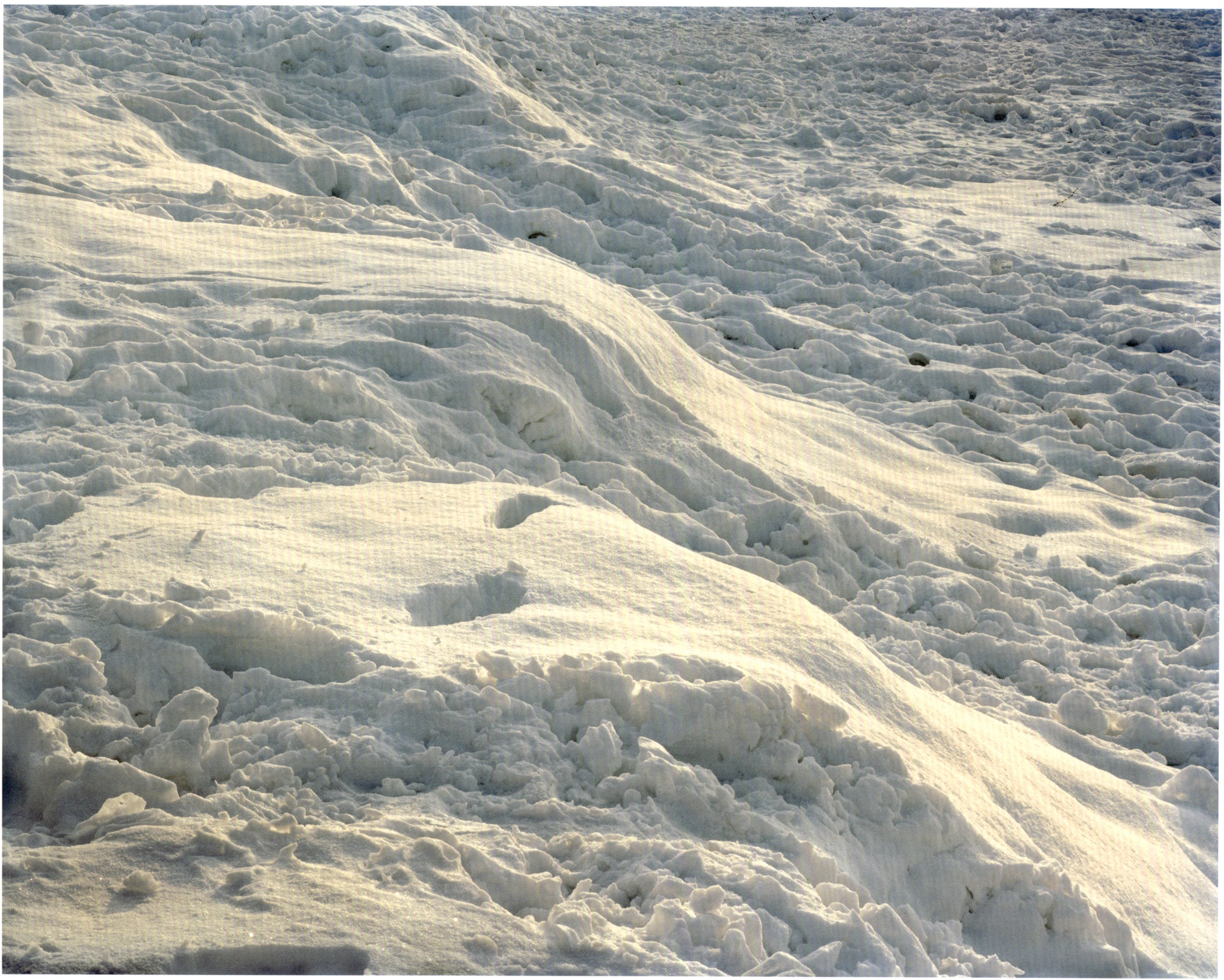

Simon Norfolk

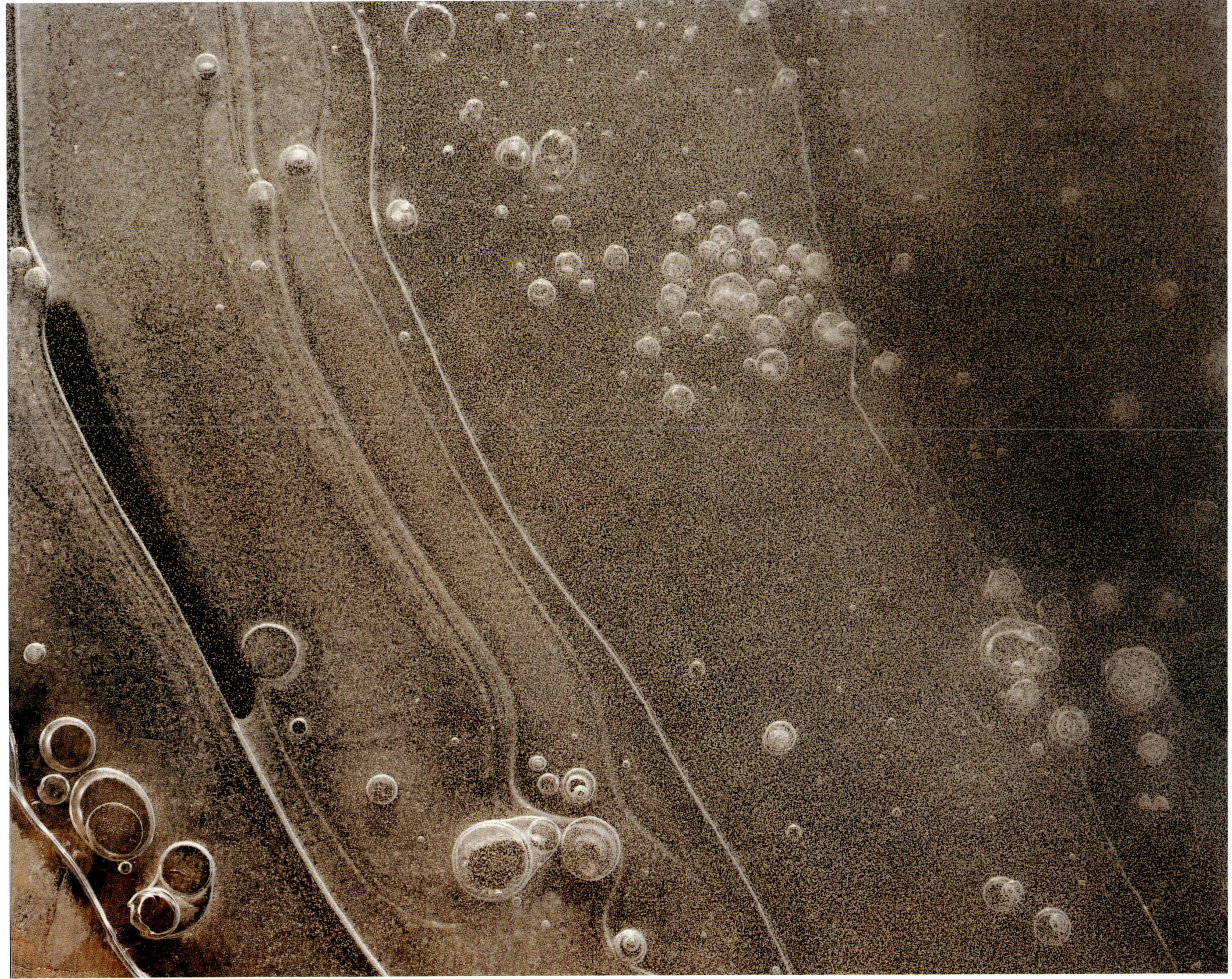

Simon Norfolk

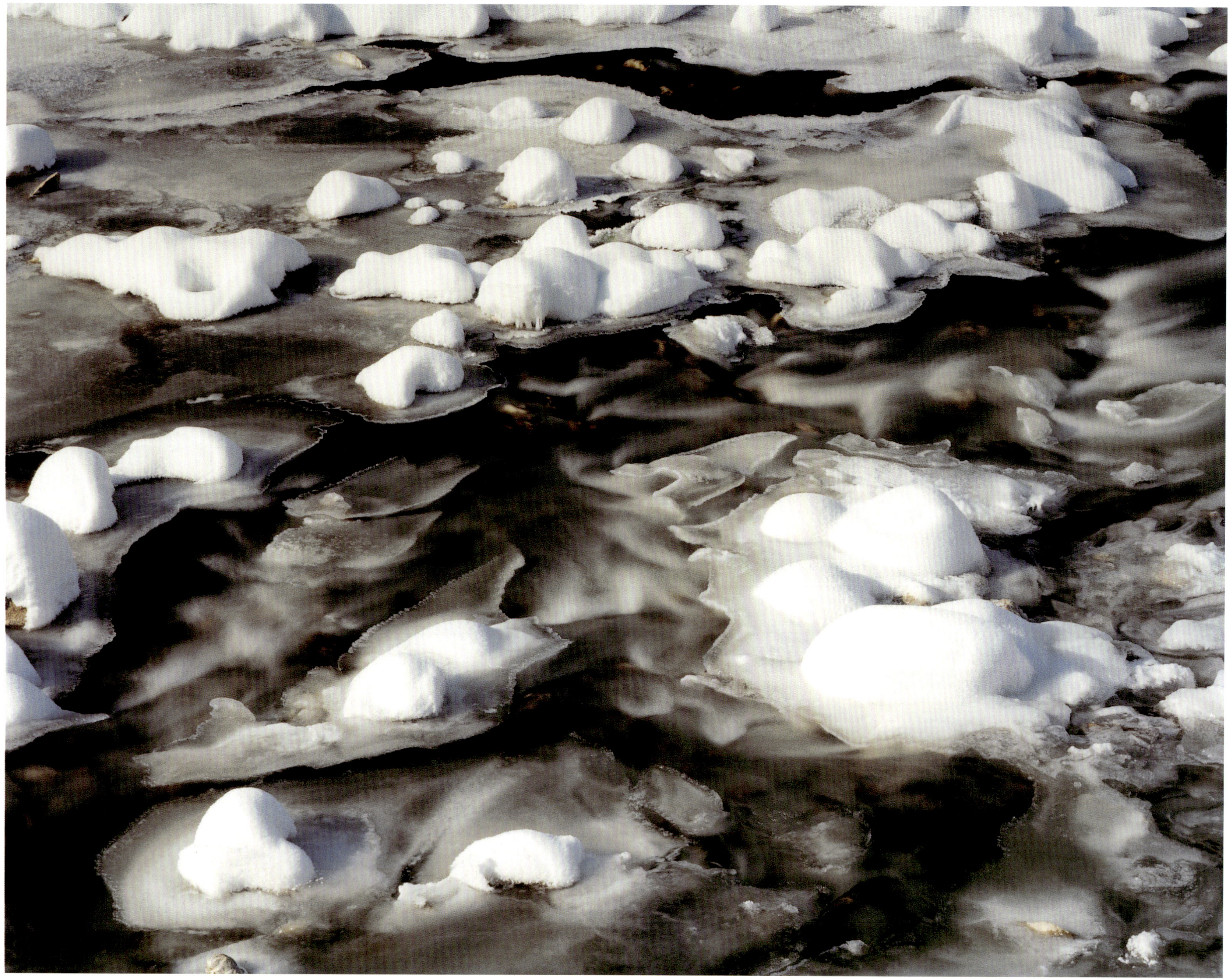

Simon Norfolk

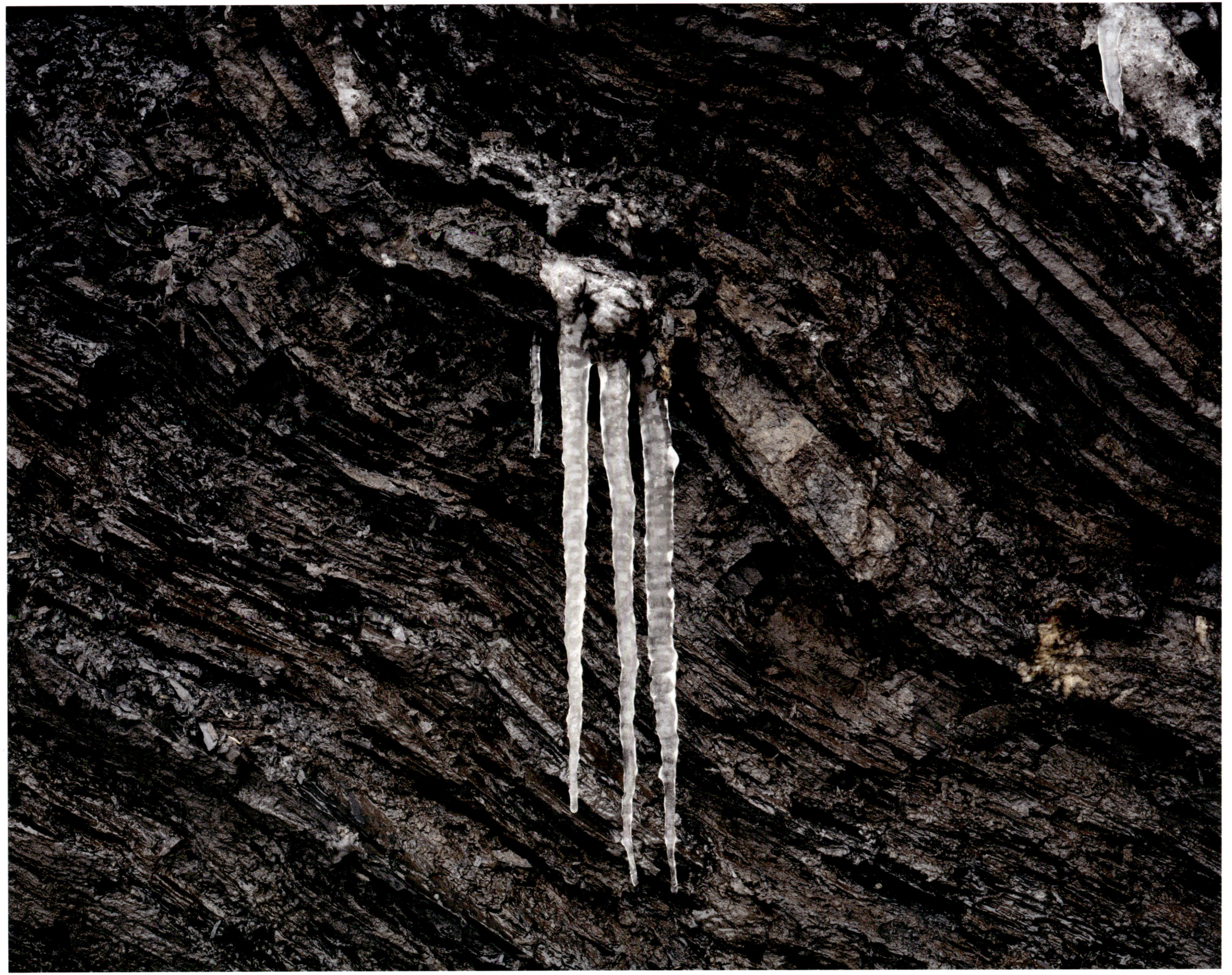

Simon Norfolk

Simon Norfolk

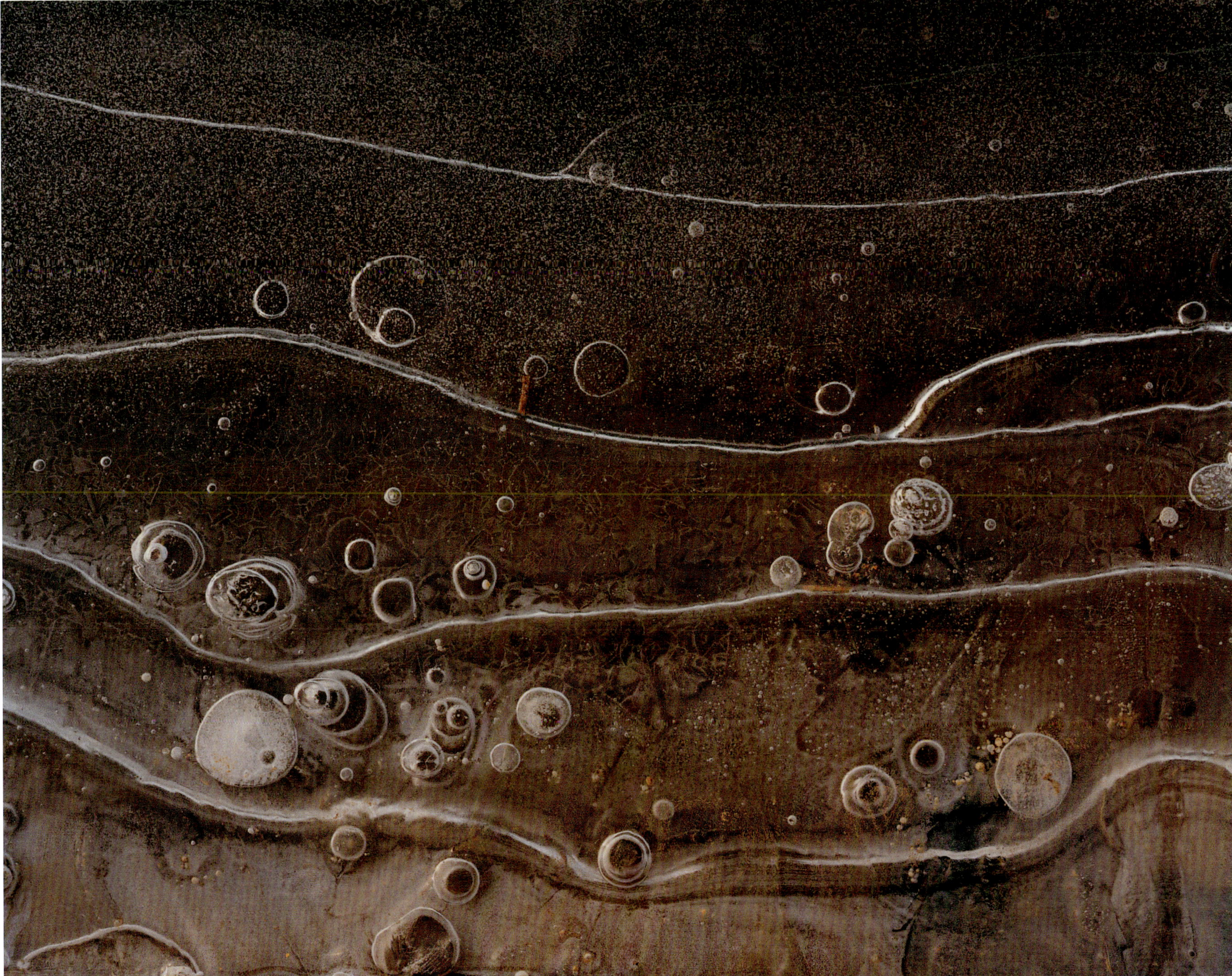

Bleed

In many ways the war in Bosnia in the early 1990's seemed pioneering. It raised to common currency the terms 'ethnic cleansing,' and 'humanitarian intervention;' it brought back to Europe a barbarism not seen since 1945; and it was said to be the first war fought right under the eyes of the world's media. But what was really exceptional was that it was the first conflict fought by killers who knew, before the hostilities had even finished, that a War Crimes Tribunal awaited them.

A peculiar consequence of this development can be found along a pot-holed track through unpeopled forests in the Serbian controlled part of Bosnia, at a place known as Crni Vrh. Here there is a large 'secondary' mass grave. This term is a technical one and needs explaining. 'Primary mass graves' are tragically common, not just in Bosnia. When villages were captured or there was a quick shift in the frontlines, prisoners were taken. These captives were often killed and buried nearby.

But when the Serb murderers realised, as the war ground on, that they might be punished for these crimes, they set about hiding the evidence. They secretly returned, often at night, to places cleared of any possible witnesses. Using digging machinery and lorries, the primary graves were excavated and the remains – mangled, decomposing bodies and clothing – were taken away and re-buried in remote and secret locations. These are 'secondary mass graves;' they are unique to the war in Bosnia, and the lush valleys and wooded hills northwest of Srebrenica are full of them. Crni Vrh is the largest secondary mass grave to be discovered to date.

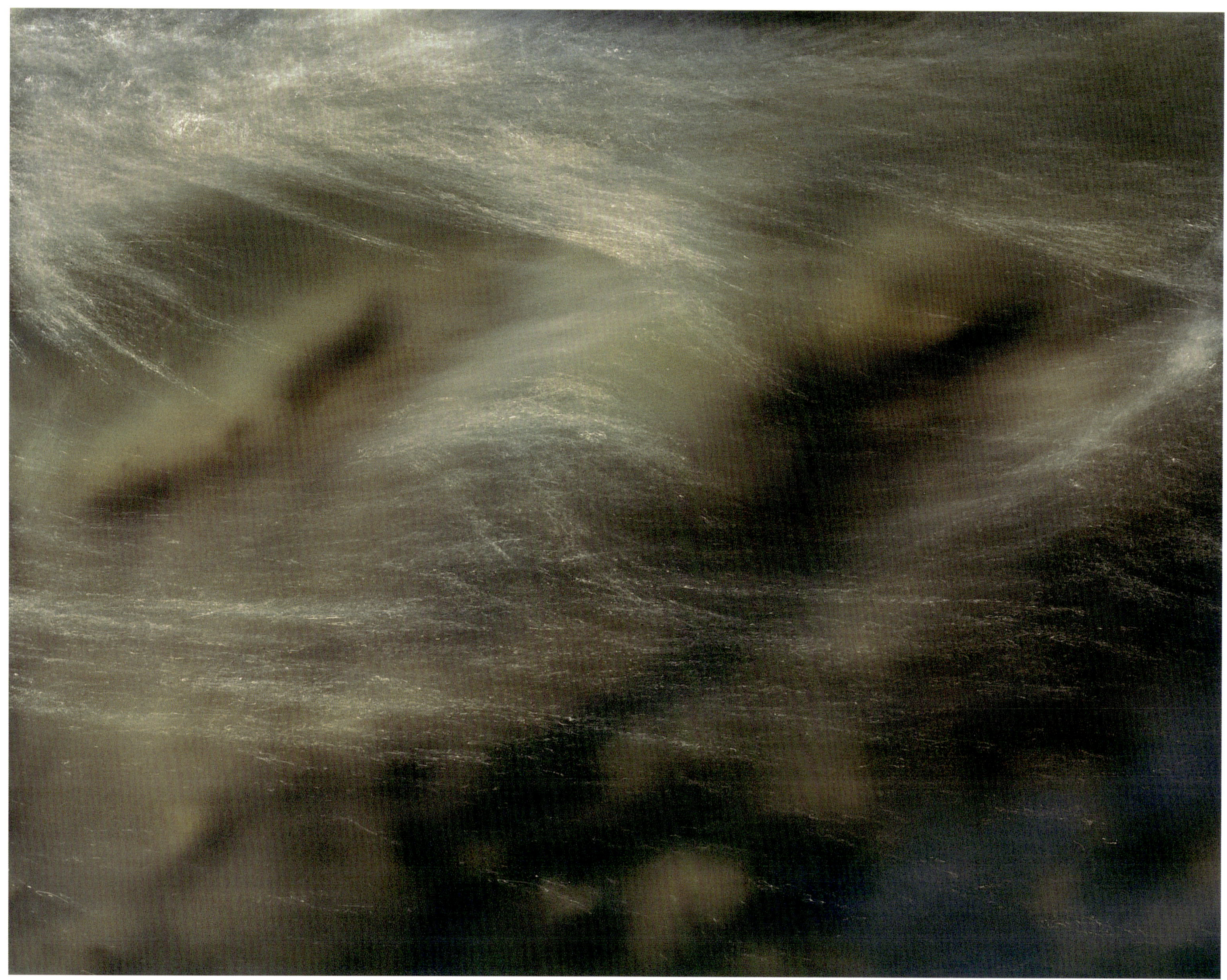

The rivers and streams around Srebrenica flow down into the bright green waters of the River Drina which, near Zvornik, is dammed by a large hydro-electric plant. There is a common rumour, that is at least plausible, that in July of 1995 when the killings after the fall of Srebrenica were at full flow, the Director of the dam phoned the Bosnian Serb Army to request that no more corpses be thrown into the rivers. He complained that the bodies were blocking the intake pipes to the dam.

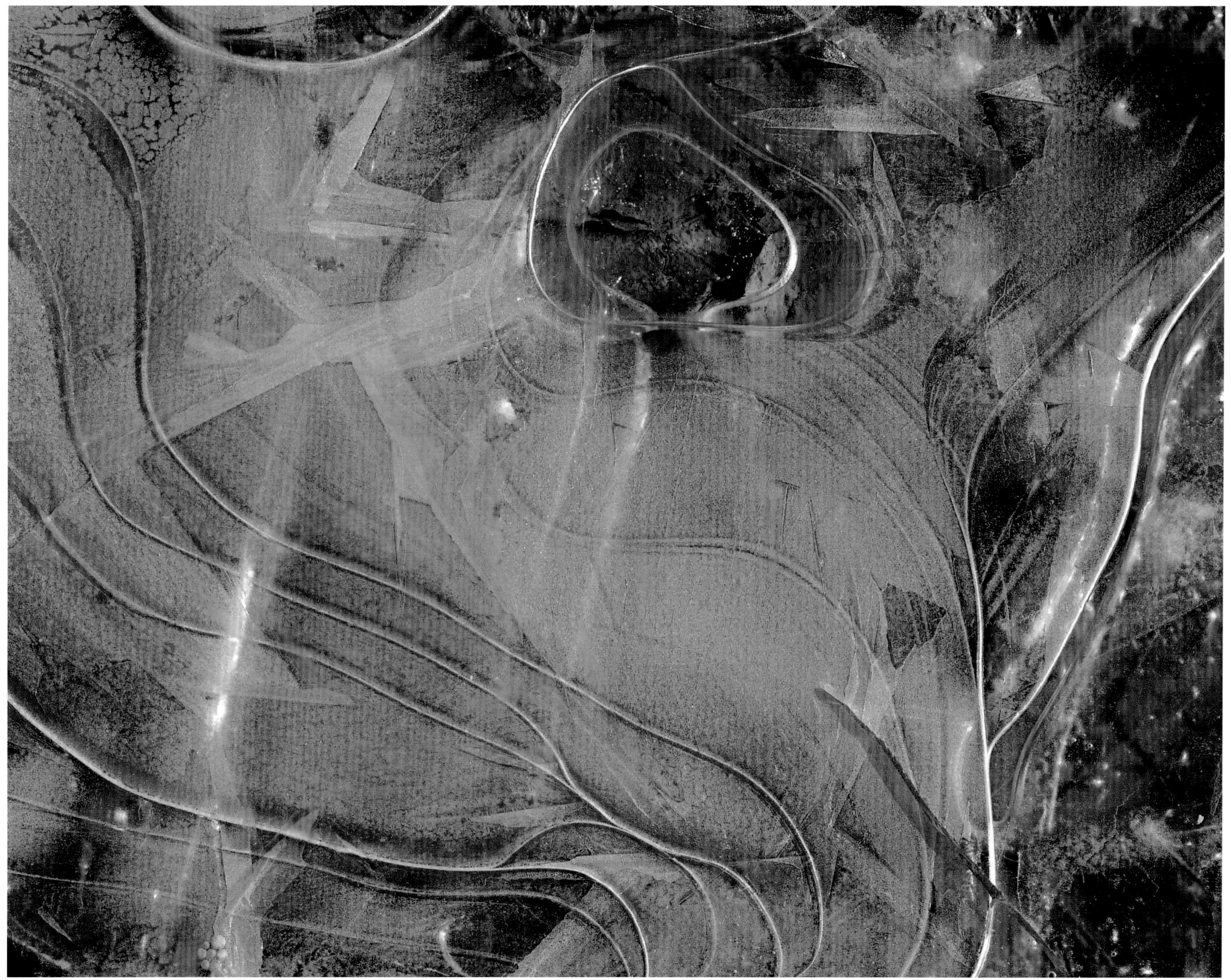

Simon Norfolk

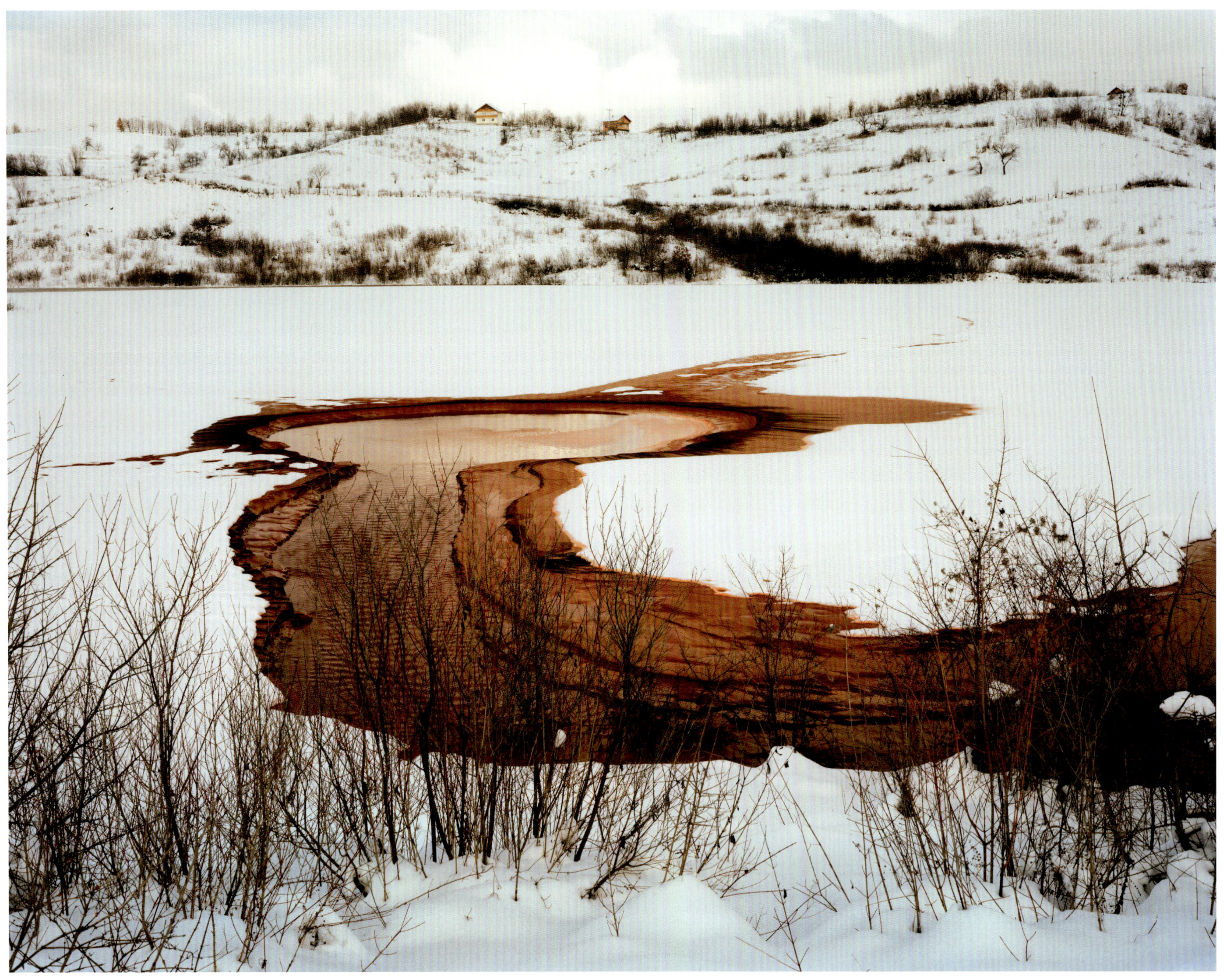

I have little to add to the much-documented discussion about what happened at Srebrenica: how it could have been prevented, who was to blame and what the massacres mean for the rest of us. But I am intensely interested in the devious, cold-blooded ideas of men who went to extraordinary lengths to try to hide the evidence of their appalling crimes. They thought that by intimidation or subterfuge their sly, dirty secrets could be preserved, held, trapped.

Simon Norfolk

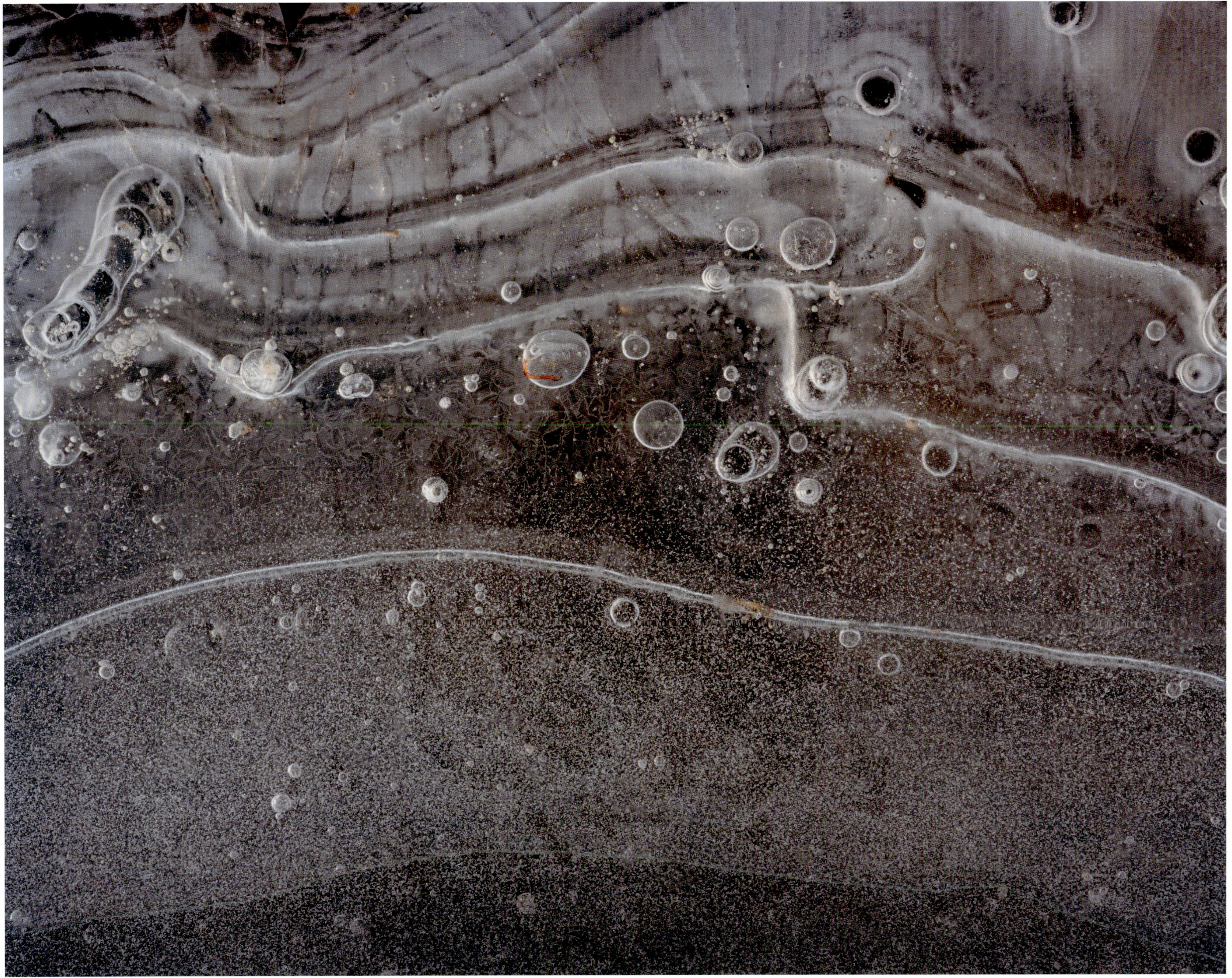

Simon Norfolk

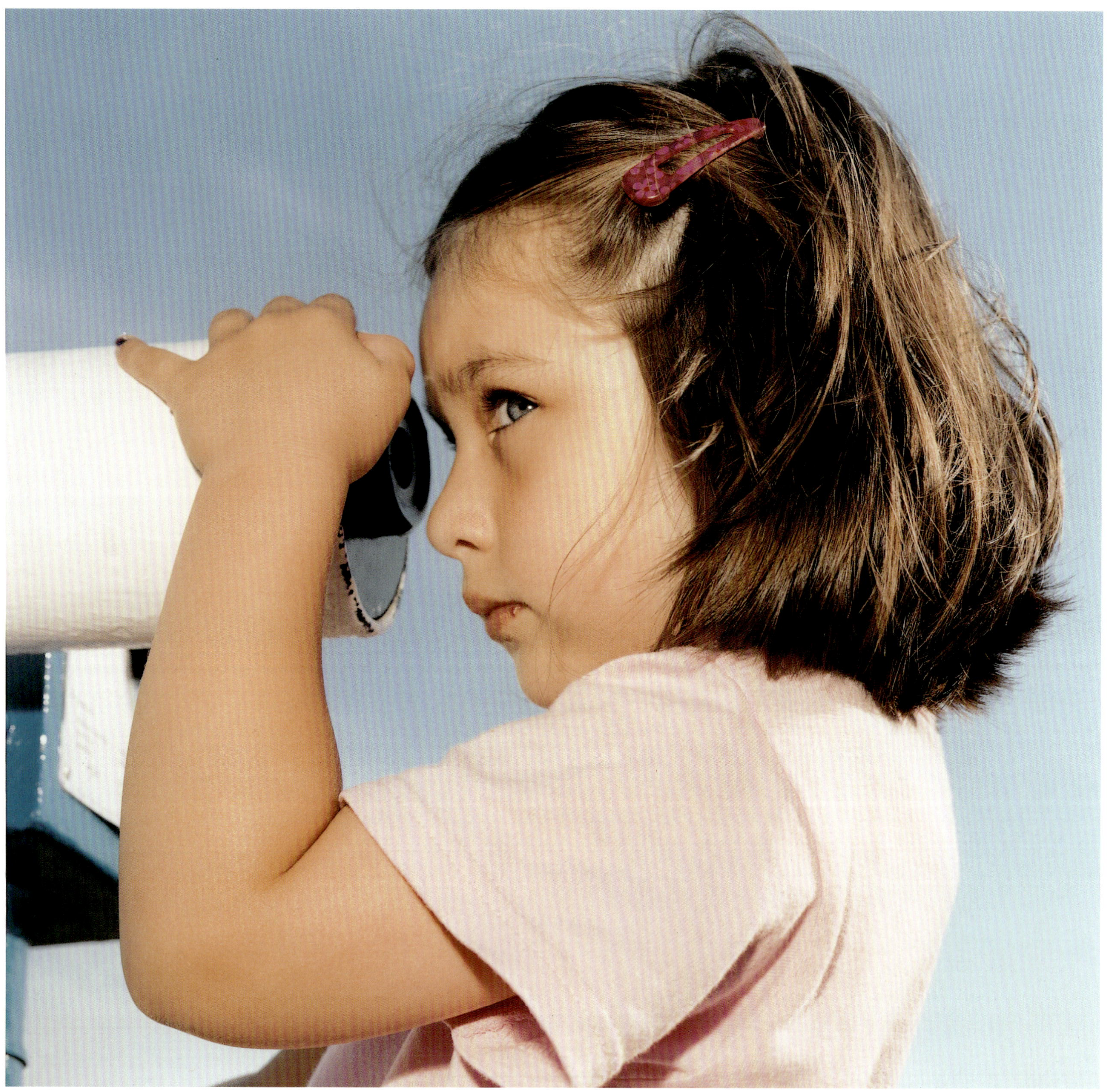

Magali Nougarède

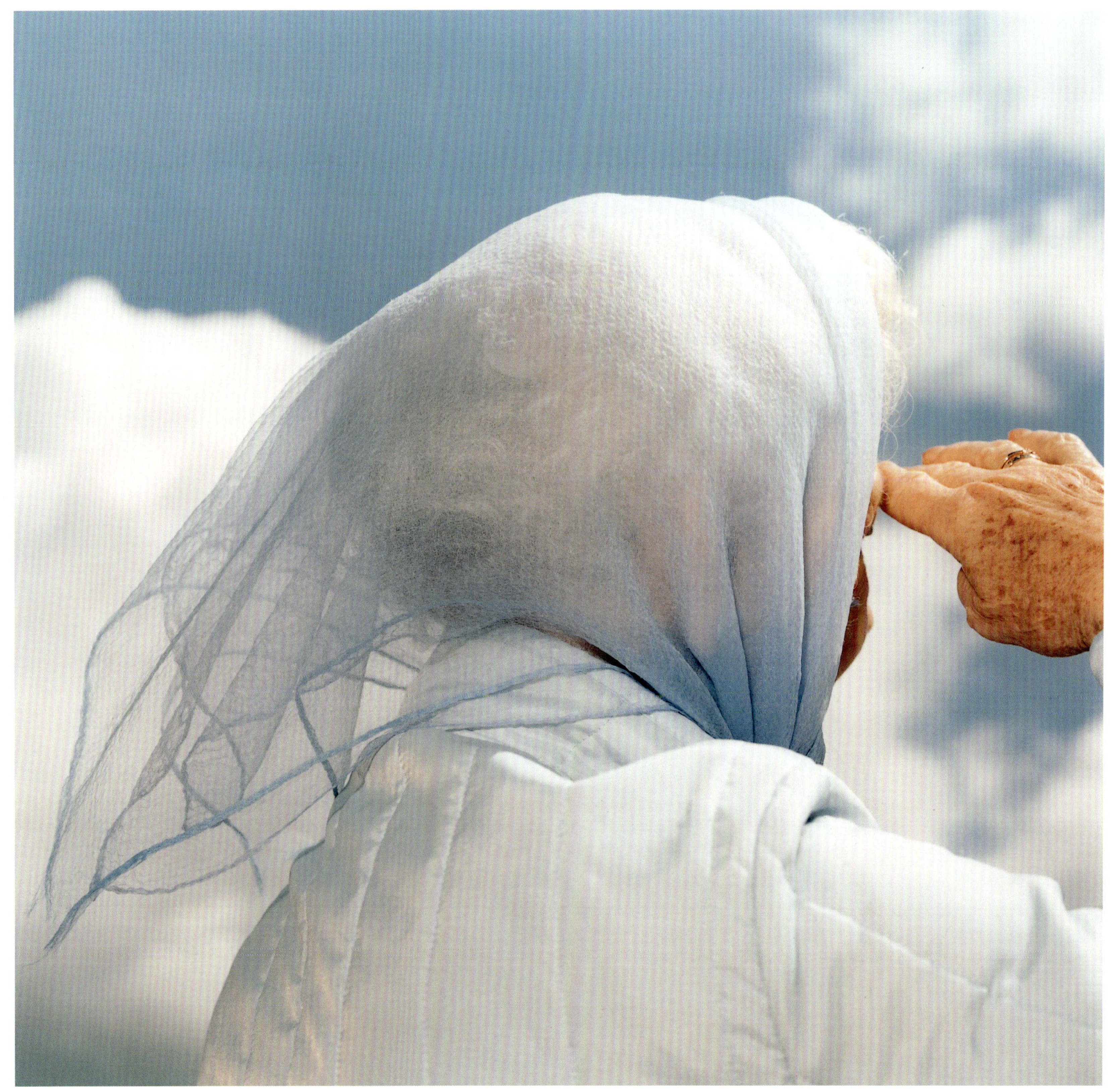

Magali Nougarède

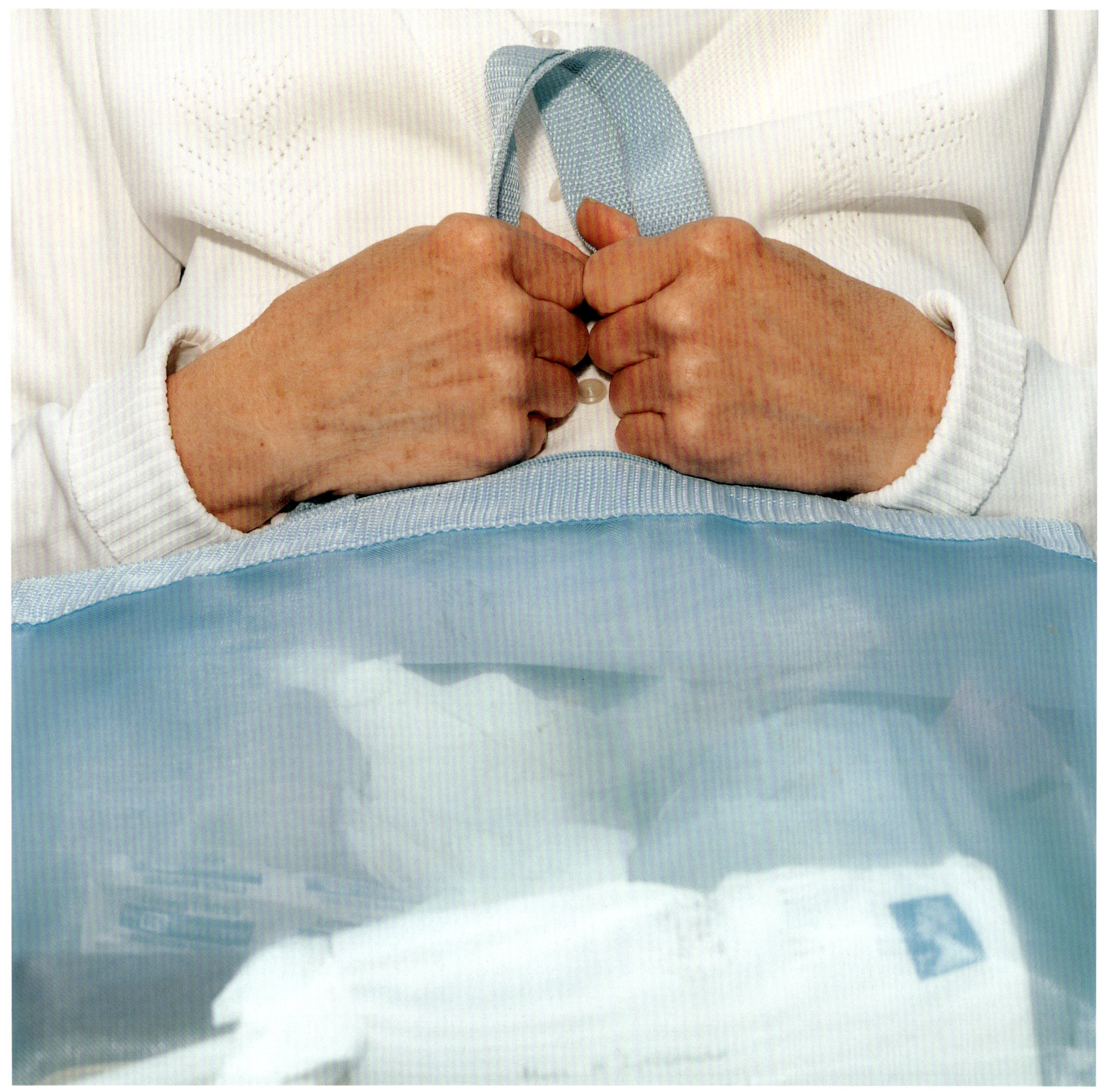

Magali Nougarède

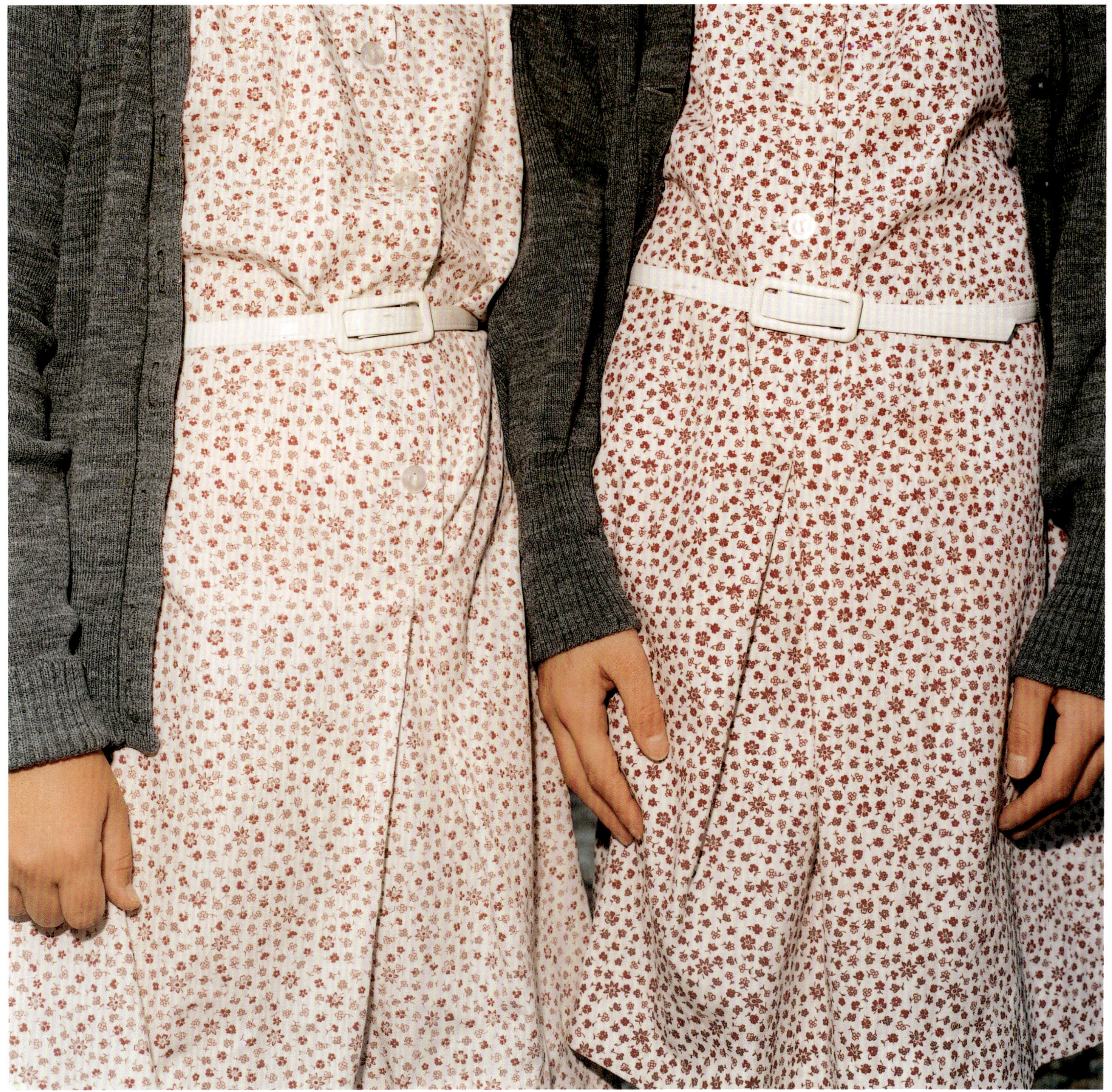

Magali Nougarède

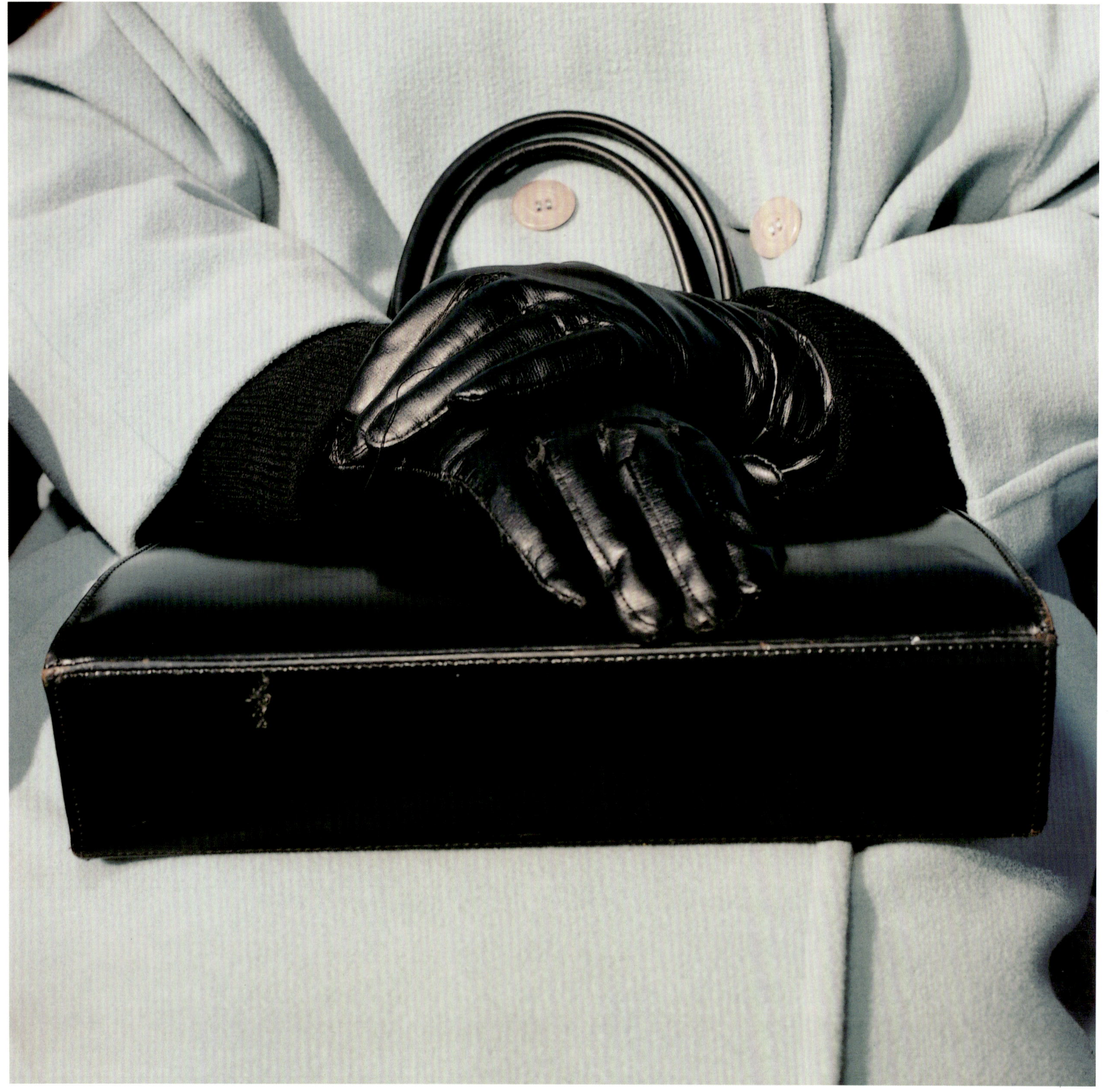

Magali Nougarède

The series "Toeing The Line" (2000) portrays women and girls encountered during repeated walks in the seaside landscape of an English south-coast town (Eastbourne). None of the subjects are known to the photographer prior to photographing them. She approaches people in the street or on seafront promenades and requests permission to photograph them. This often establishes a dialogue between them. The resulting portraits are a combination of her own experience and elements of the subjects' lives revealed to her during the photographic process (often alluded to in the titles).

Inherent to the title "Toeing The Line" are both the notions of obedience and competition (as in athletes toeing the line before the race starts). By extension this work is an attempt to speak of the values of the middle-class, especially in relation to the lives of women. The images flutter between two opposite female representations: the repressed woman and her principles on one side and the free child on the other. Women's handbags become containers of concerns and emotions, thus representing the female mind.

The work as a whole shows disregard for the subjects' real age, adopting a more psychological notion of age akin to the idea of Russian dolls. It tries to articulate the tension between inner world and external reality. As well as exploring physical and psychological passage this series is also about geographical passage: the passage of women in the landscape as well as territorial passage, based on the photographer's own experience of migrating from France to England.

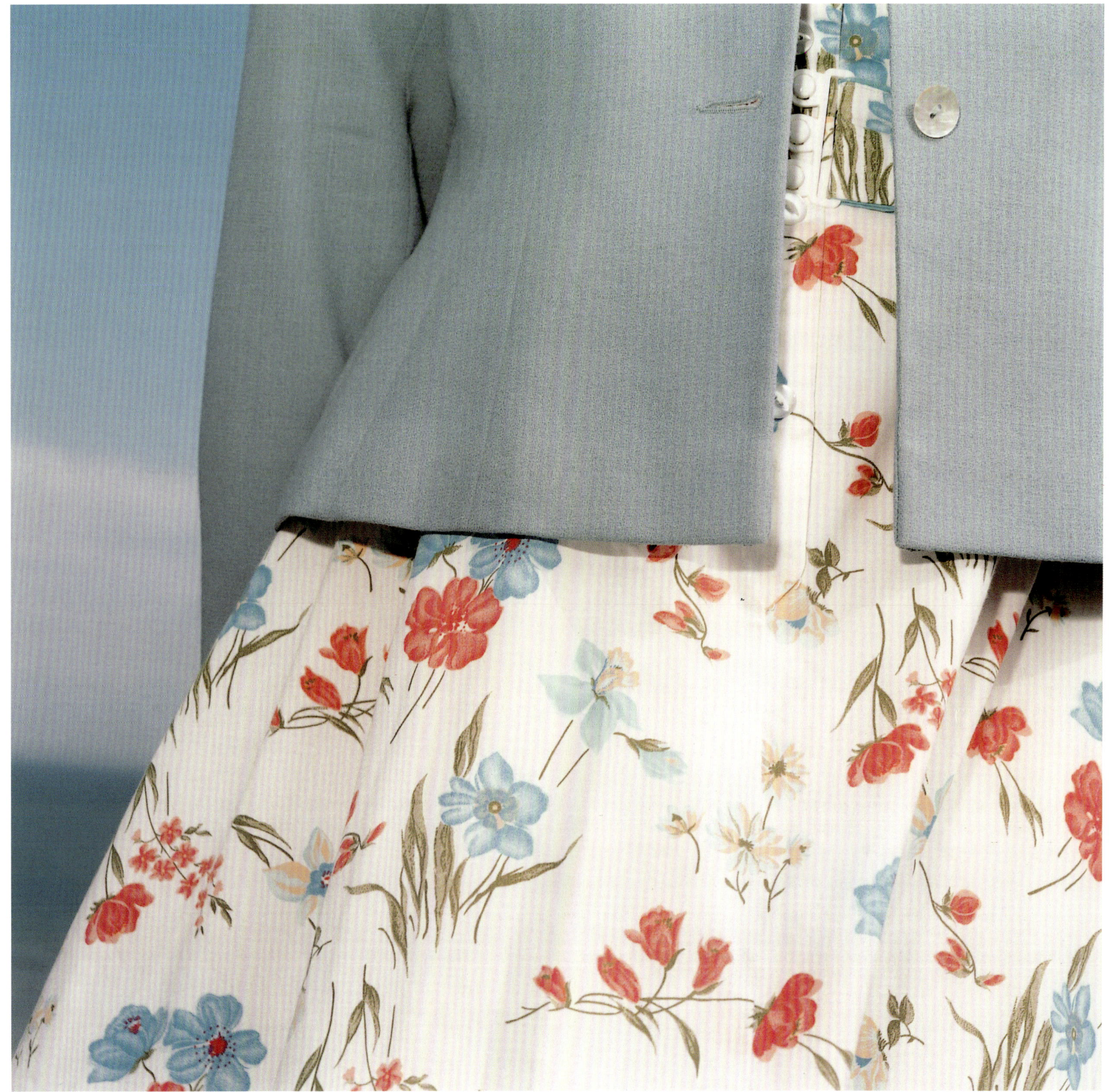

Magali Nougarède

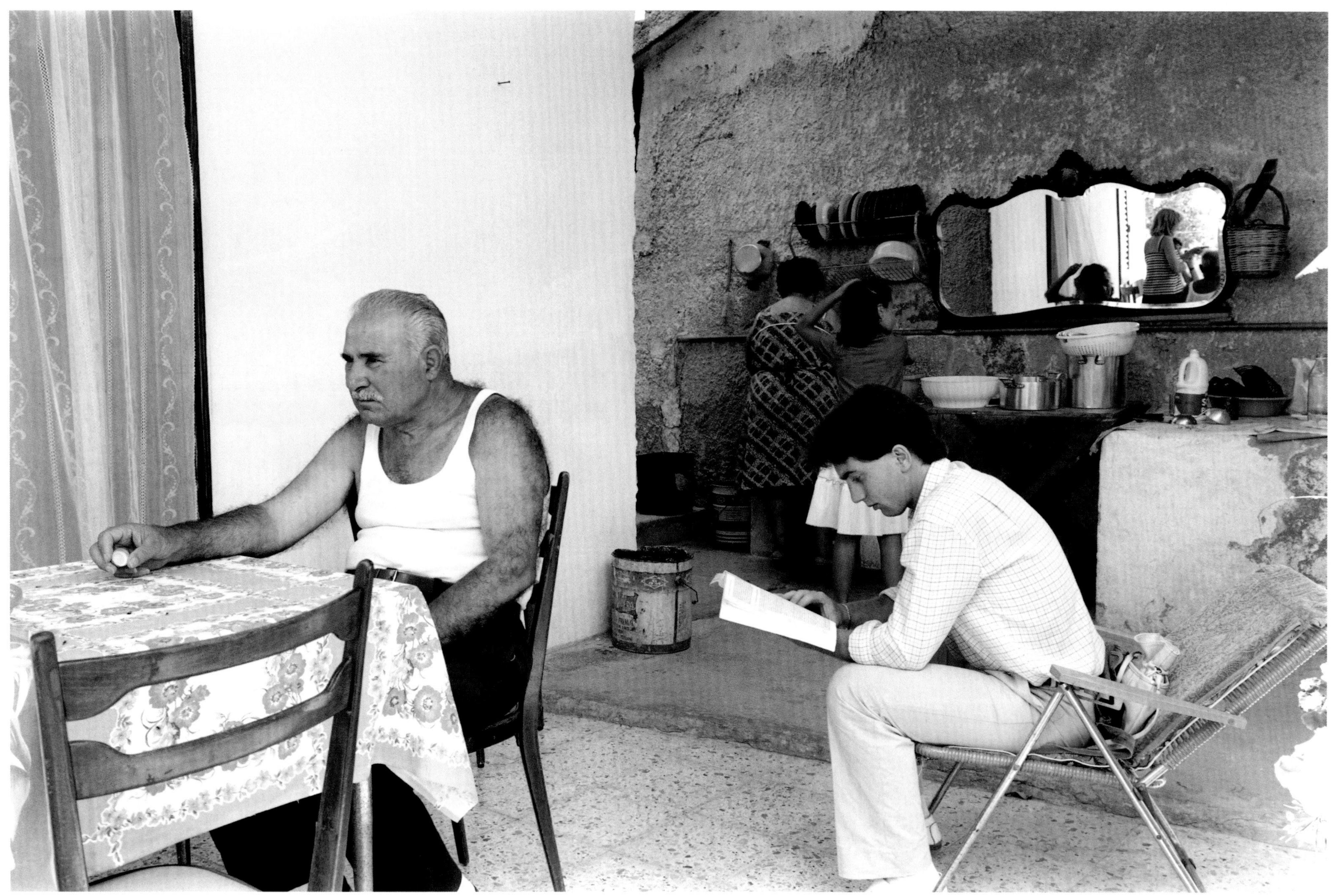

Thomas Roma

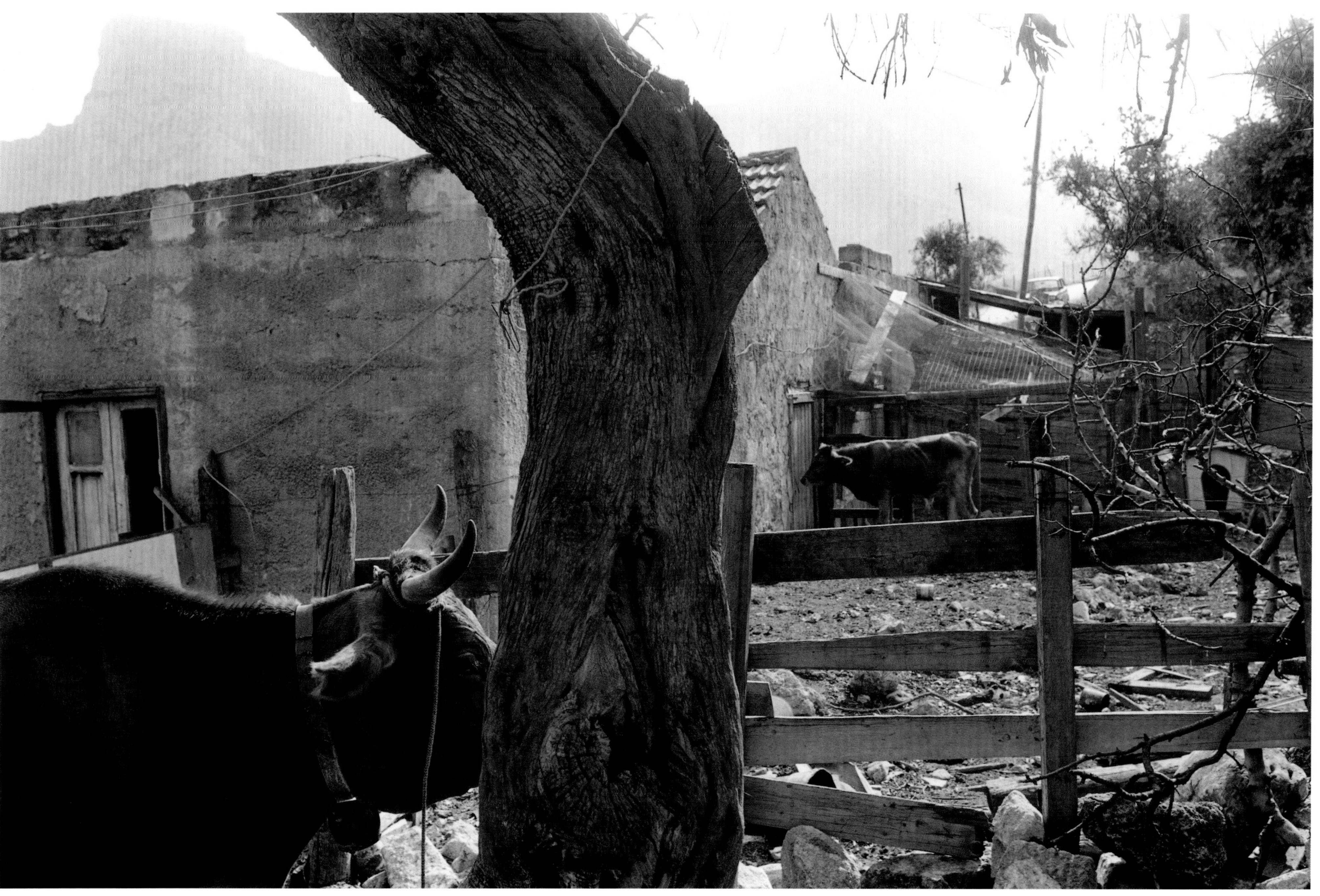

Thomas Roma

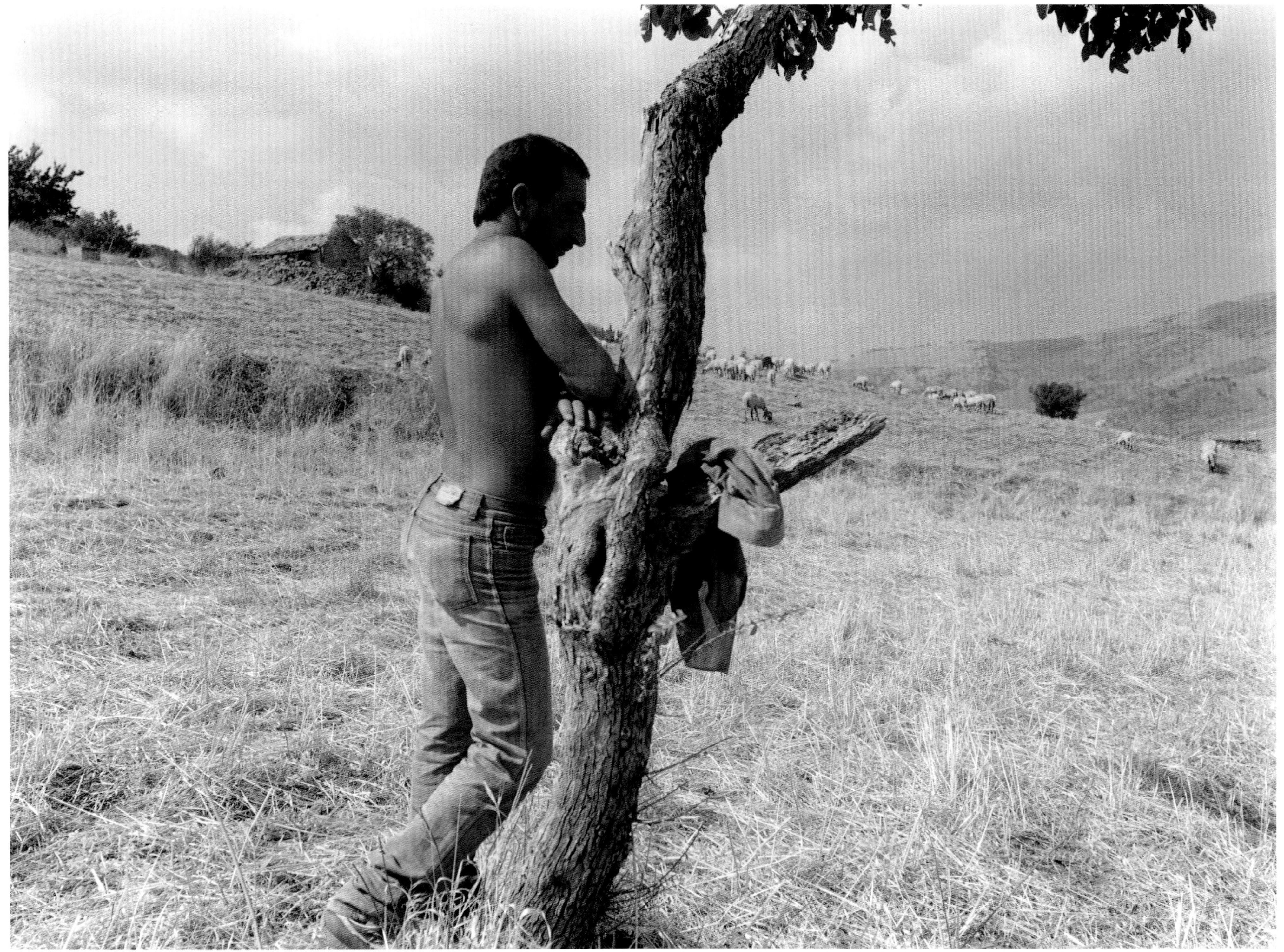

Thomas Roma

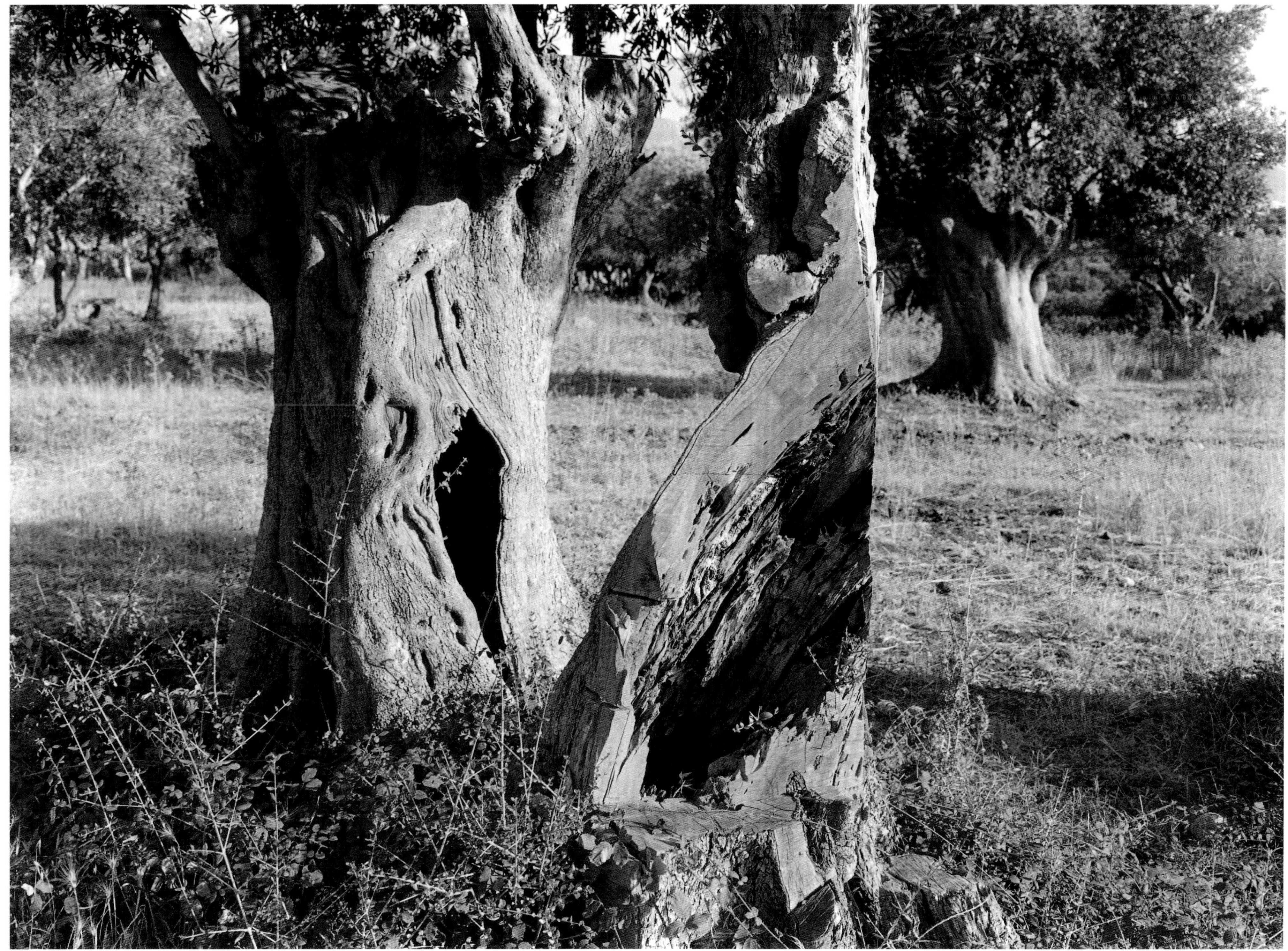

Thomas Roma

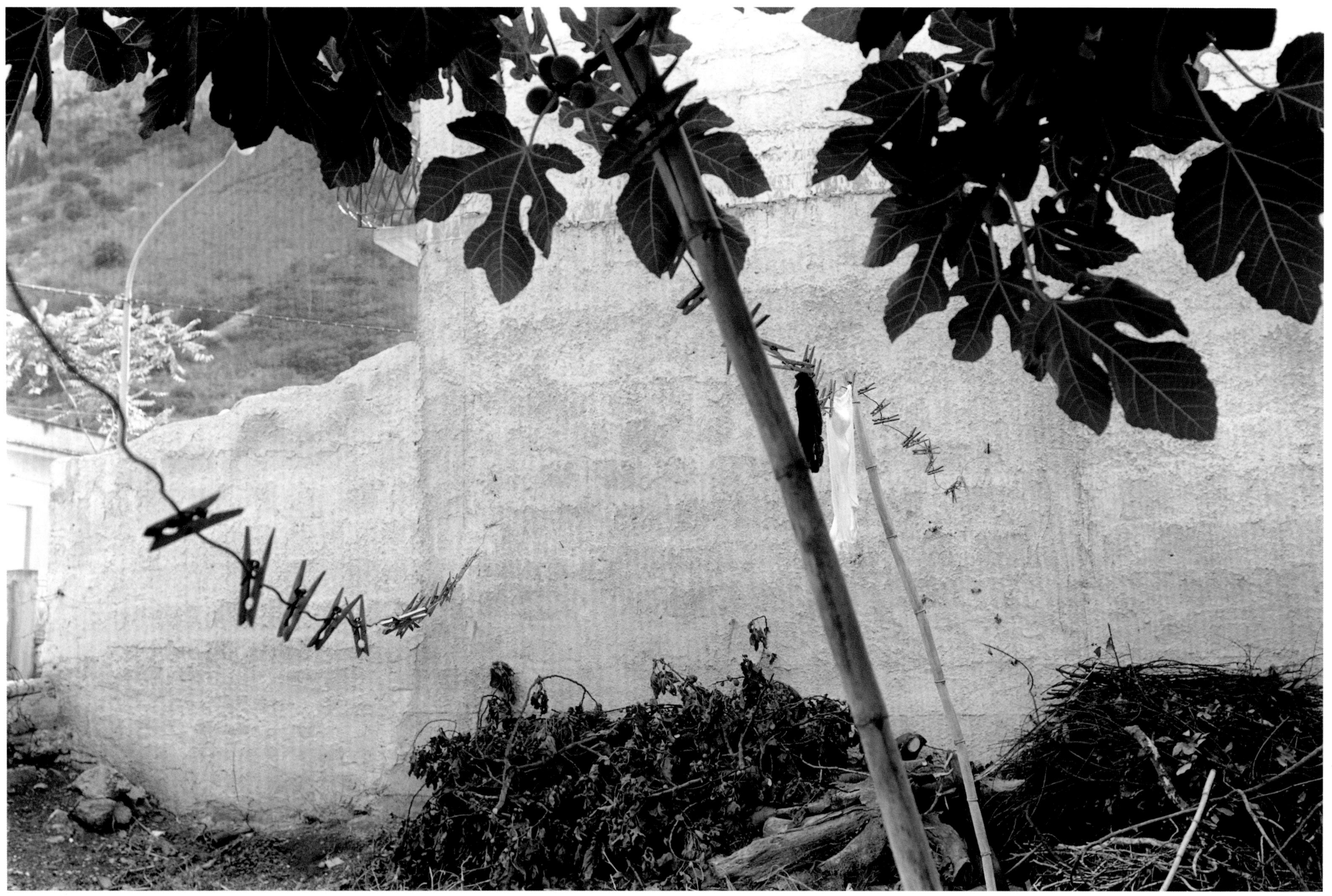

Thomas Roma

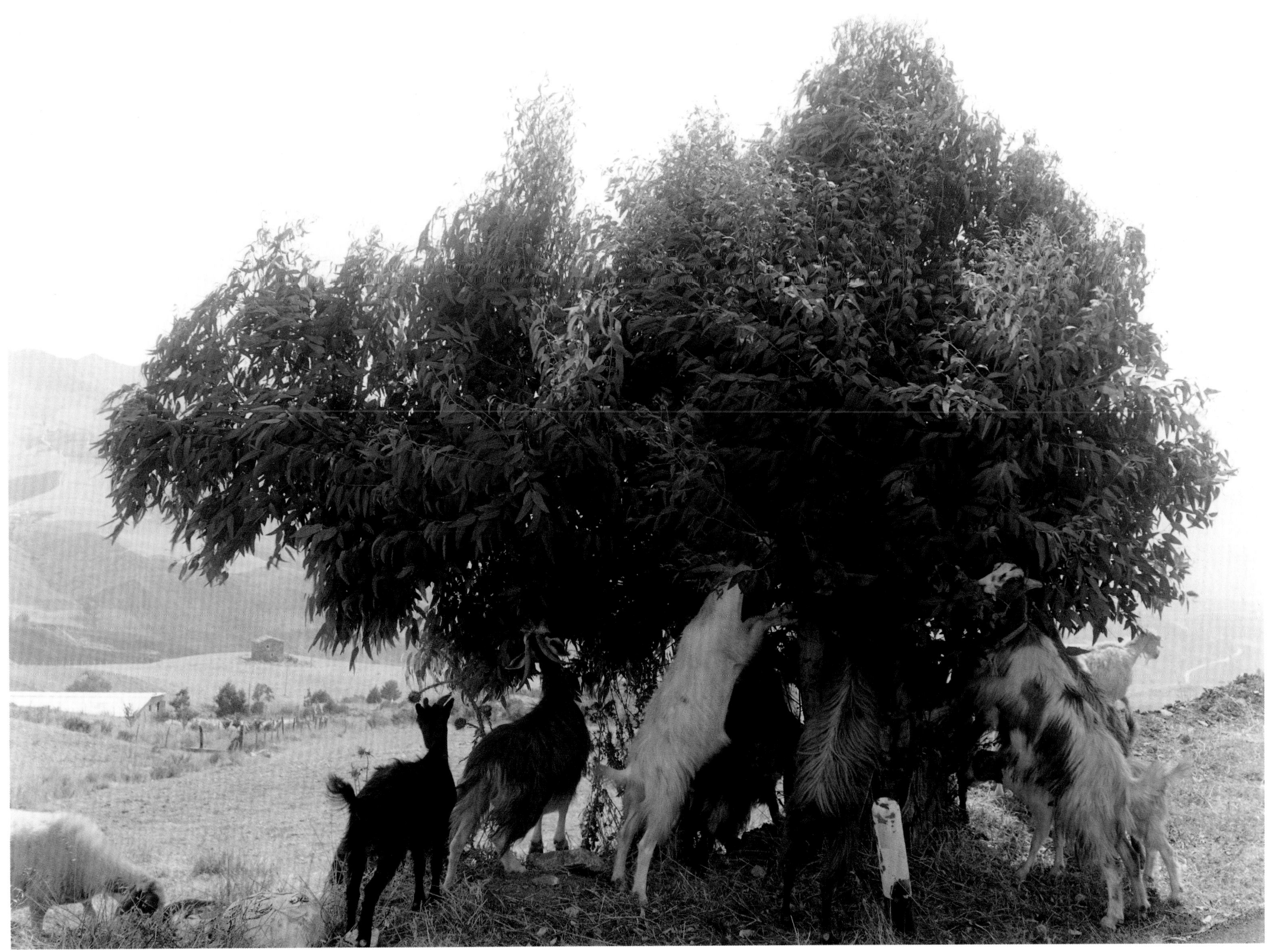

Thomas Roma

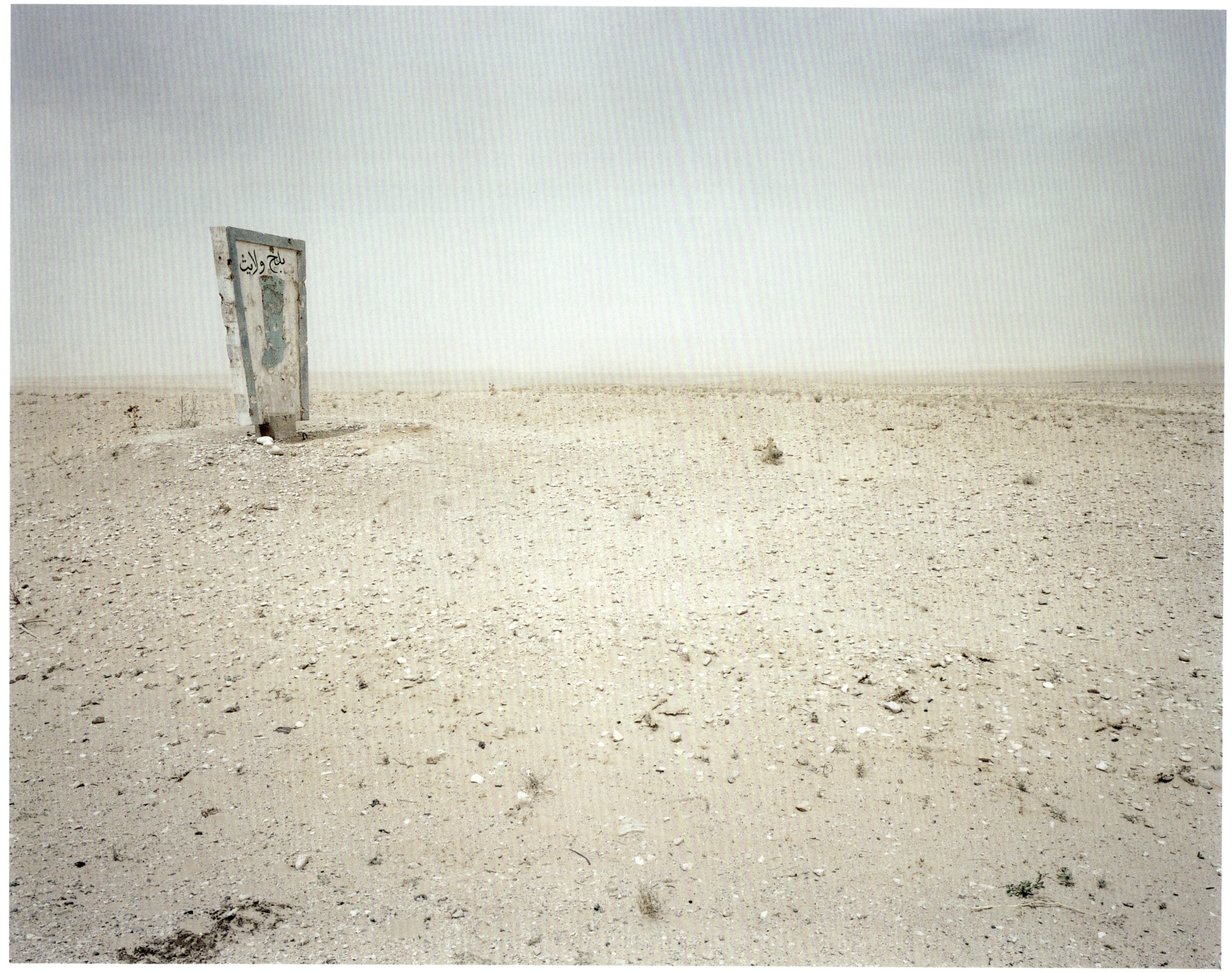

Paul Seawright

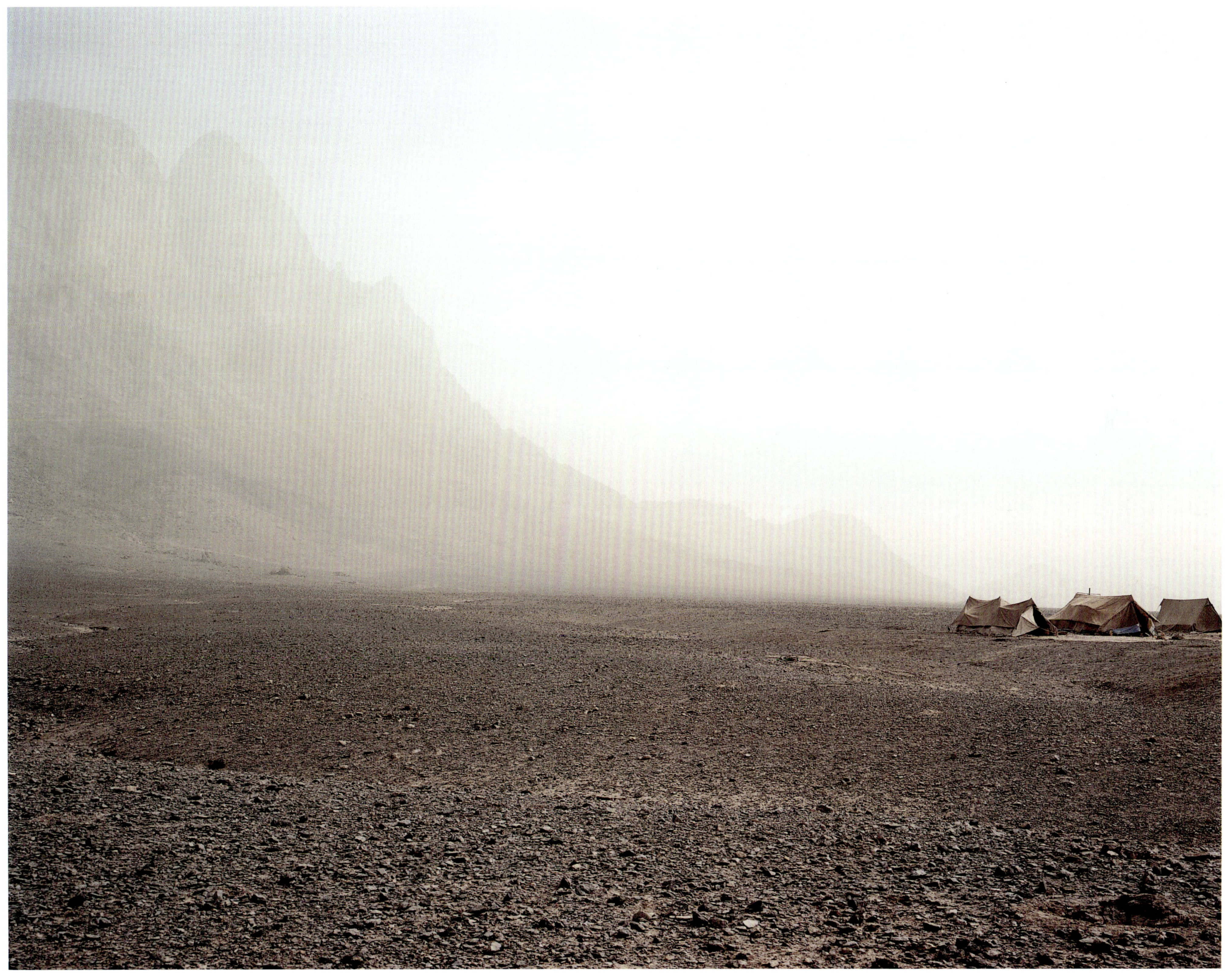

Paul Seawright

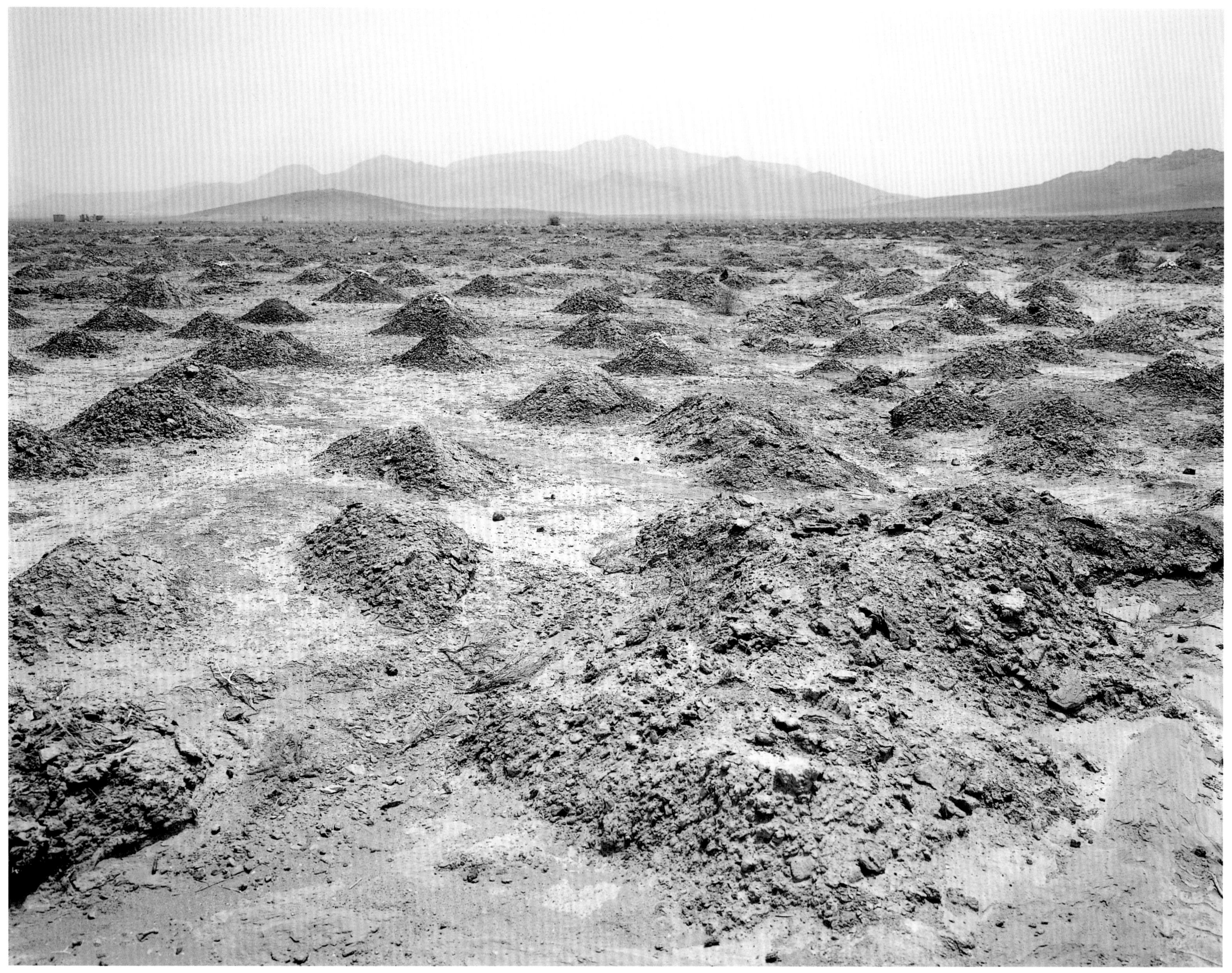

Paul Seawright

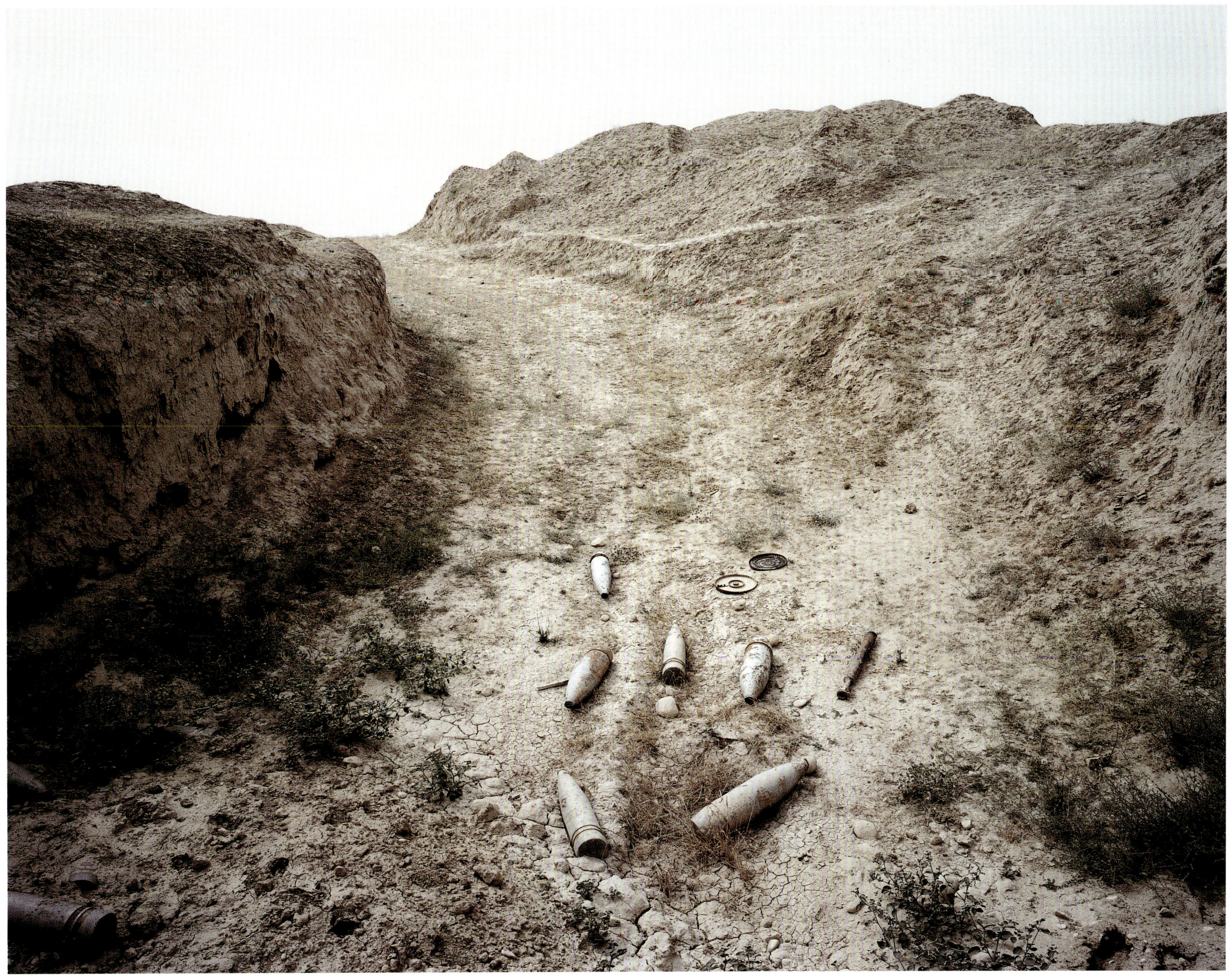

Paul Seawright

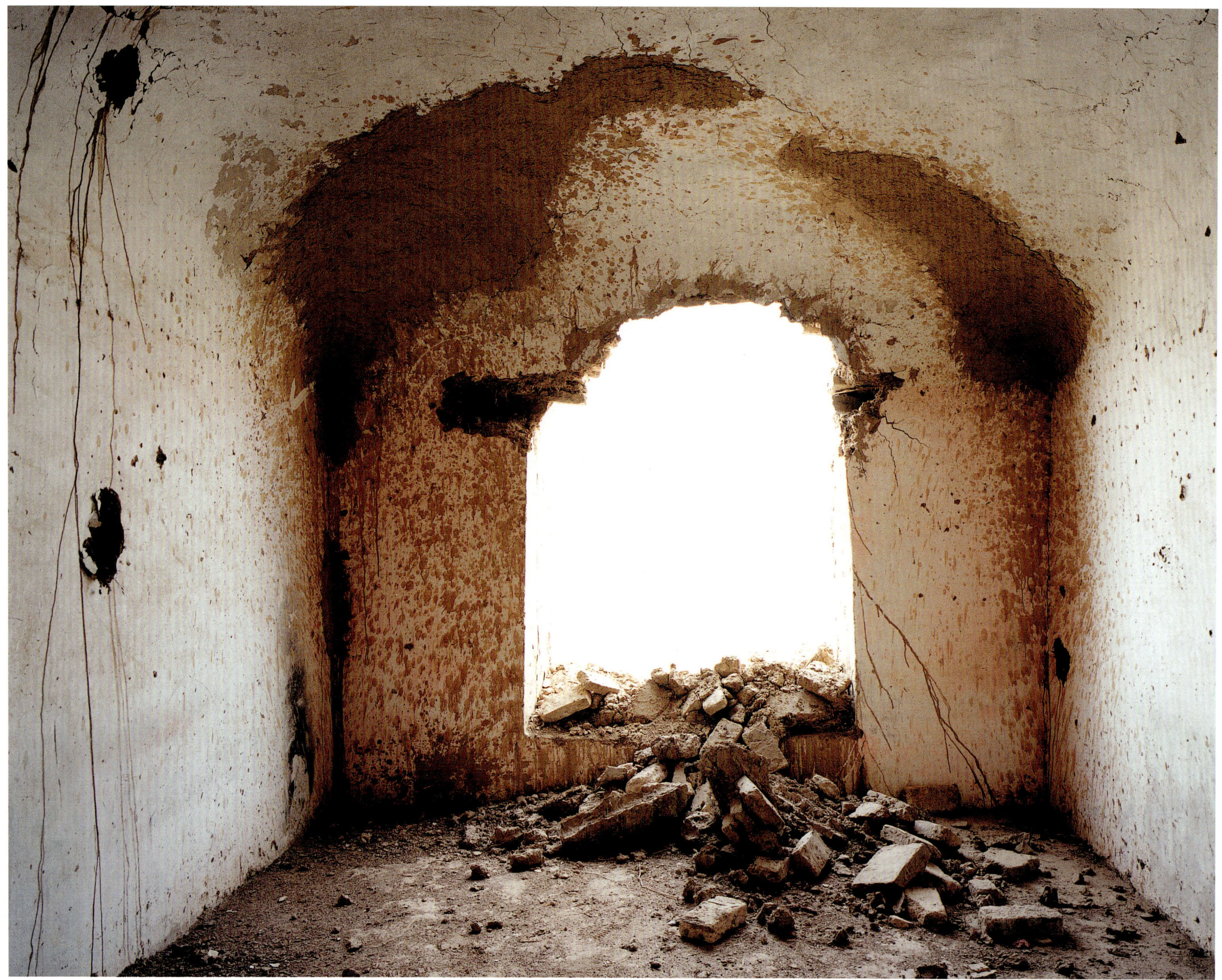

Paul Seawright

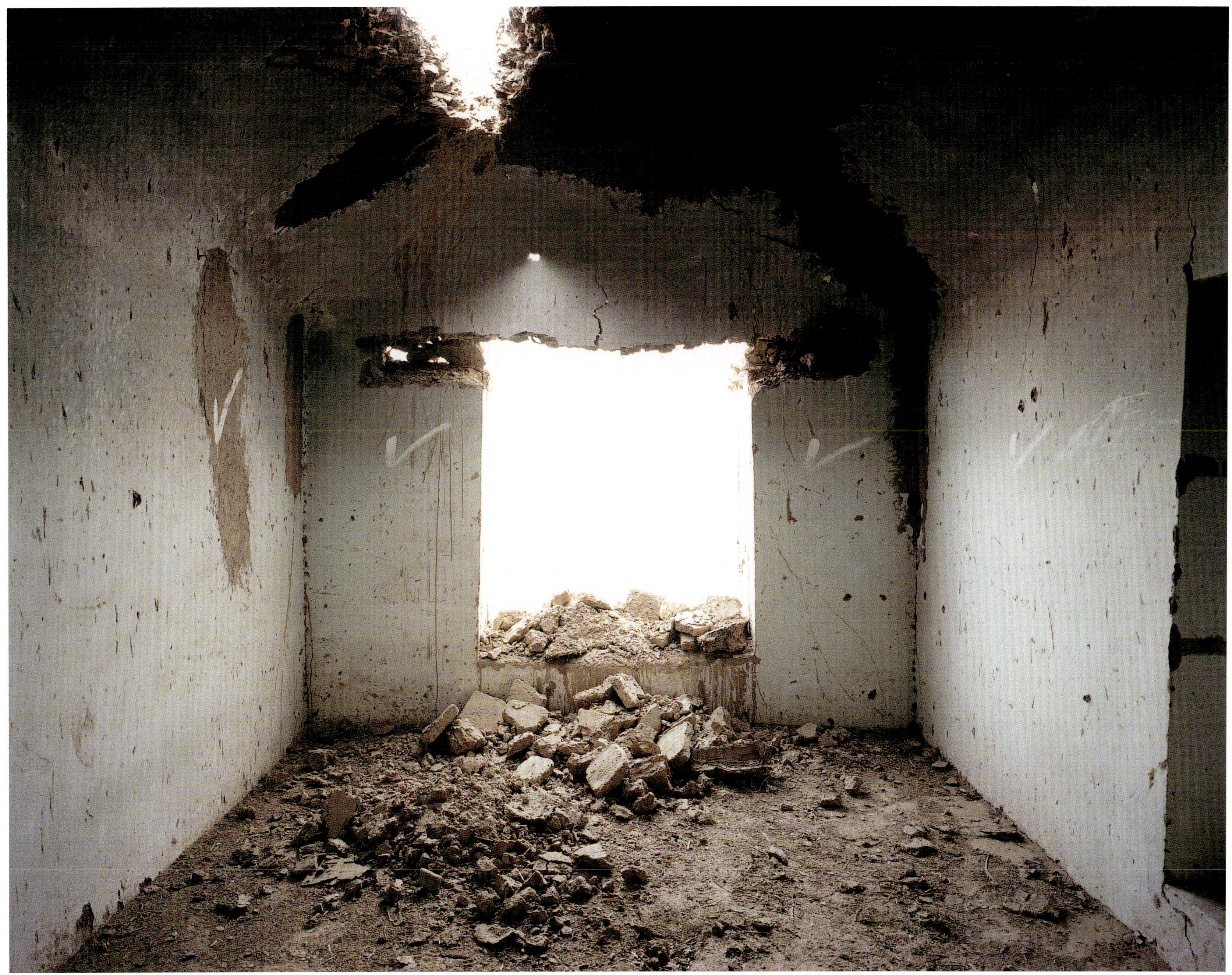

Paul Seawright

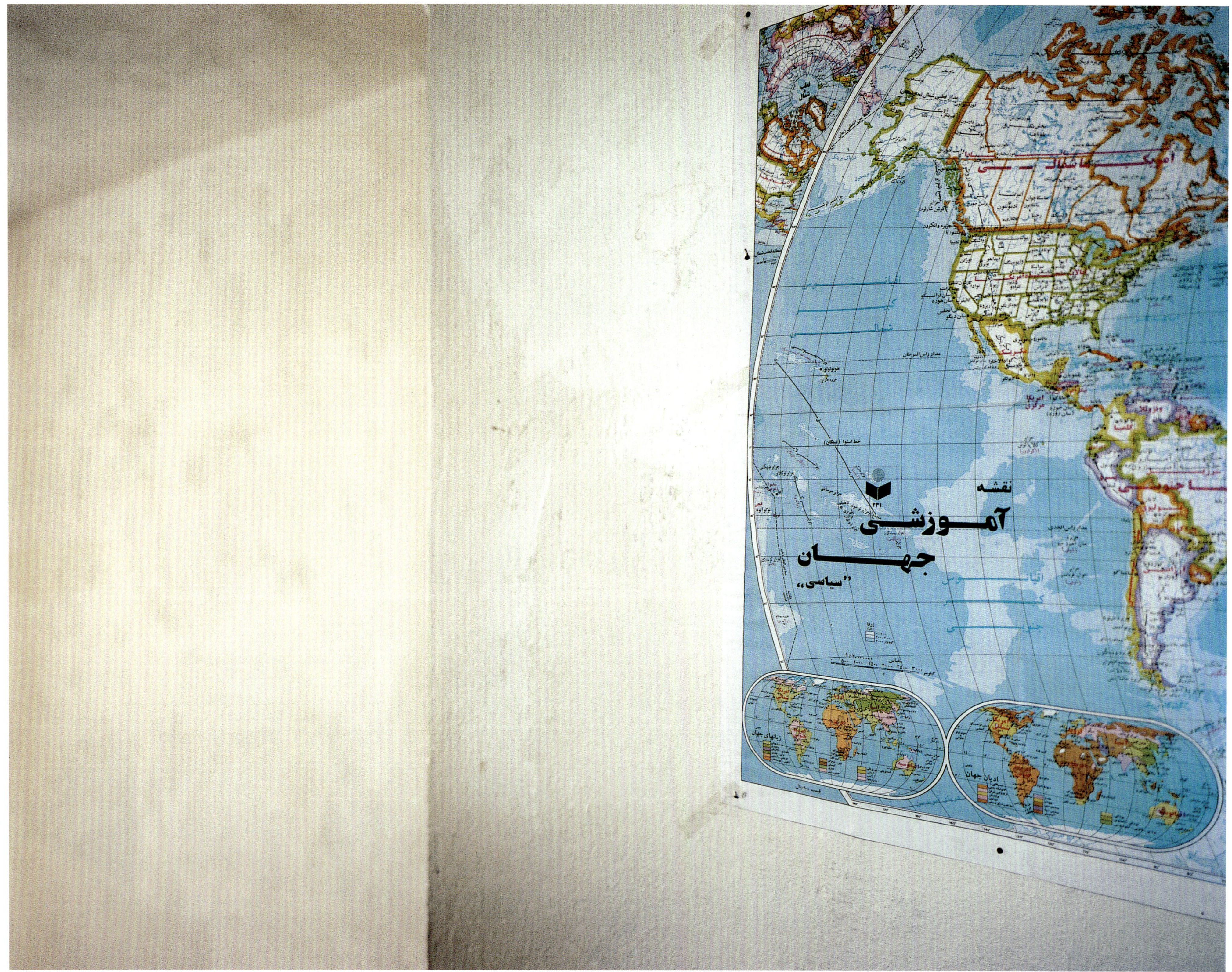

Paul Seawright

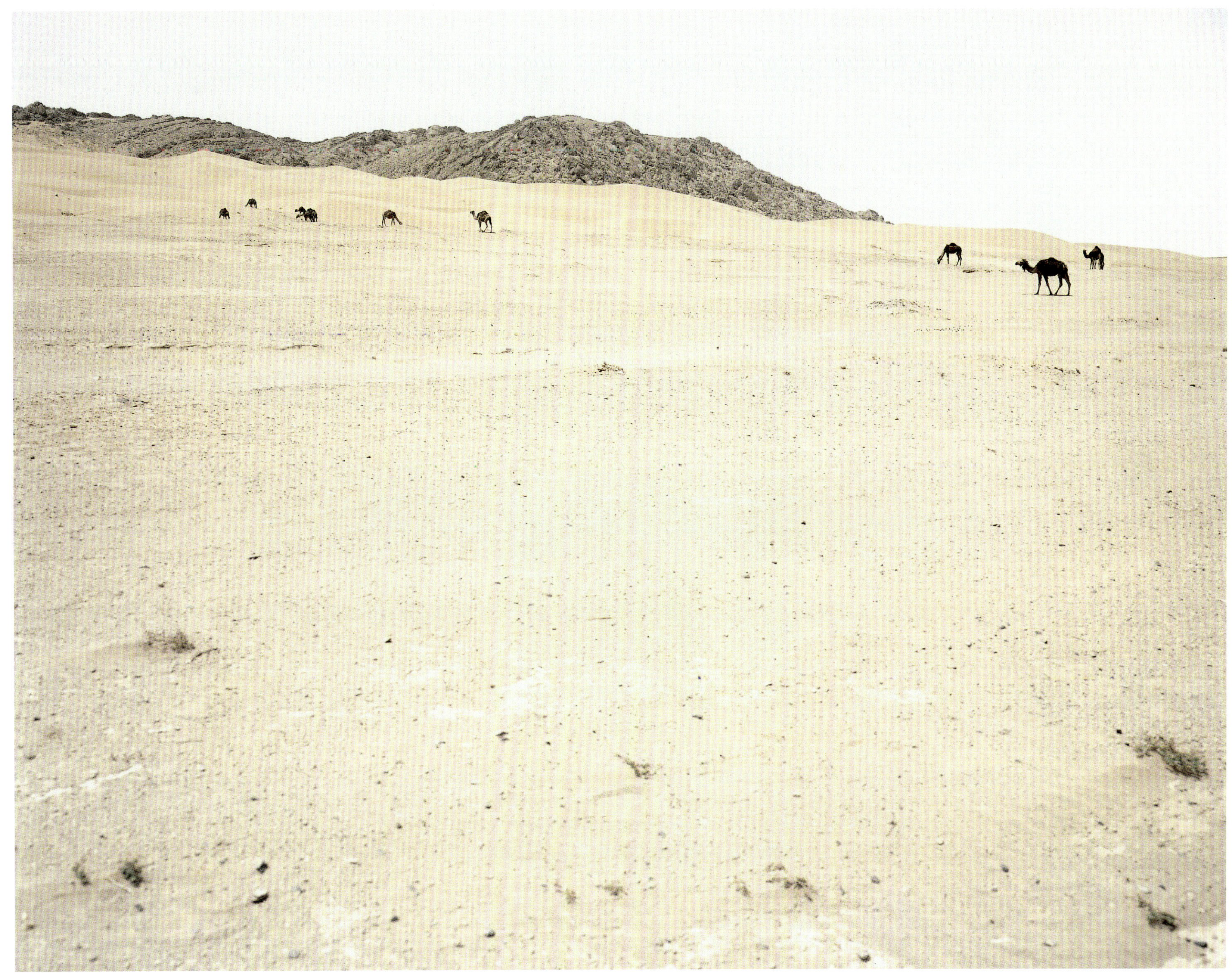

Paul Seawright was commissioned by the Imperial War Museum, London, to respond to the attacks of Sept 11th and the war in Afghanistan. He went to Afghanistan after much of the devastation had been unleashed on the country, after most of the fighting that had seen the country's liberation from the Taliban was over. Avoiding the trappings of an exoticizing vision, best typified by the photojournalist's portrait of Afghanistan as a spectacle of ruins, his series of pictures are spare, subdued, understated and quiet. Seawright's responses to the terrain of the destroyed and heavily mined desert landscapes of the country both draw upon, extend and rework the distinctive aesthetic and conventions he had established through earlier landscape photographs, made first within his home city, Belfast, and more recently on the fringes of a number of European cities. In war-torn Afghanistan, Seawright is less concerned with the visible scars of war, but instead the hidden malevolence of its landscapes.

Paul Seawright

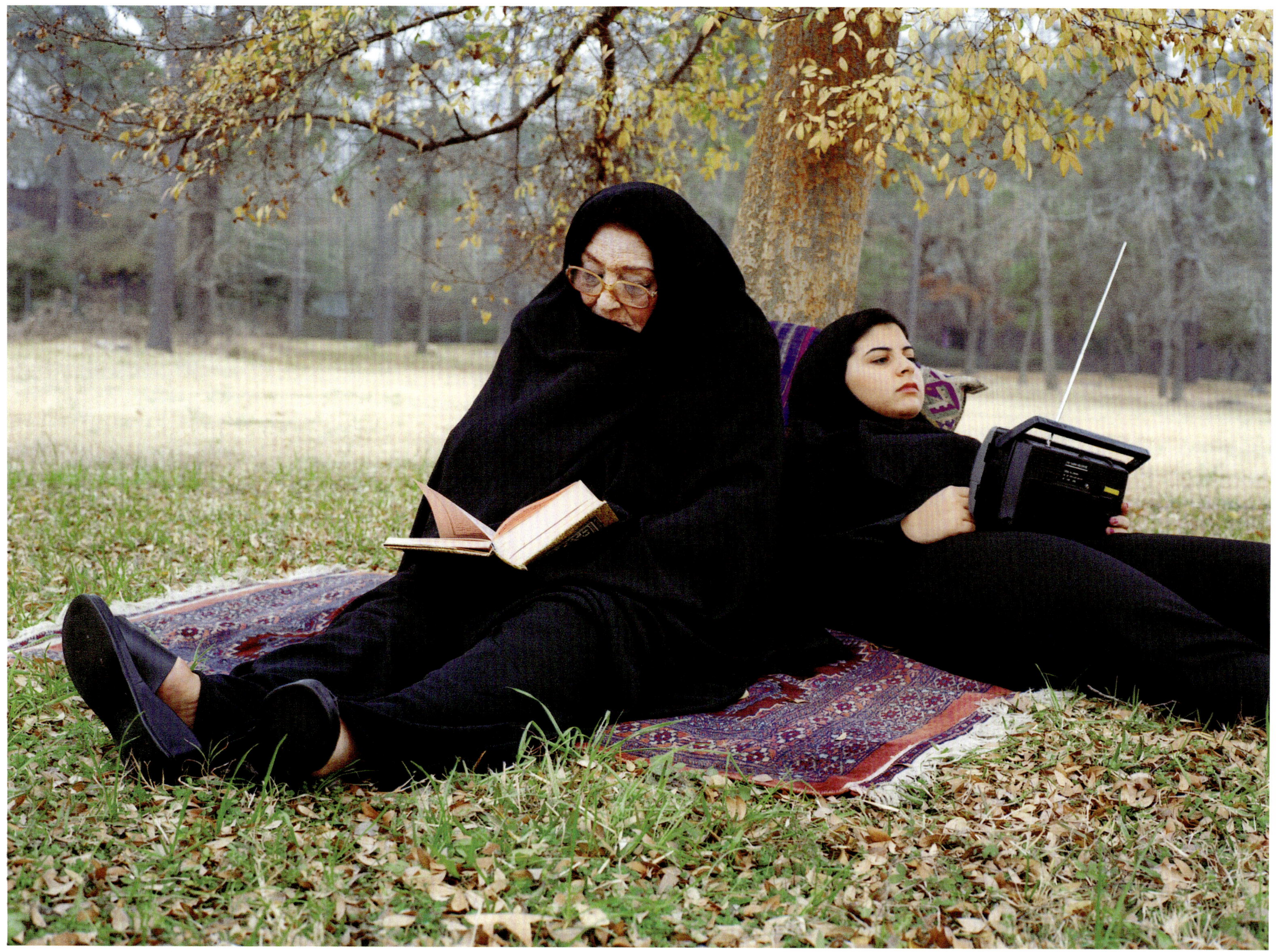

Soody Sharifi

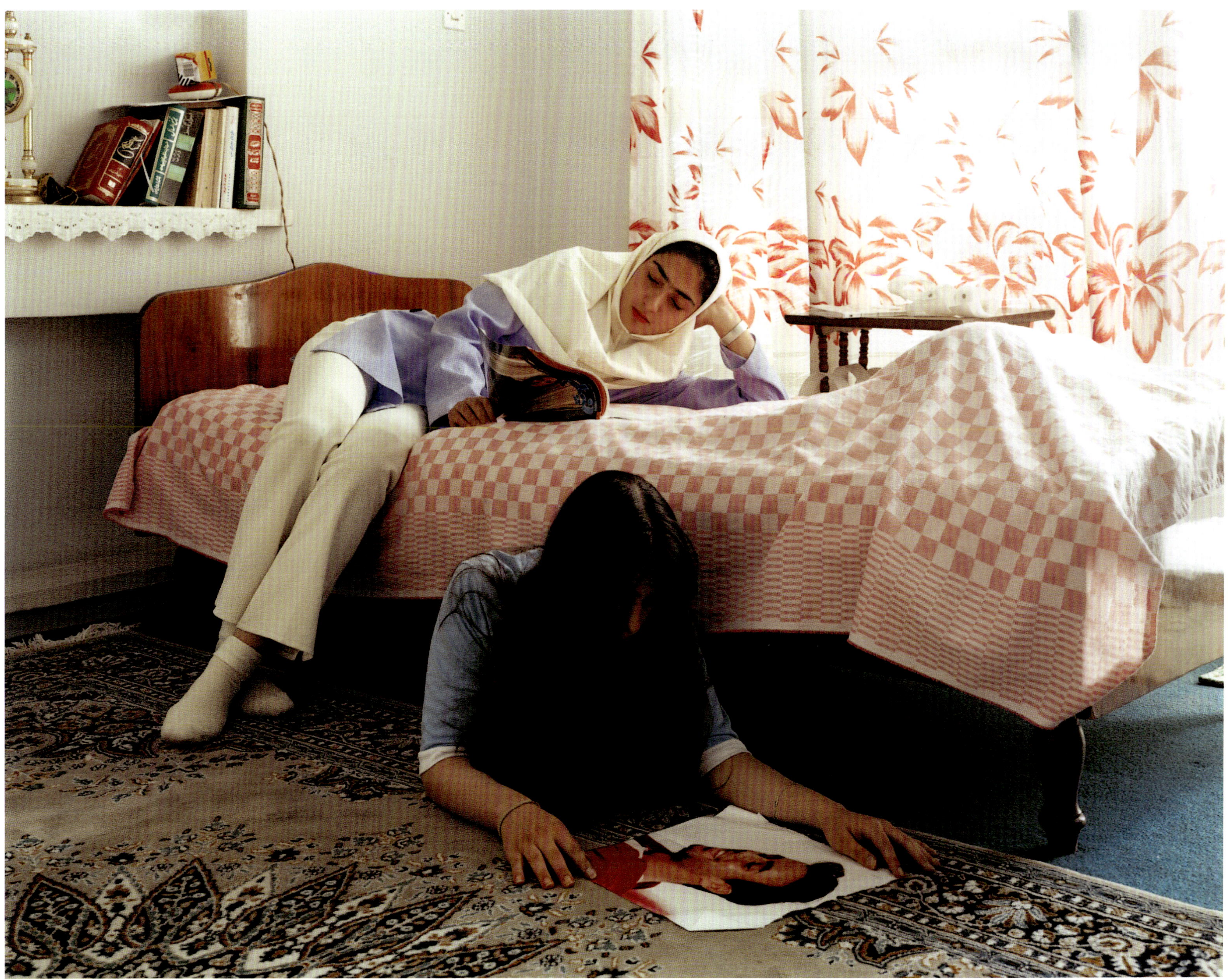

Soody Sharifi

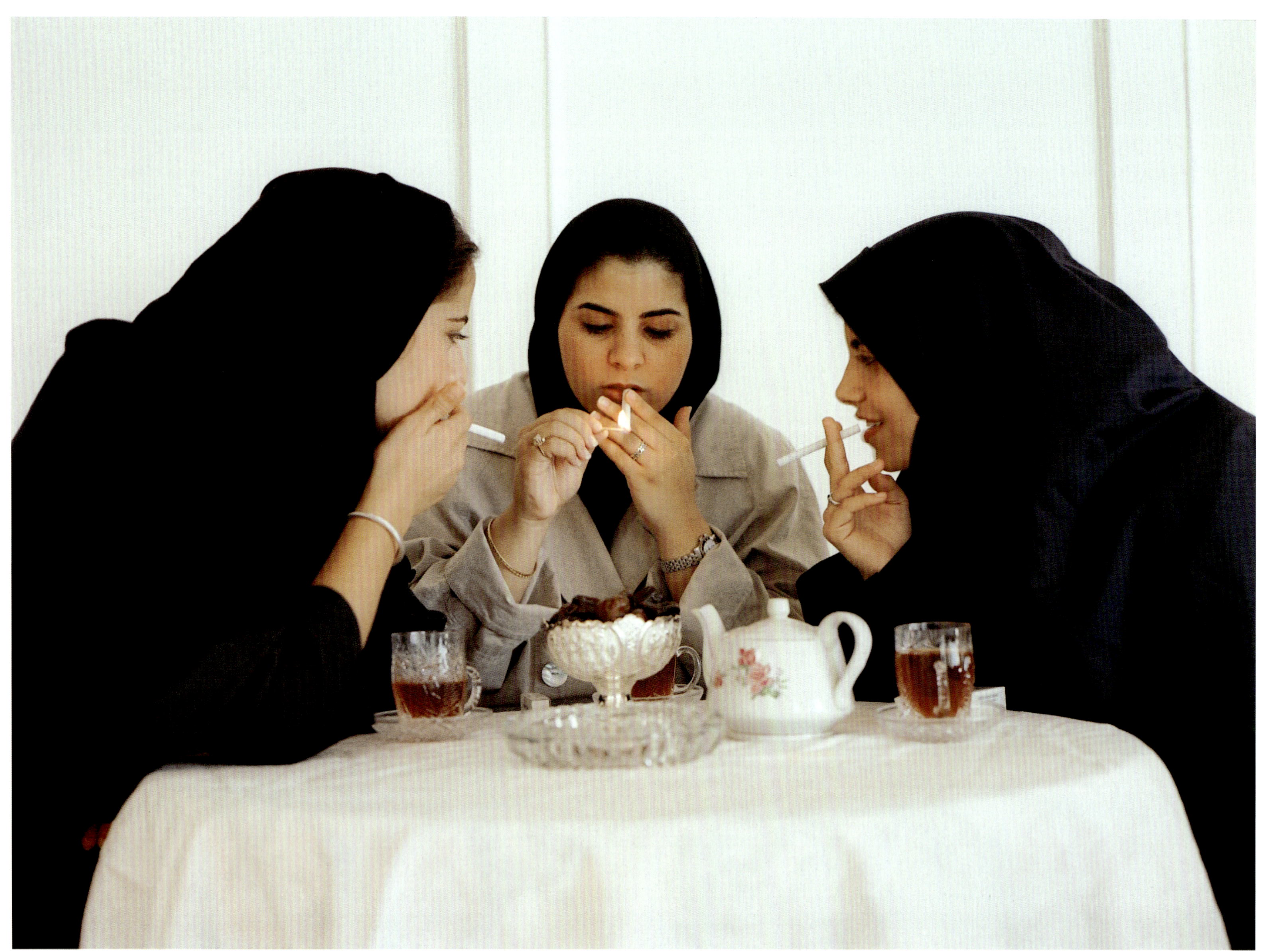

Soody Sharifi

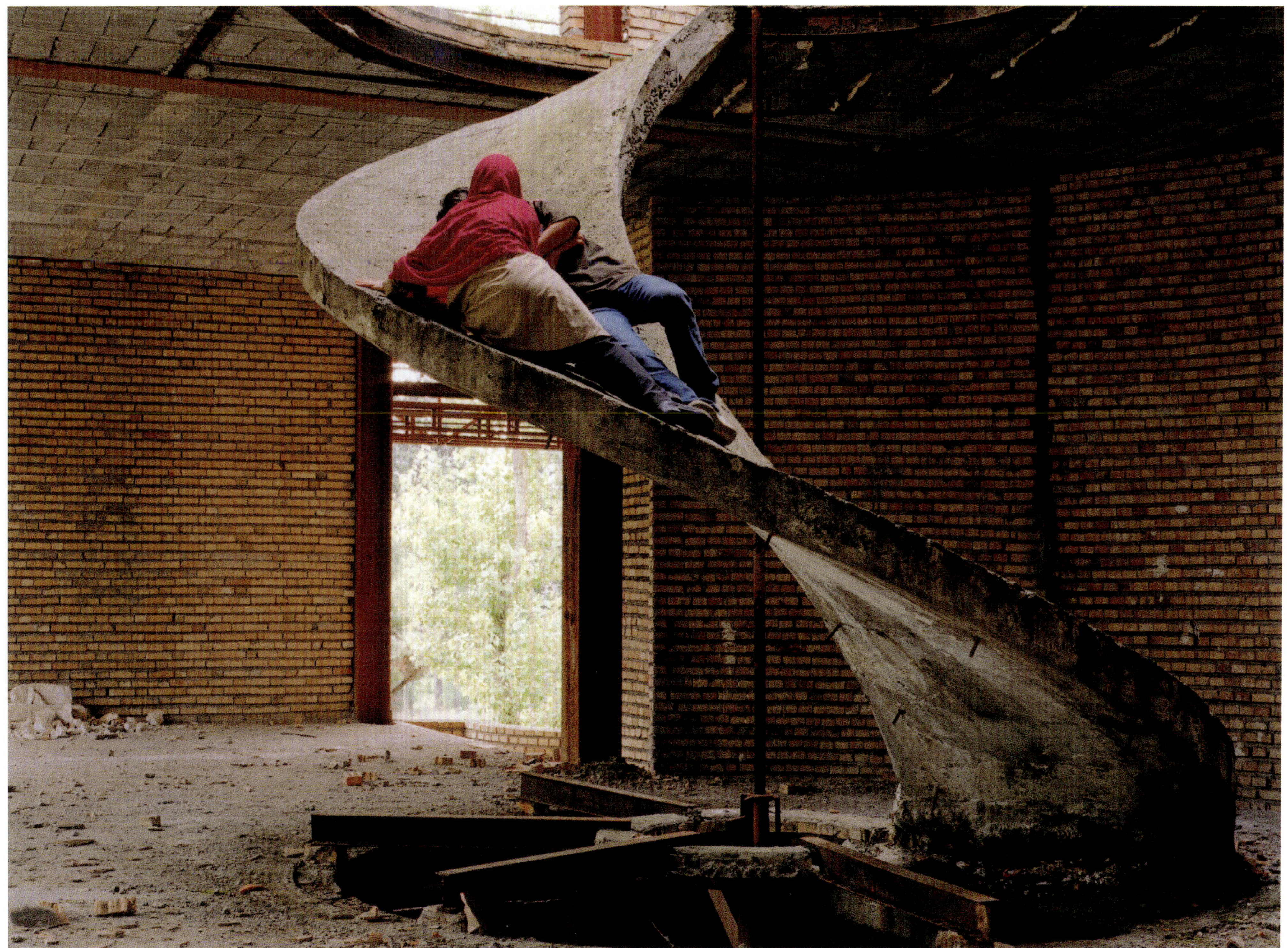

Soody Sharifi

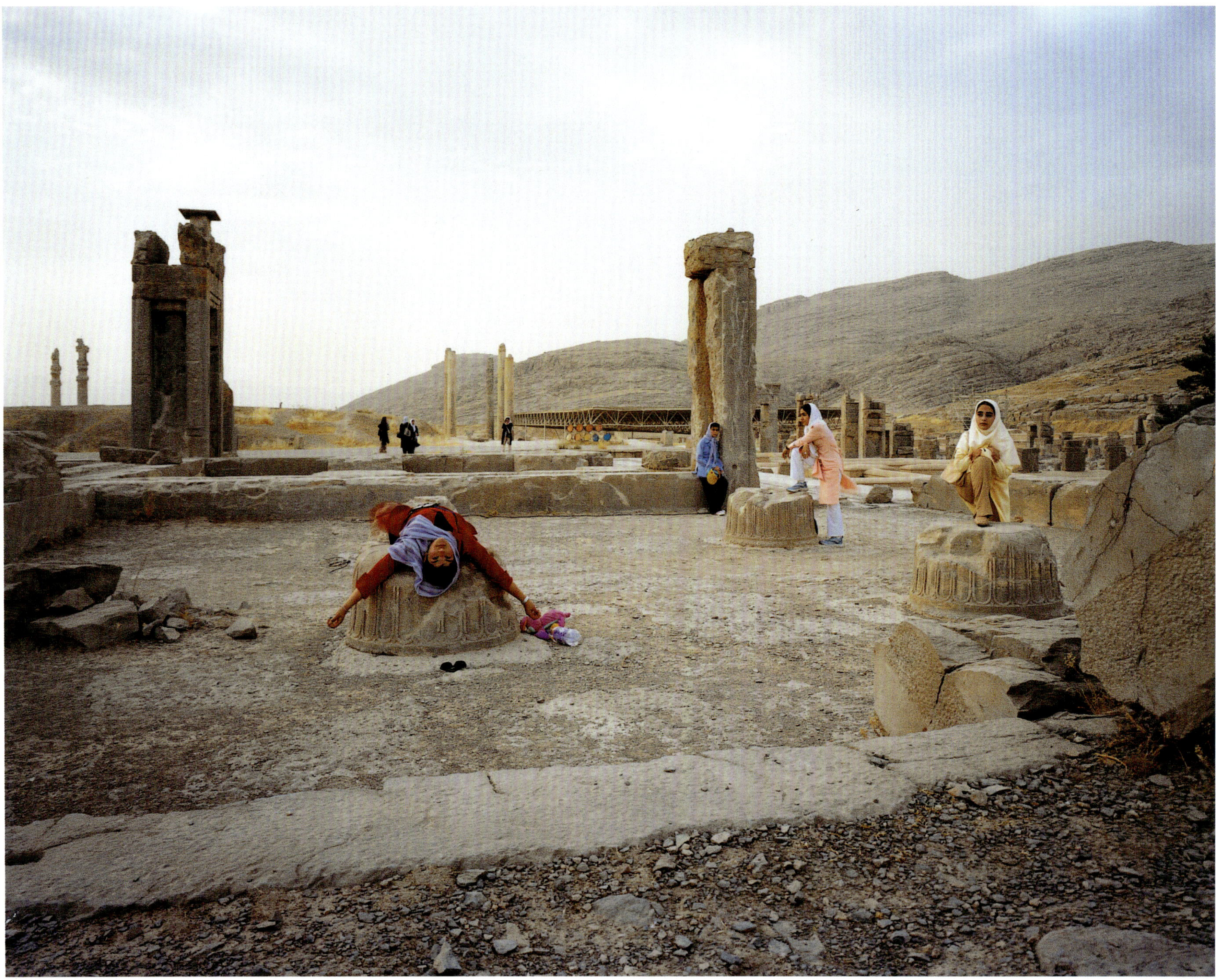

For several years, through my photography, I have attempted to question the role of women under Islam as well as my own position as an Iranian-American woman. Drawing on my dual identity, I have sought to explore issues of oppression, exile, and integration that reflect the position of women as simultaneously inside and outside their respective cultures. In a larger context this can be seen as the position of women worldwide, a struggle between the conflicting demands of cultural and personal identity, specifically the tension between traditional and non-traditional roles for women.

These images are part of my series entitled "Moslem Teenagers." This series confounds more than it confirms Eastern and Western cultural expectations. With this group of images I delve into the unique experience of teenage girls, and more specifically the experience of teens living in the Islamic world. The lives of my teenagers defy broad characterization and resist reductive stereotyping. The majority of my images are staged because I believe in emphasizing the delicate fiction underpinning them, these images come closer to 'reality' than what is seen in most news media. Because of this theatrical tendency in my work, when shooting I try to make my camera and myself as transparent as possible. Teenagers are capricious and fanciful by nature; they are frequently daring and willing to improvise, despite any cultural or religious considerations. This is exactly what I'd like to communicate to my viewers. Once I give them the props, they often create the tableau themselves, and this element of spontaneity and naturalism nicely balances the dramatic tendency in my work.

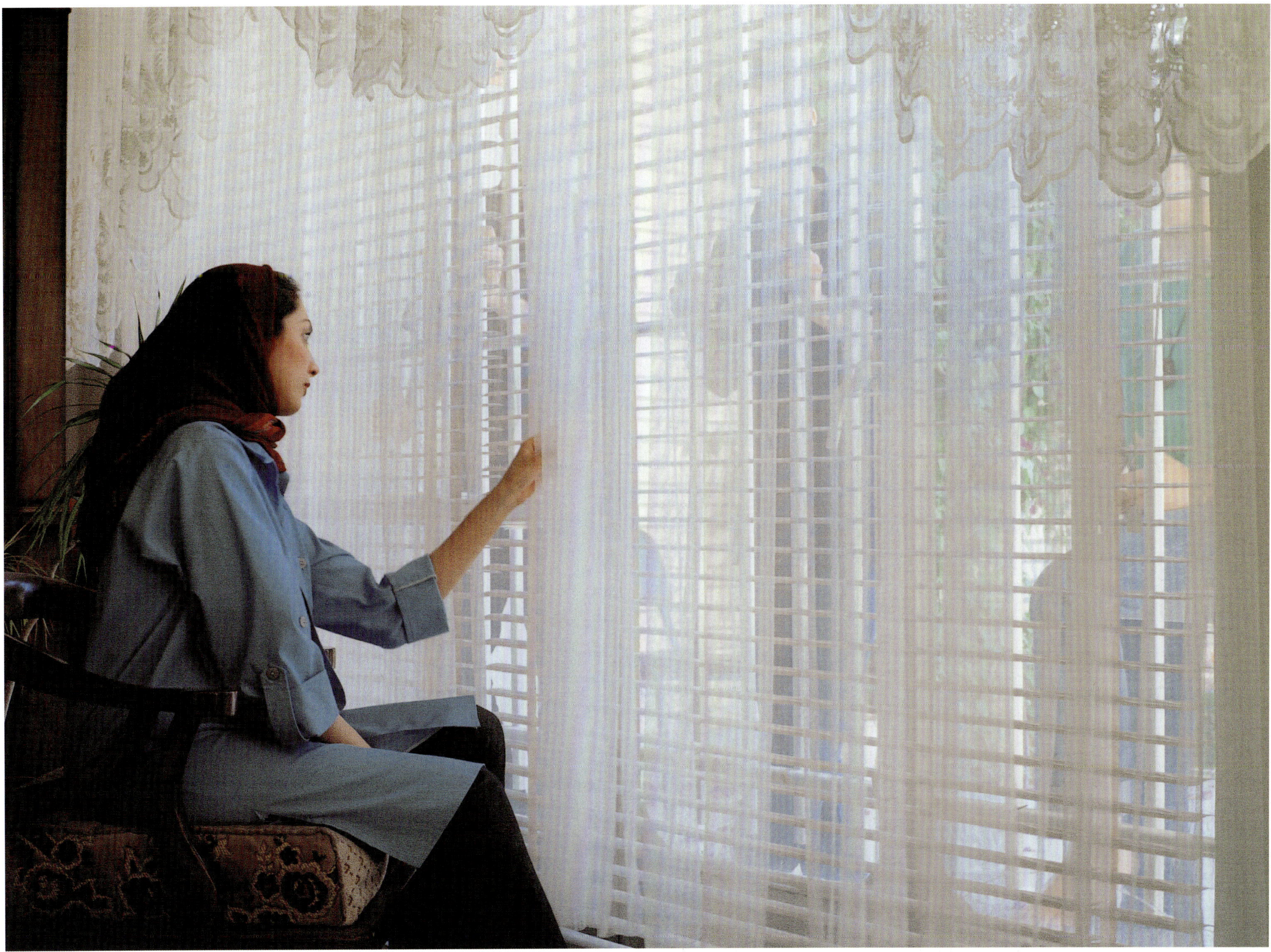

Teenagers as a group are constantly aware of themselves, especially as individuals between cultures. In Iran in particular, these teens exist in and partake of the larger adult culture that surrounds them, while participating in another culture exclusive to teens. The two worlds are not mutually exclusive; the teens are at home in multiple cultures simultaneously. The teen years bring an awareness of the body and a new sense of self-consciousness. Teenage girls in particular become extremely focused on matters of appearance and spend a good deal of time trying to create a visual self-image. They eagerly imitate what they see in popular culture, drawing on images from magazines, Internet, and TV to express themselves. There is certain theatricality inherent to this adolescent performance which I play up in my work. Since they are covered, the viewer gets a chance to peek into the room and observe their mundane life—the details of which escape and undo any commonly held preconceptions.

Through these images, I explore the tension between public and private spaces, depicting images which undo the images of Islamic stereotypes represented through the narrow focus of the daily media. Moreover, they challenge the Muslim expectation of propriety. By using a fictive strategy and a documentary style, I have created a body of work that hovers between photographic realism and fantasy.

Soody Sharifi

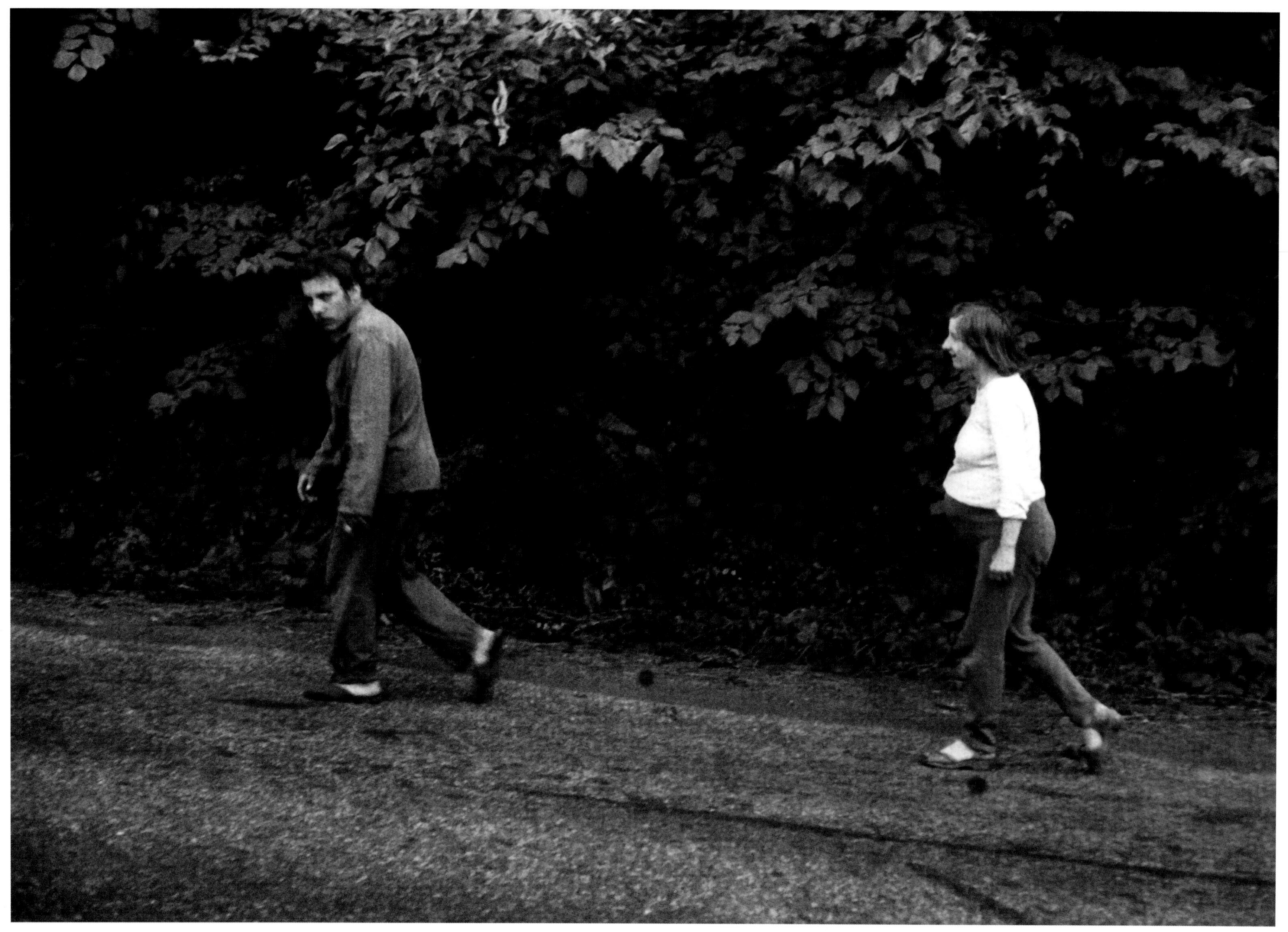

Jindrich Streit

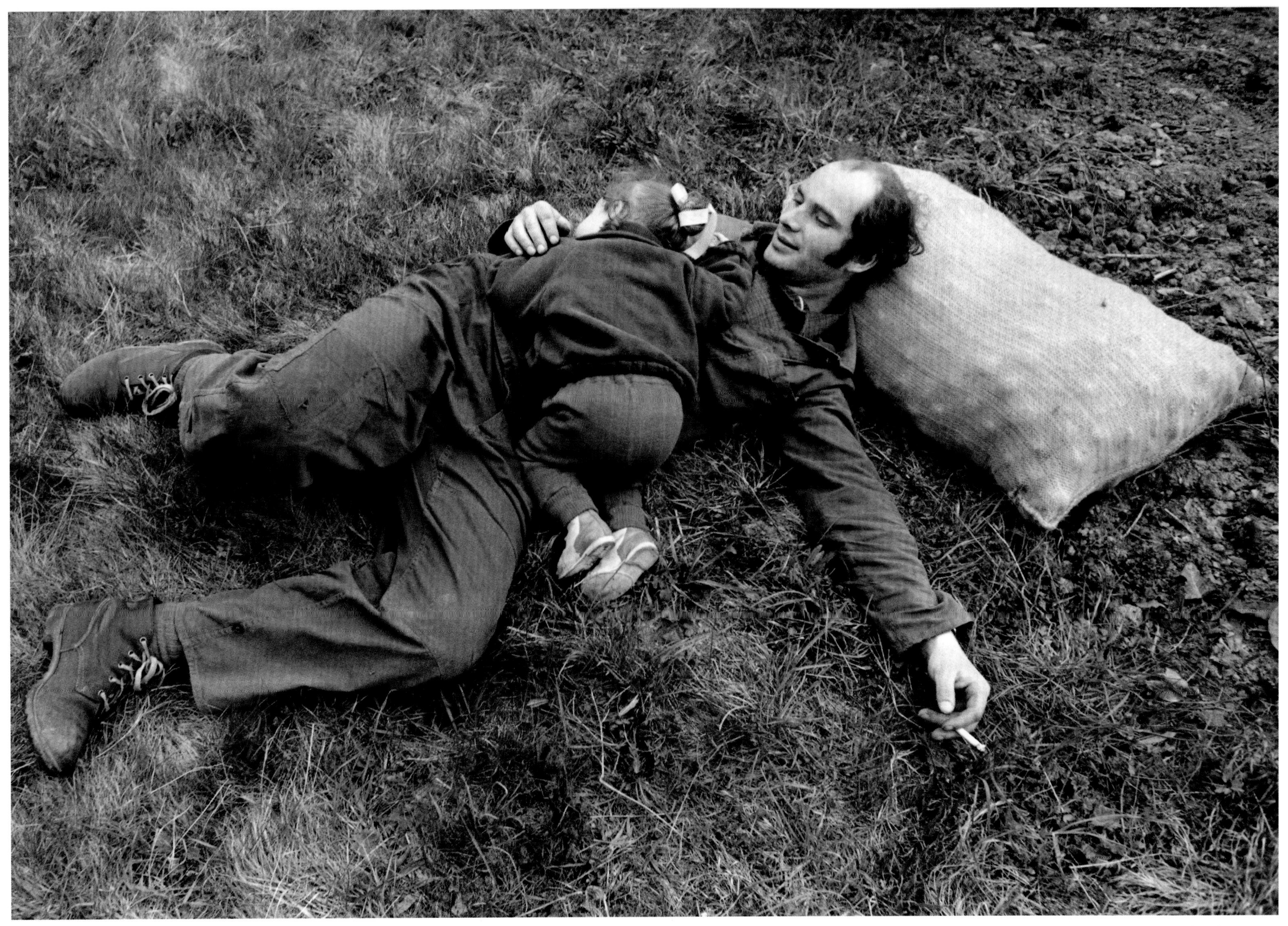

Jindrich Streit

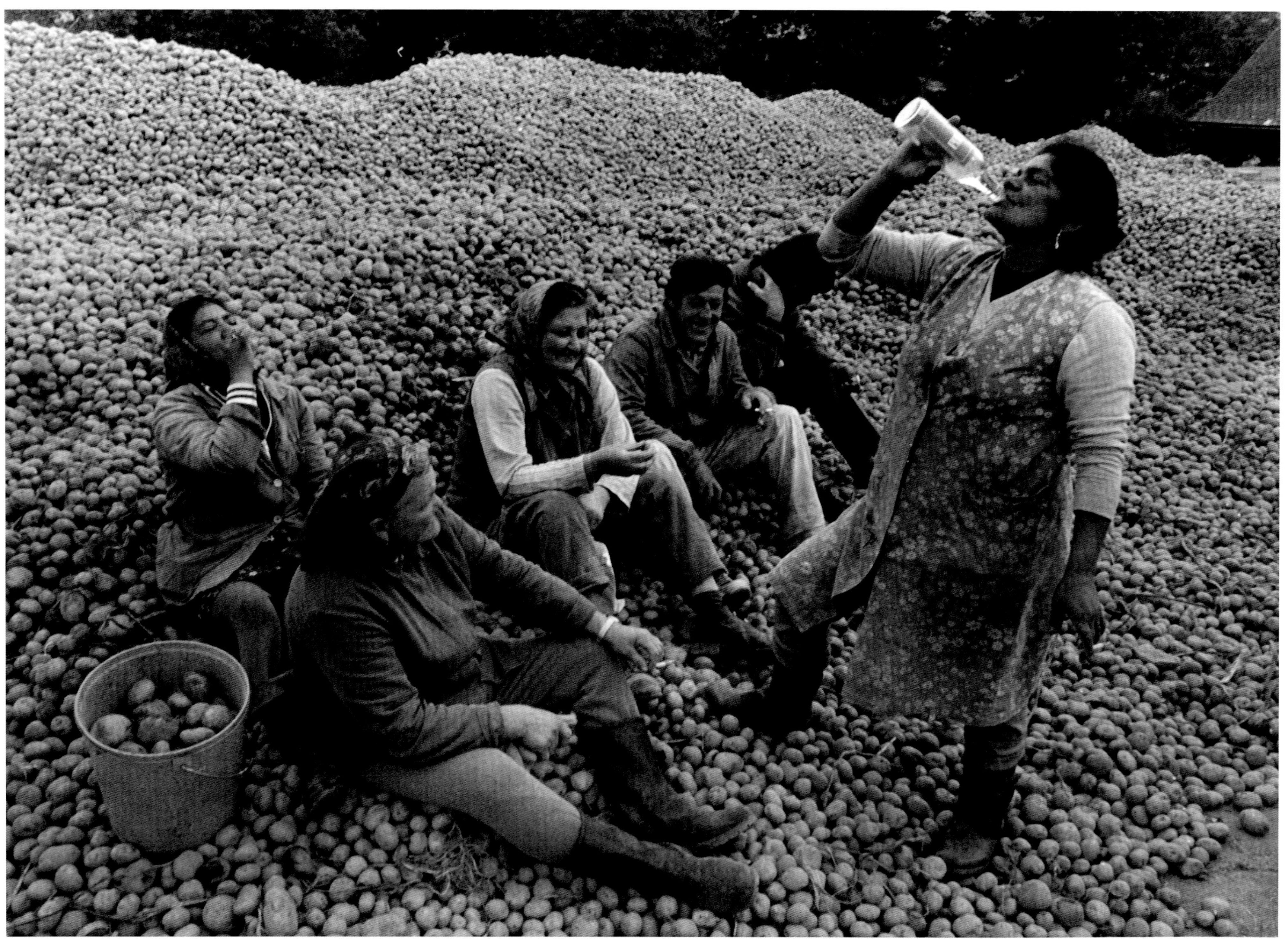

Jindrich Streit

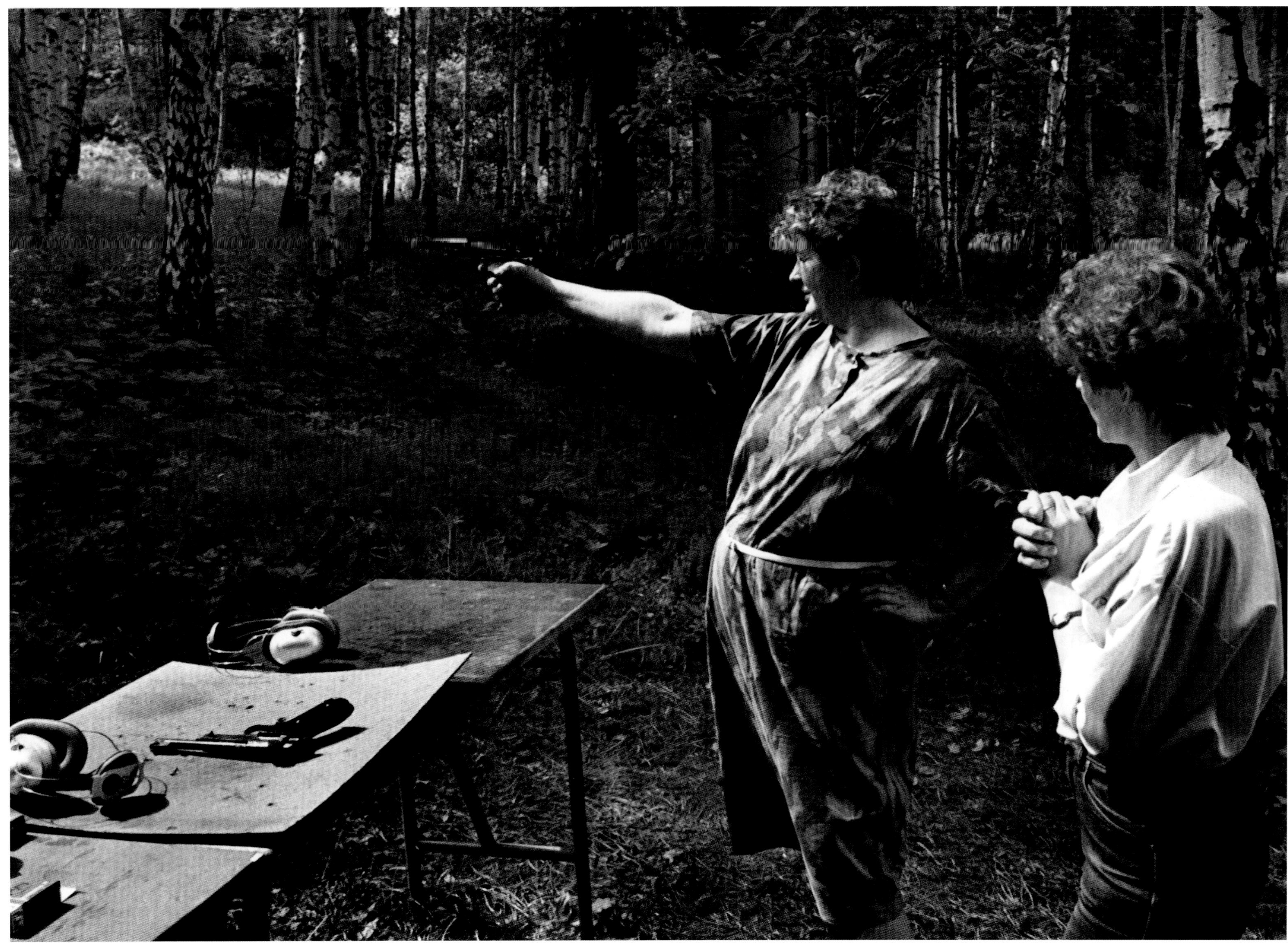

Jindrich Streit

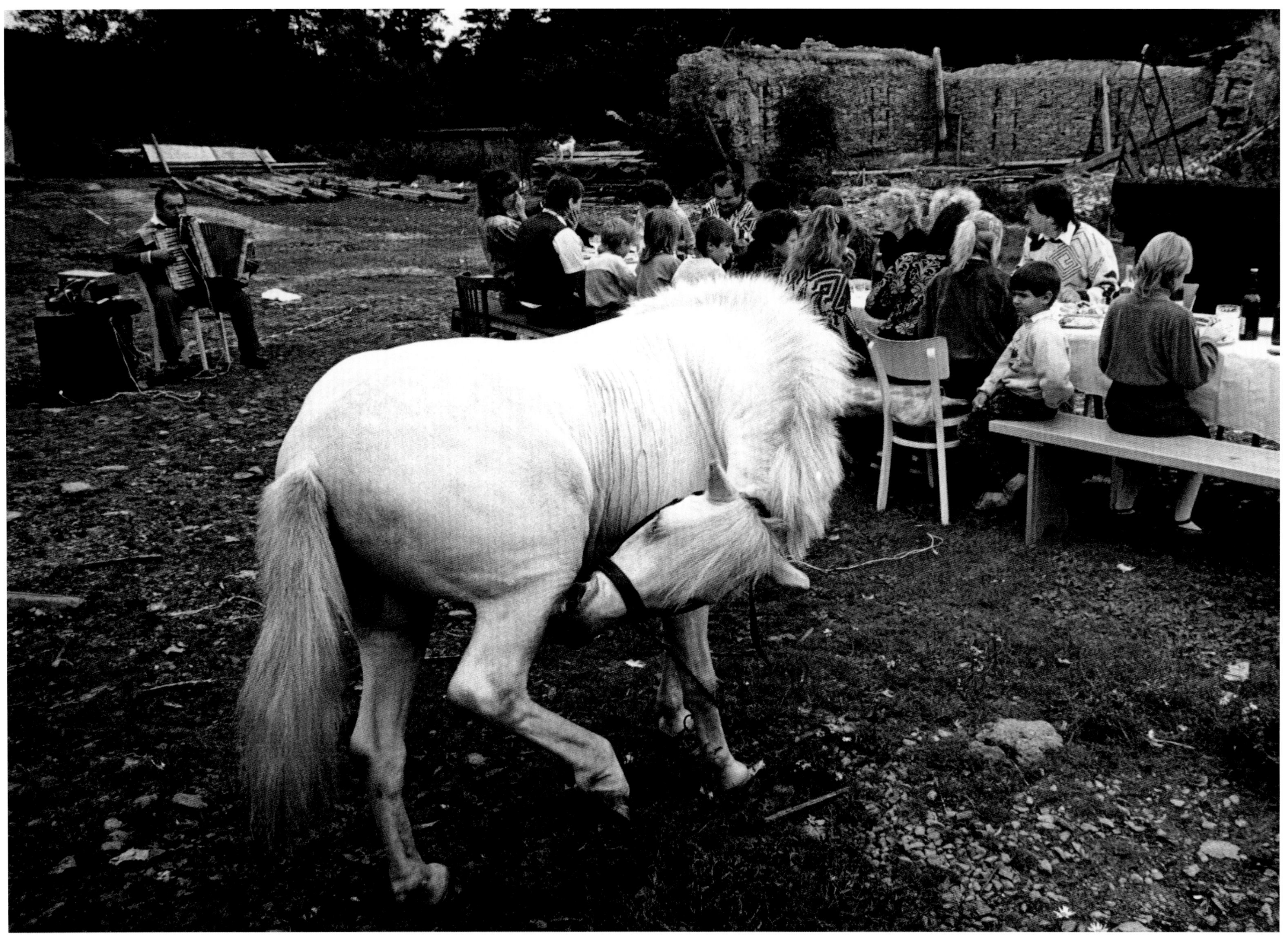

Jindrich Streit

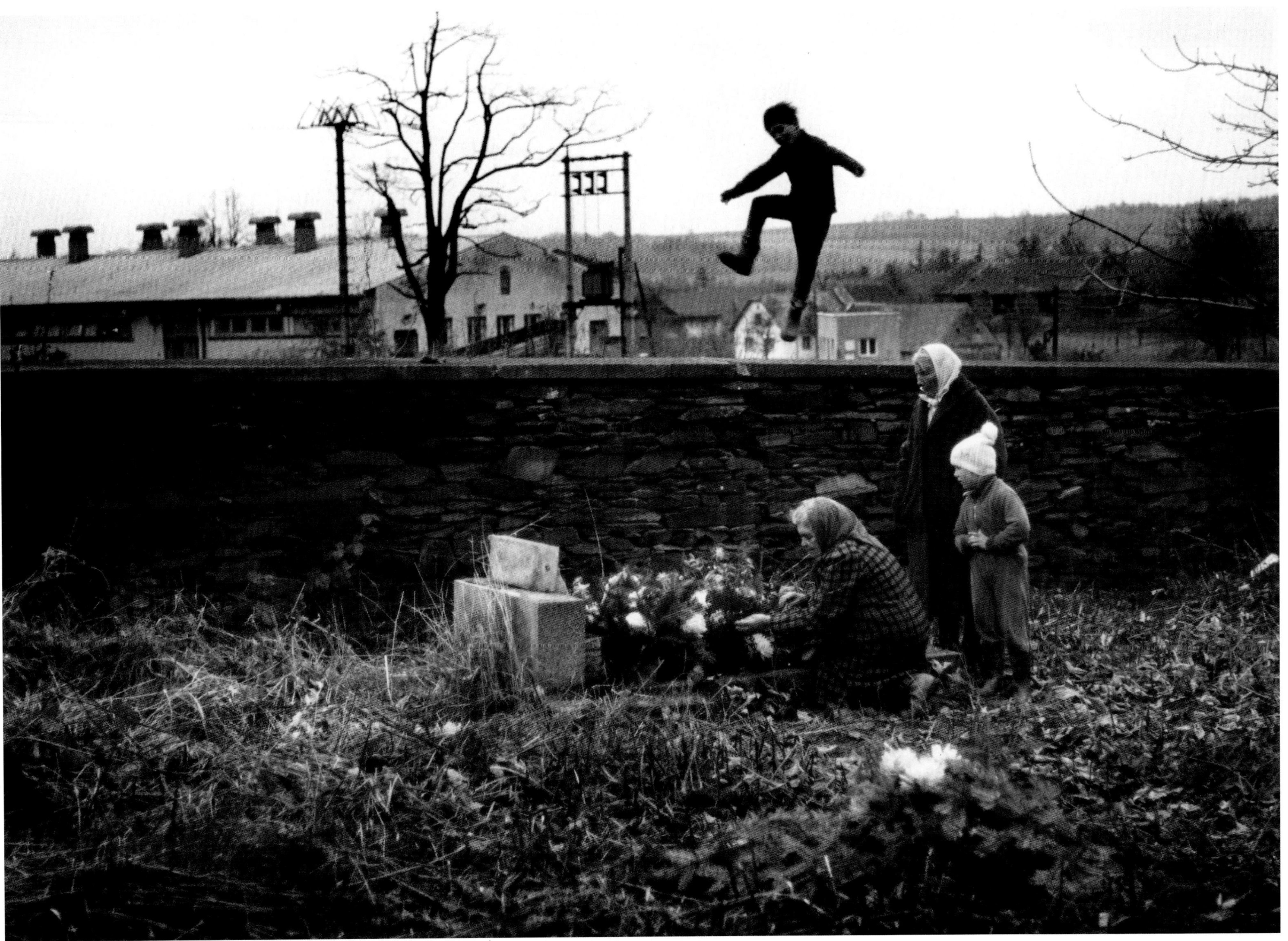

The concept of concerned photographer acquired a new meaning in Streit's case. He was not a globetrotting reporter who courageously recorded conflicts wherever they occurred, but an idiosyncratic chronicler aiming not at preserving the world he was recording but of changing it by being an integral part of it. He did not think of reconstructing the whole world but wished to participate, not only as a photographer but also as a man of action, in the life of the few villages that represented his home – his world. Unlike the hundreds of reporters who constantly take the risk which springs from their desire to be "on the spot" when dangerous political crises occur (and sometimes pay for it with their lives), Streit is perhaps the only photographer who has ended up in jail on the basis of an arbitrary interpretation of his essentially non-political engagement. He was judged on the basis of his photographs, only some of which were actually exhibited. In the history of photography this seems to be a unique case. – AntonIn Dufek

Jindrich Streit

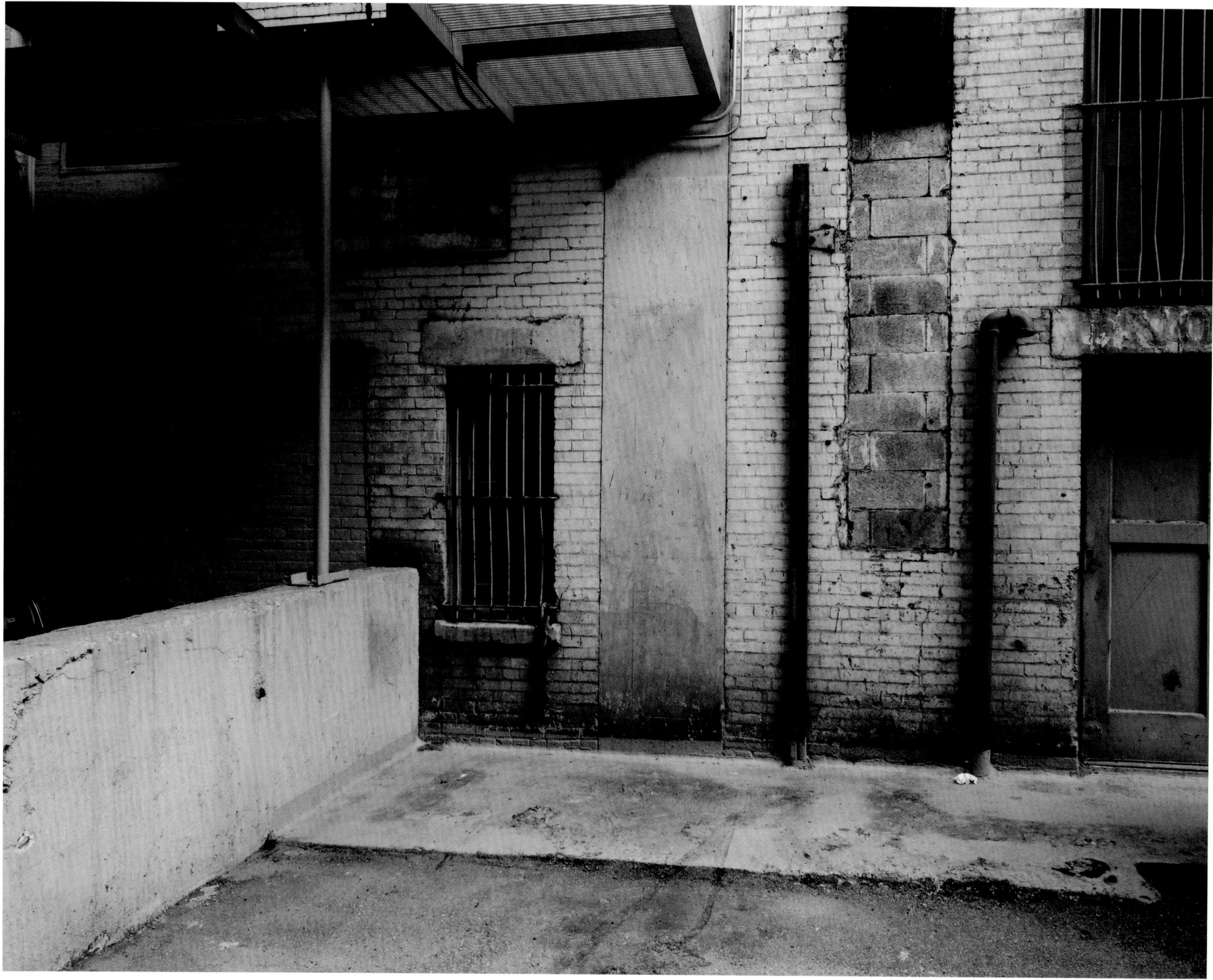

Bob Thall

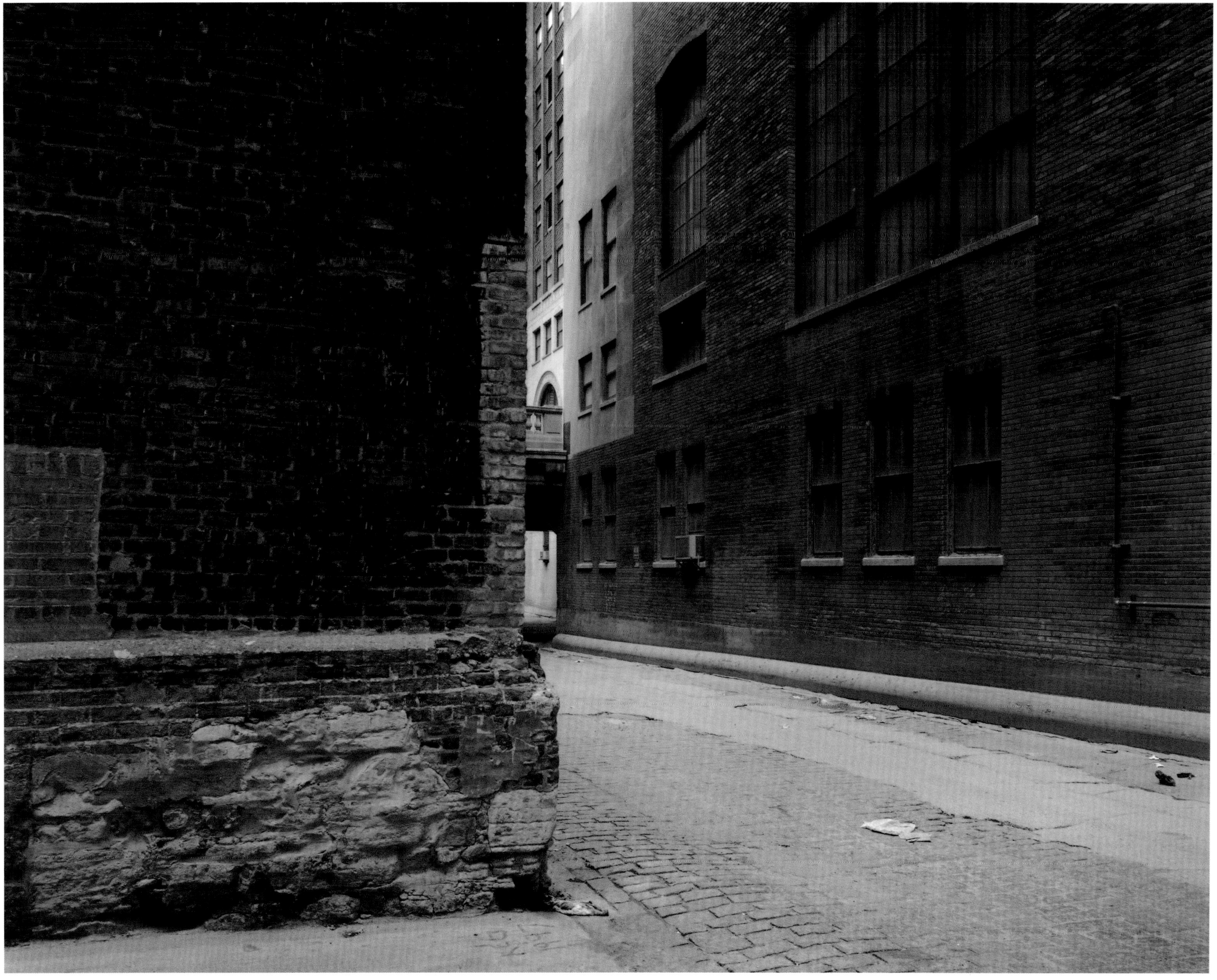

Bob Thall

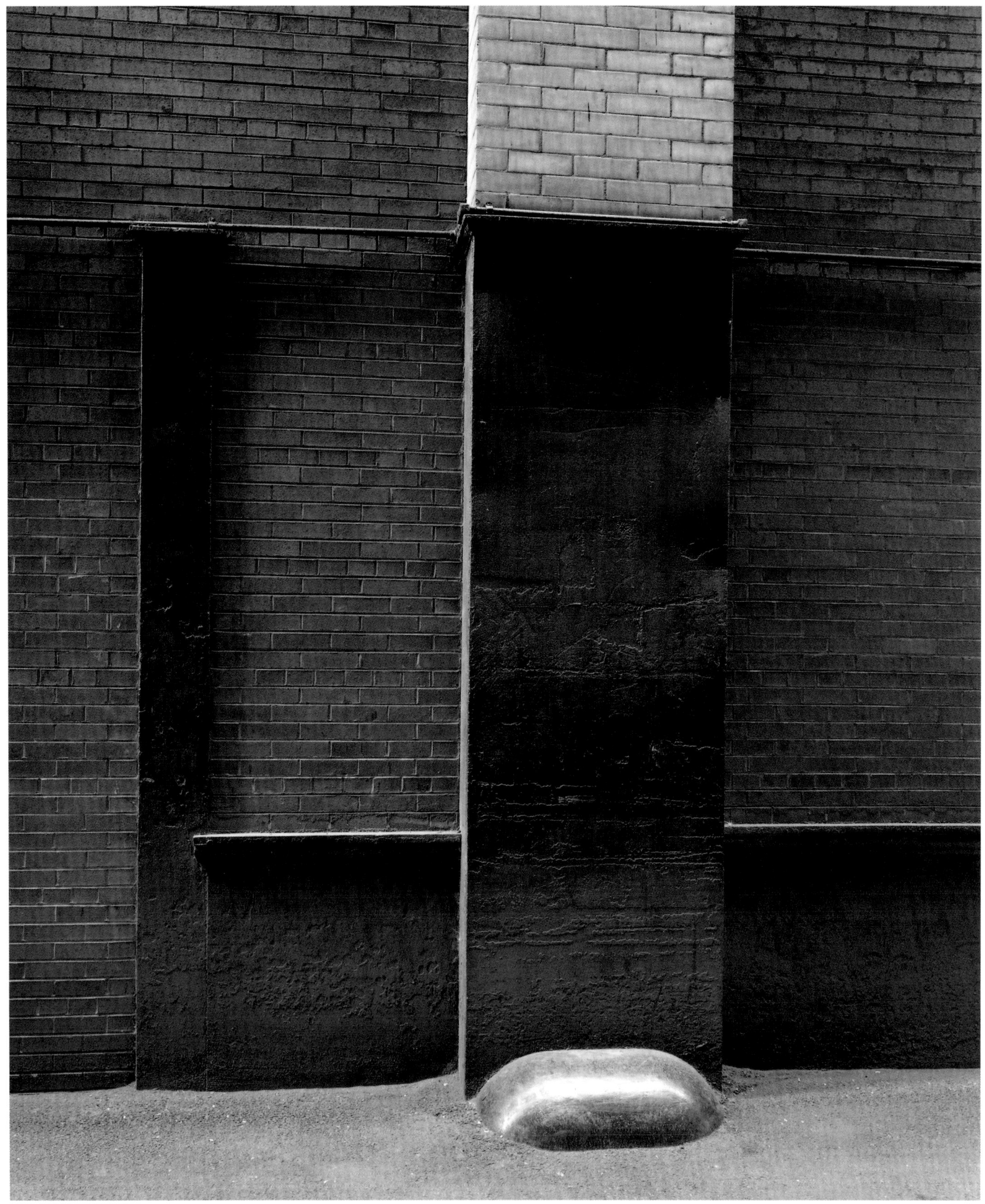

Bob Thall

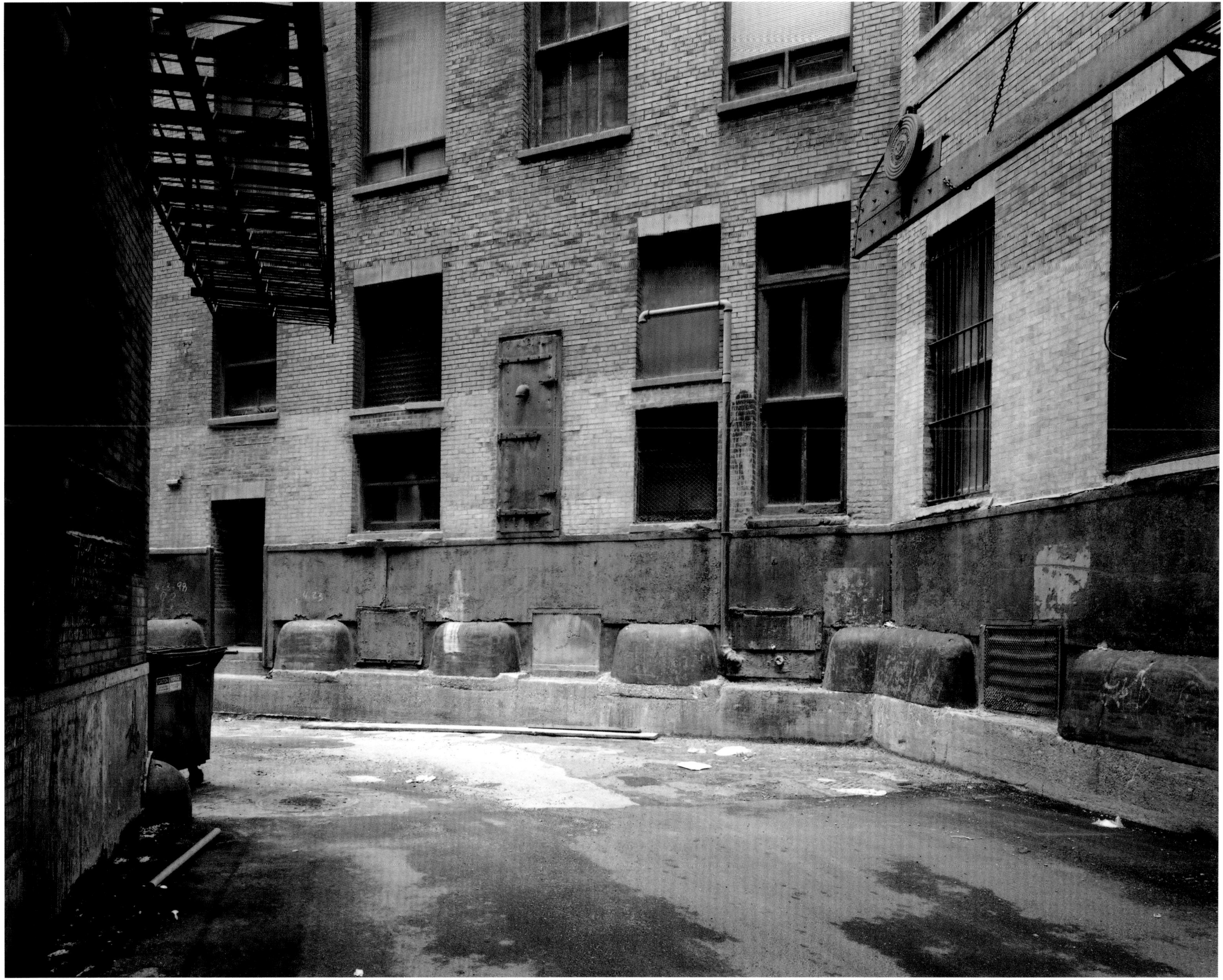

Bob Thall

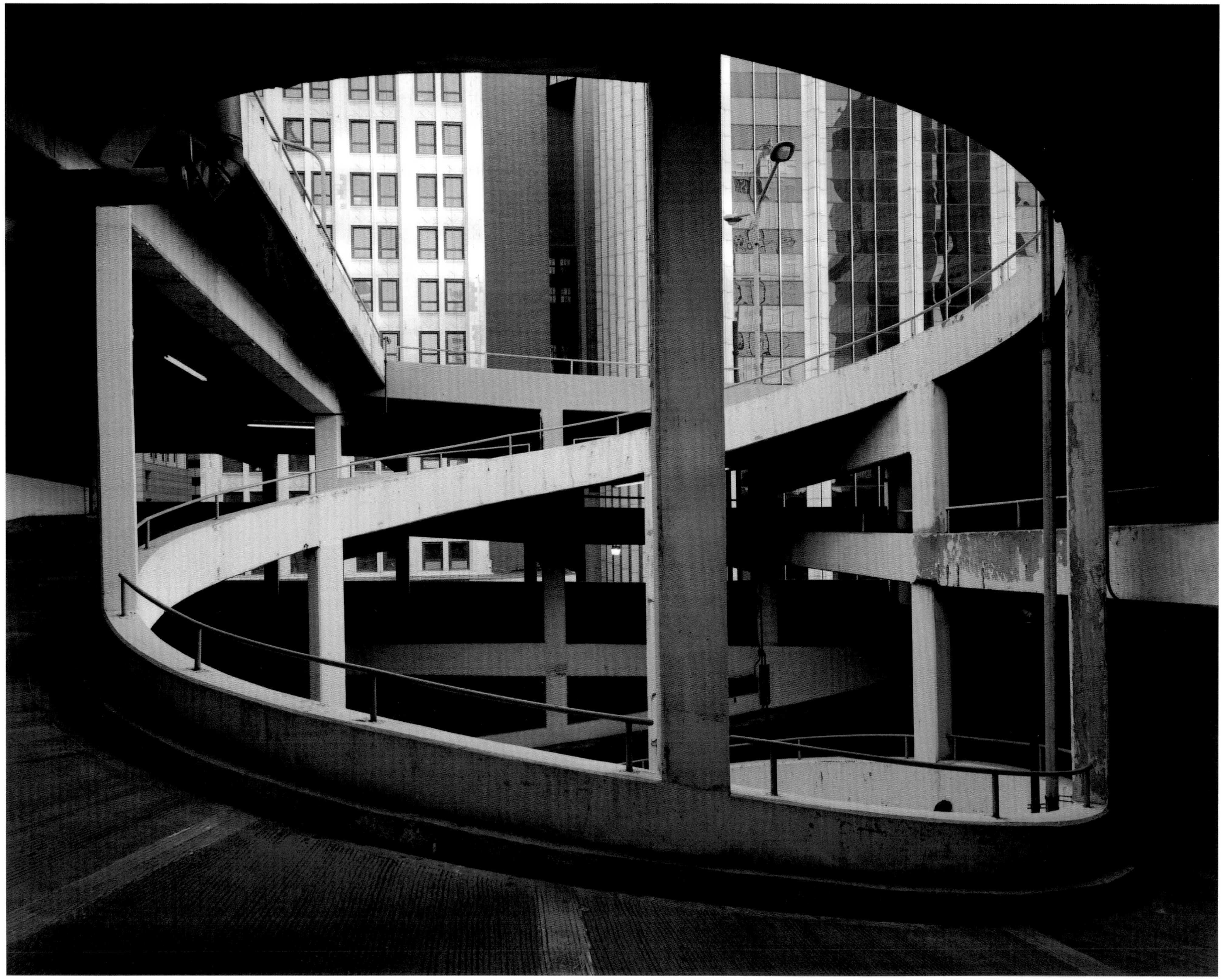

Bob Thall

The heart of my work as a photographer has always been photographing the Chicago landscape. I have spent many years photographing older neighborhoods, the downtown area, the industrial region to the south, and finally the new suburbs. In 1996, as I was shaping that suburban work into my second book, The New American Village, I chanced on a scene on the near west side and casually took a picture, using the last sheet of unexposed film I had with me. That photograph, of an alley near the Chicago River, intrigued me. It didn't fit in with anything I was planning to work on. I couldn't really decide if it was even a good picture, but I couldn't dismiss it either. The image seemed beautiful, puzzling, yet resonant of some important quality of the city. In 1998 I was ready to start a new body of work. I had planned to do more photographs of the industrial area of southeast Chicago, but that odd picture of an alley stuck in my mind. I thought that I would listen to the advice I give my students: don't plan too much, just follow up on interesting pictures.

What I found as I systematically explored downtown alleys were the remnants of the old city I had once found so compelling. The fronts of these buildings may have been extensively refurbished but no one had bothered with the back. These alleys are deep urban slits, the walls twenty, thirty, or forty stories tall. Rain almost never hits the sides directly. Signs, marks, and layers of paint survive, fading slowly. The rat-control crews leave the dates of their poison drops on the walls, and the chalk marks survive five and ten years. One could see the evidence of many years of use and history.

The alleys weren't easy spaces to photograph. I needed to concentrate on the most basic elements of photography: light, space, framing, very small changes in vantage point. I felt that I had returned to my beginnings as a photographer and was forced to rediscover the elements of the medium that I had long ago struggled to control. The dim light in these places required long exposures, vulnerable to vibrations from traffic and the L trains, but I learned to see the delicate and lovely quality of a small space lit by a tiny rectangle of sky, way above me. The visual delights of the city and architecture never seem more important than when they are found in unexpected circumstances. Prompting one to see beauty and significance where it's not anticipated is one of the most important gifts of photography.

Smelly, dirty, dark, occasionally a bit dangerous, these alleys was were not physically pleasant place to work. At the end of the block I often saw people in shorts walking in the sunshine across the alley toward Grant Park and the Lake. I felt submerged in a dark, murky pool. Emerging from an alley after an hour of timing long exposures could feel like rising to the surface. Still, this project was one of the most exciting and wonderful experiences I've had as a photographer. Investigating these spaces reminded me of my earlier sense of the city as a mysterious landscape to explore. I was also reminded of all I knew about the history of photography and the history of Chicago. Without planning or anticipating it, my history as a Chicagoan, my history as a photographer, the history of the city, and-in a small way-the history of photography all came together for me in this work.

Bob Thall

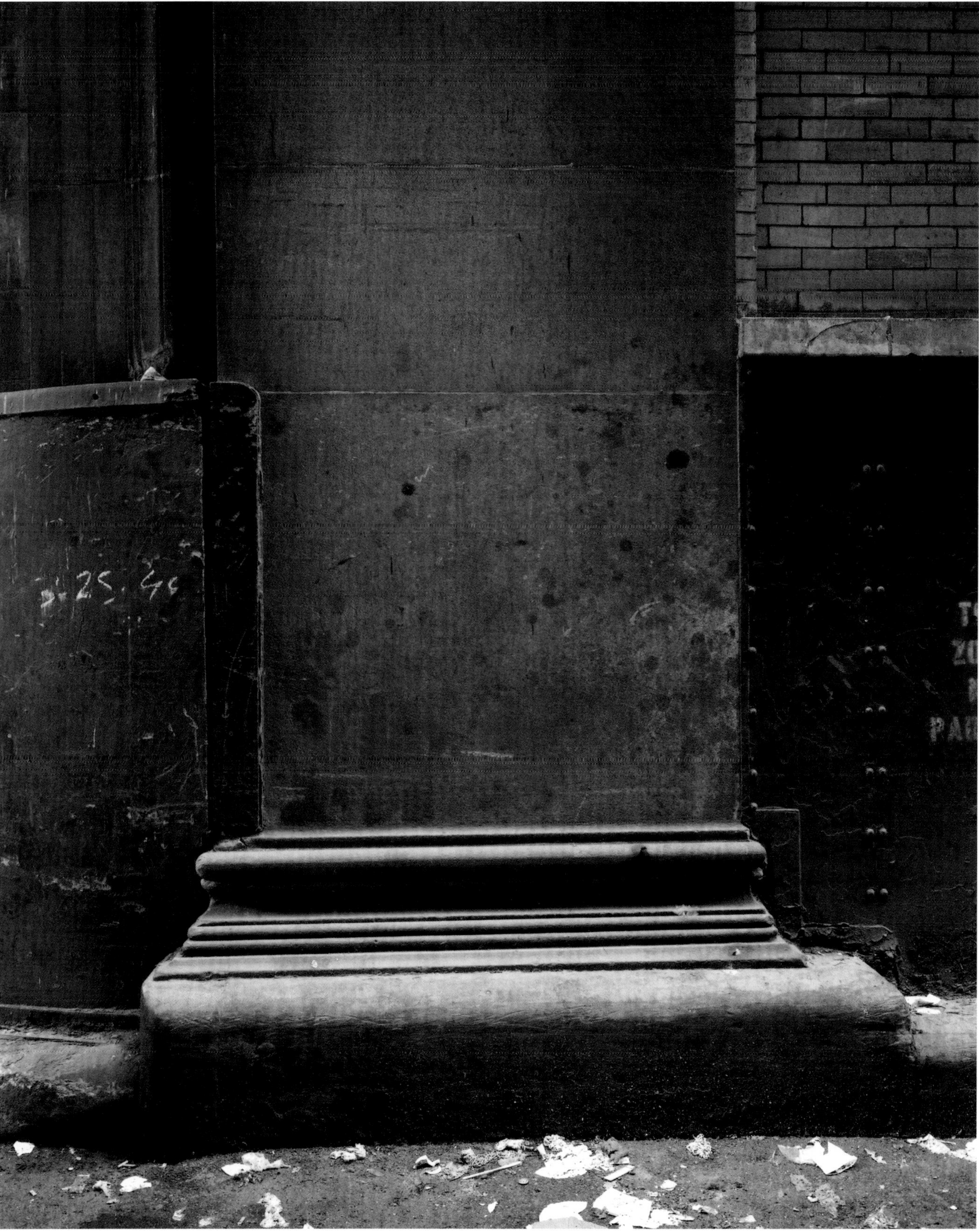

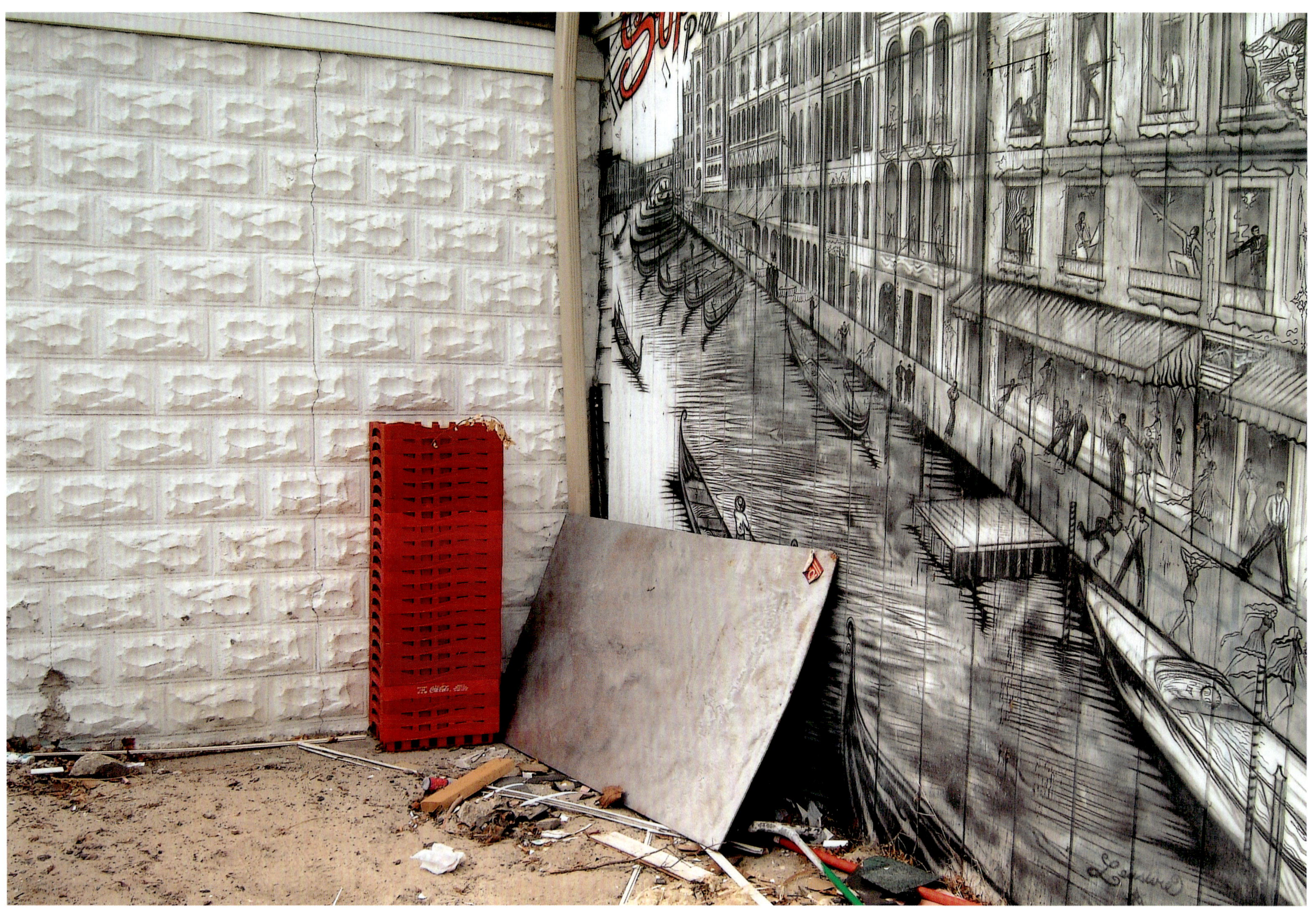

Charles Traub

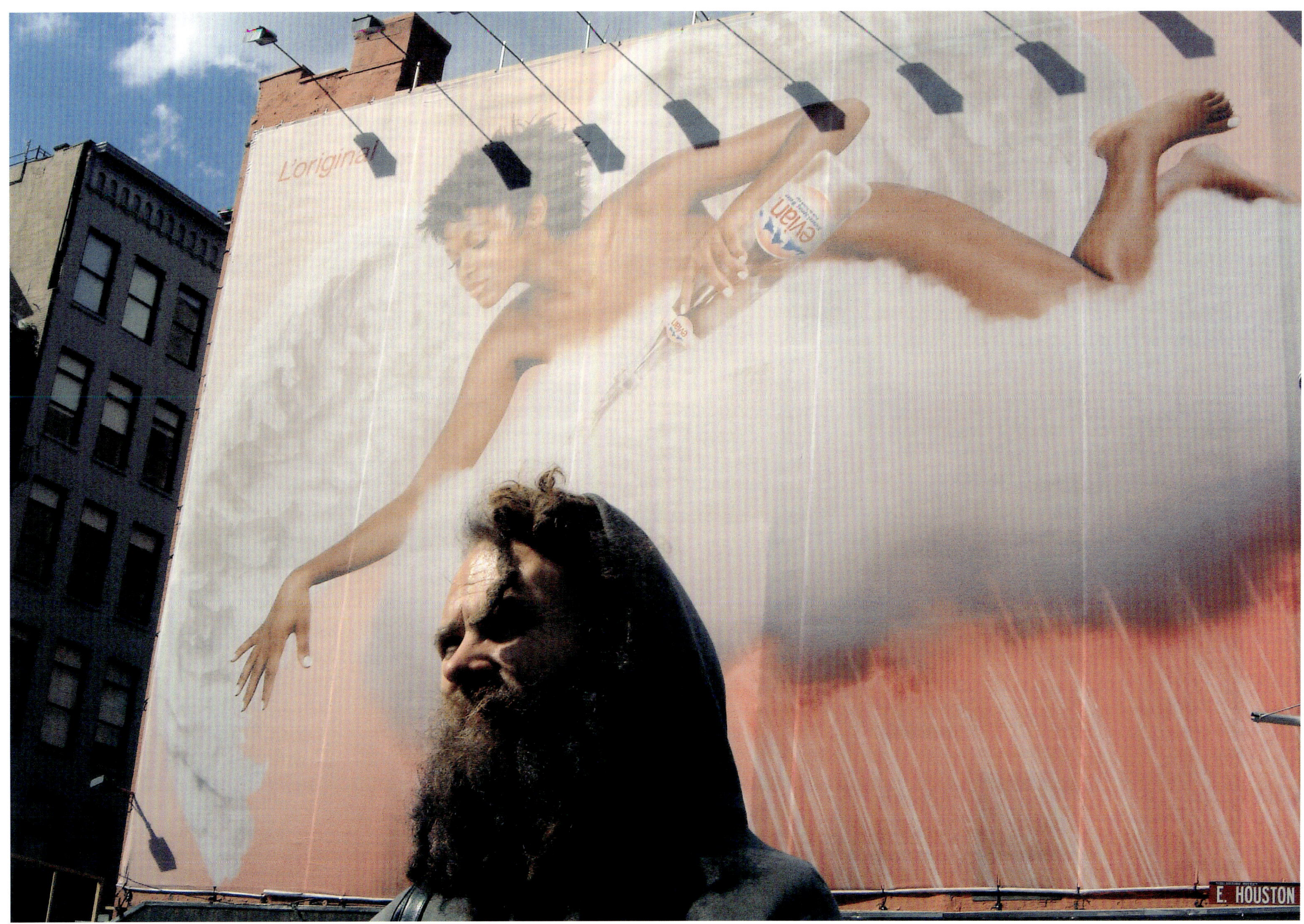

Charles Traub

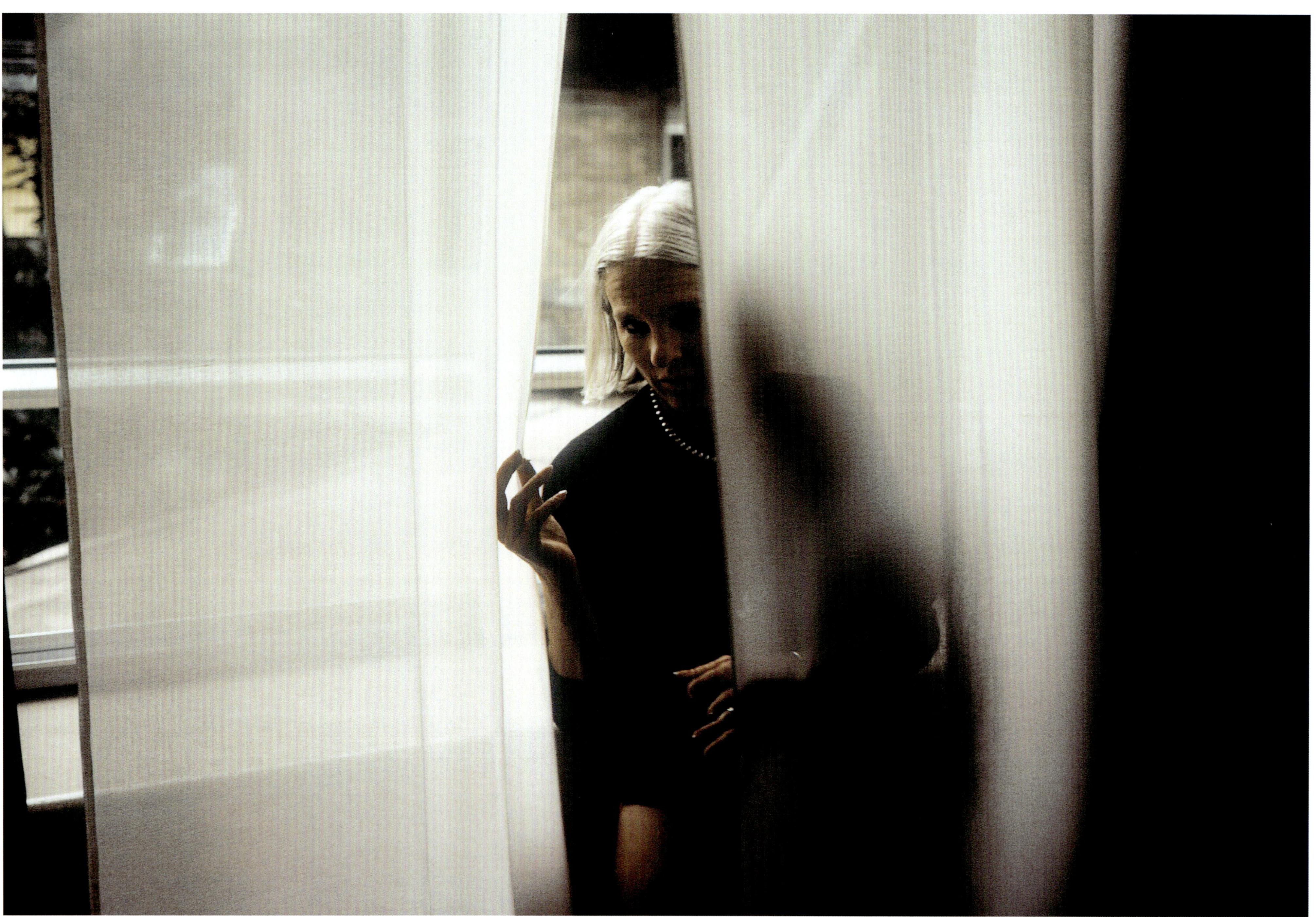

Charles Traub

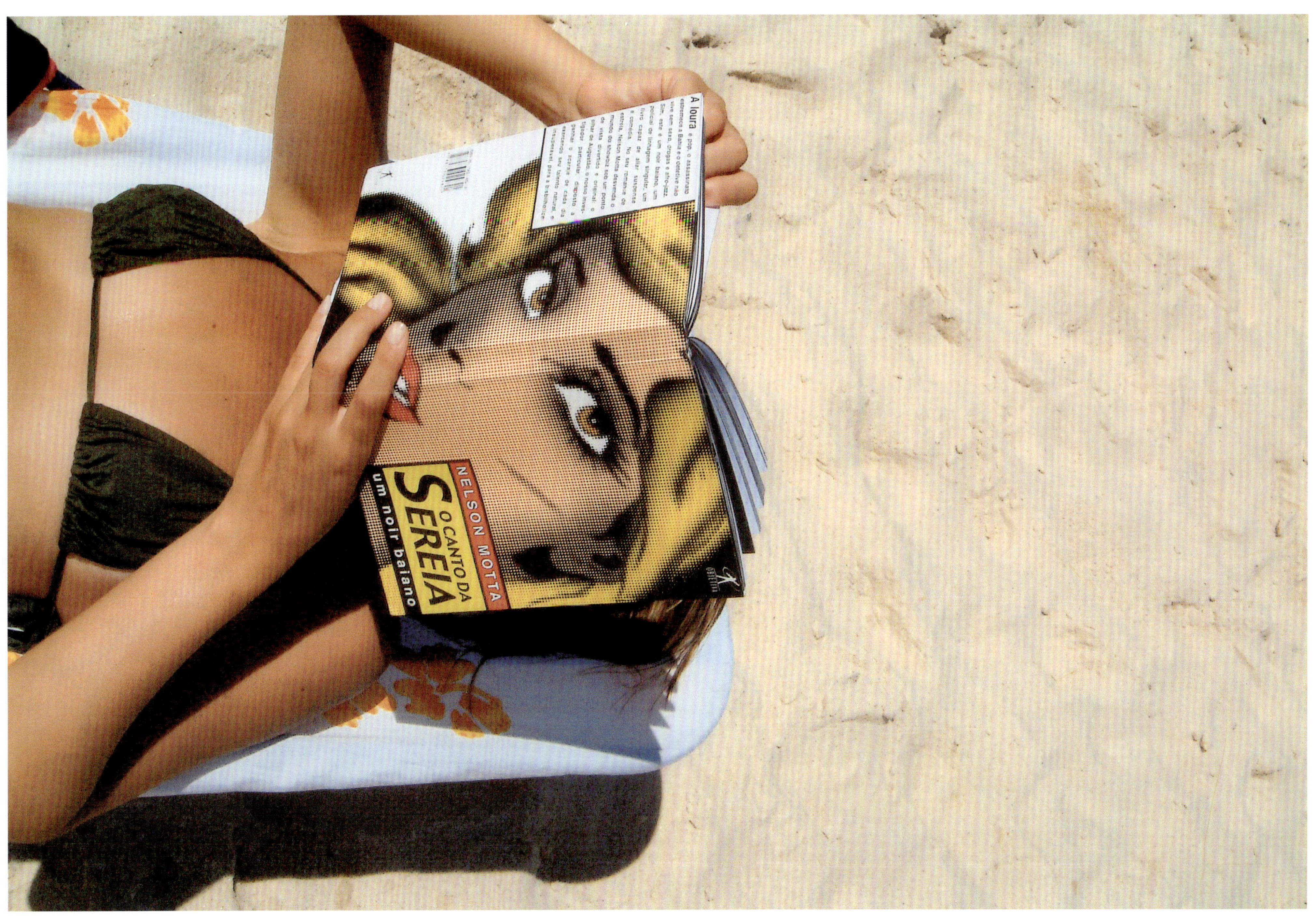

Charles Traub

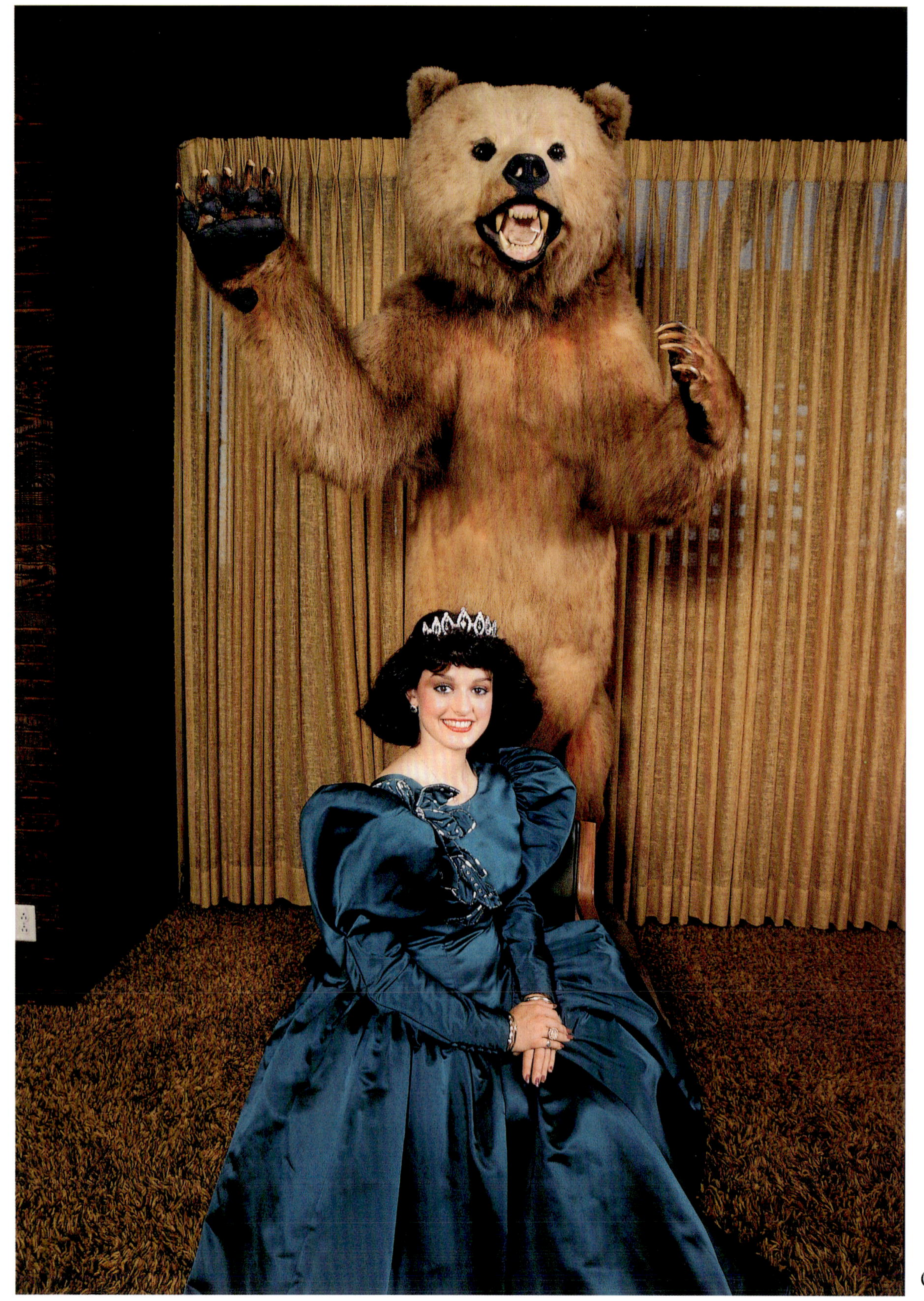

Charles Traub

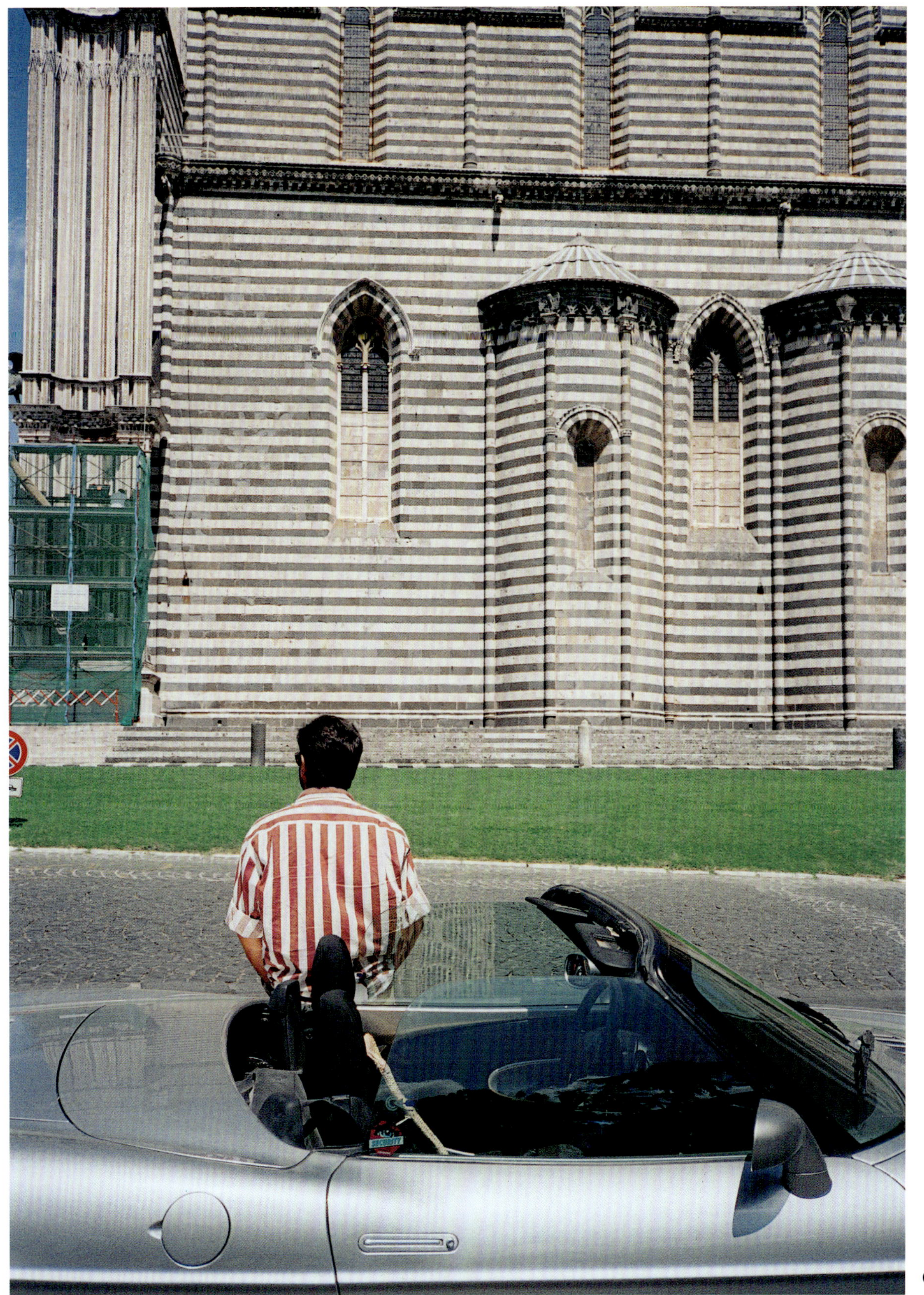

Charles Traub

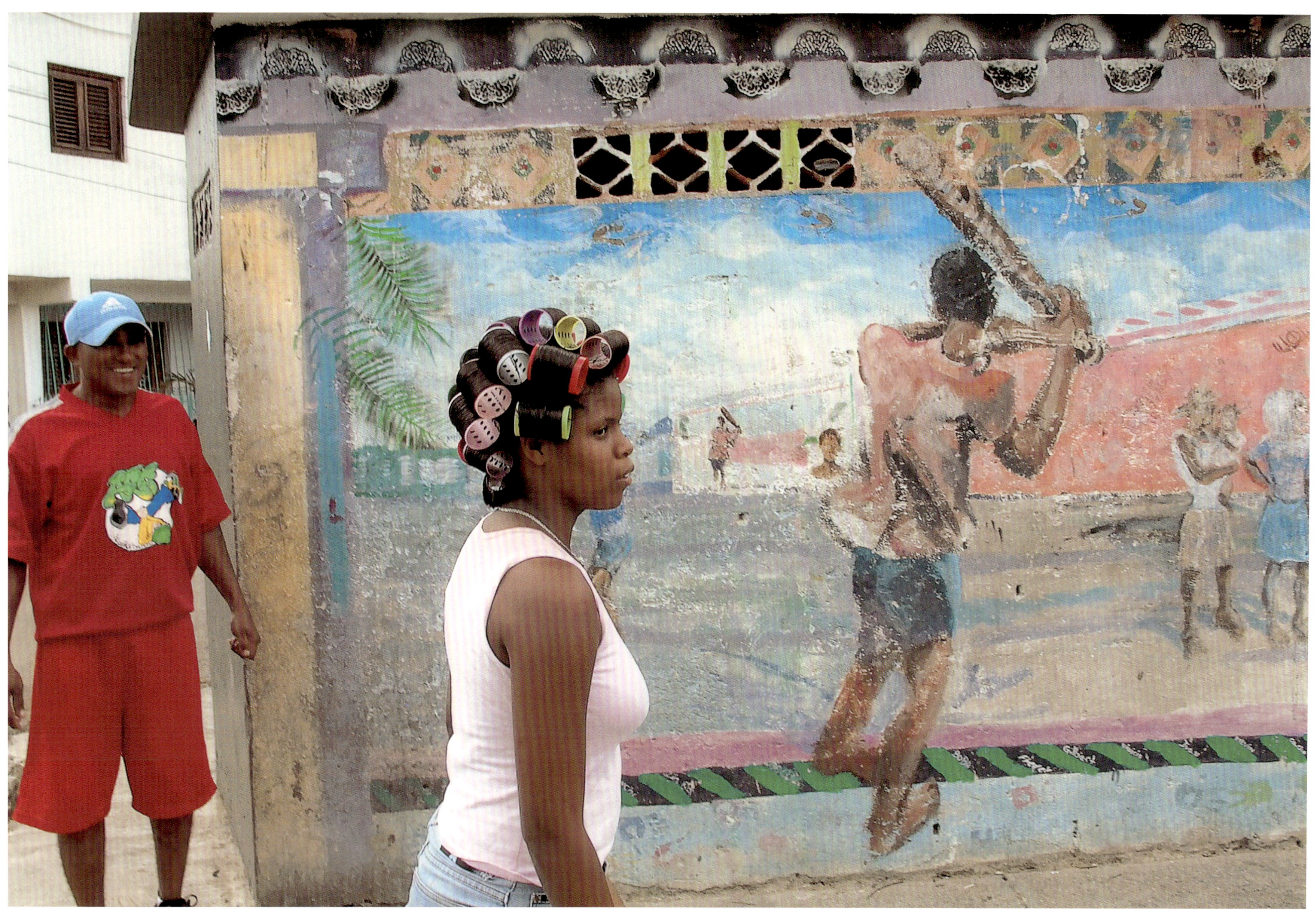

Charles Traub

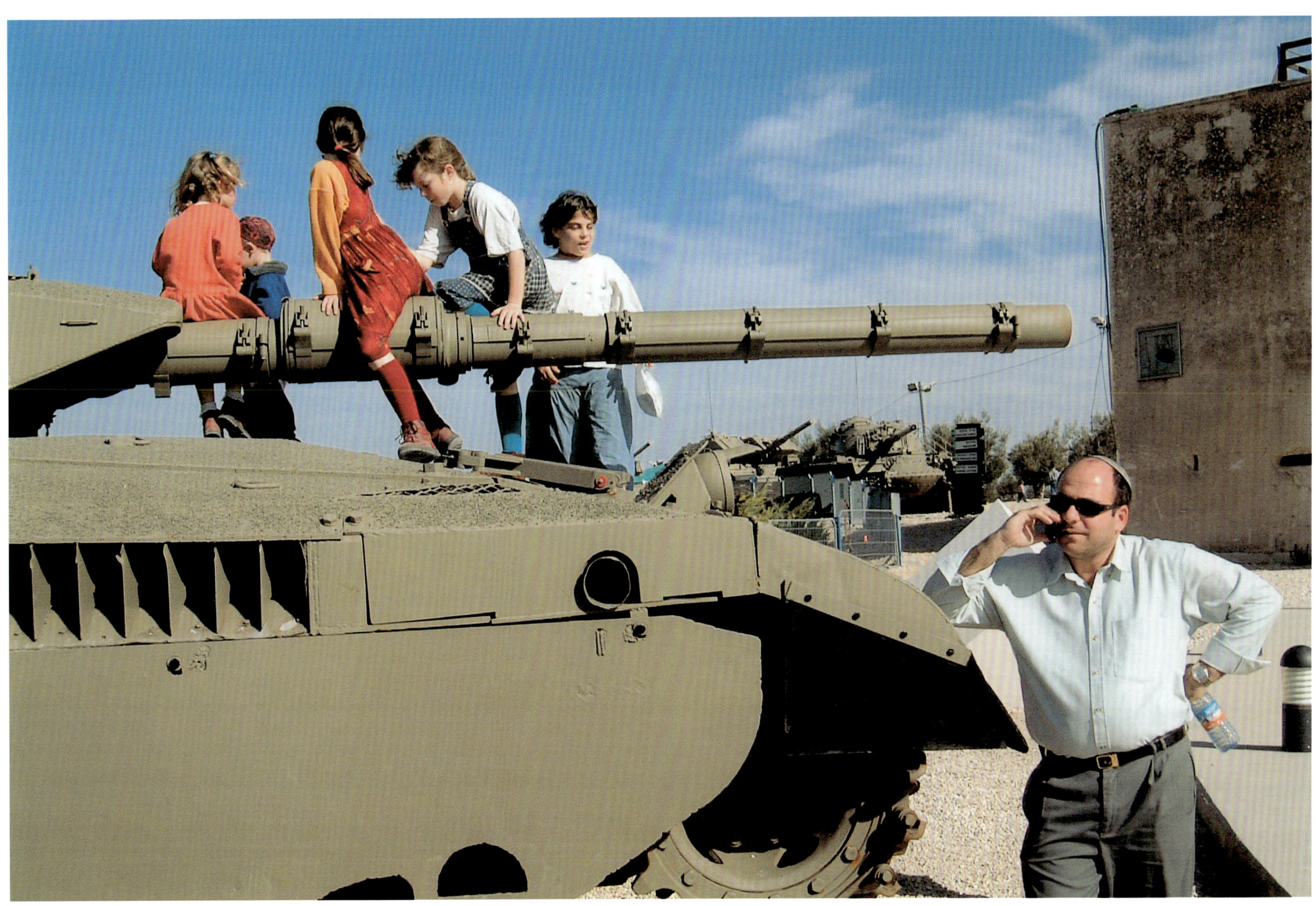

Charles Traub

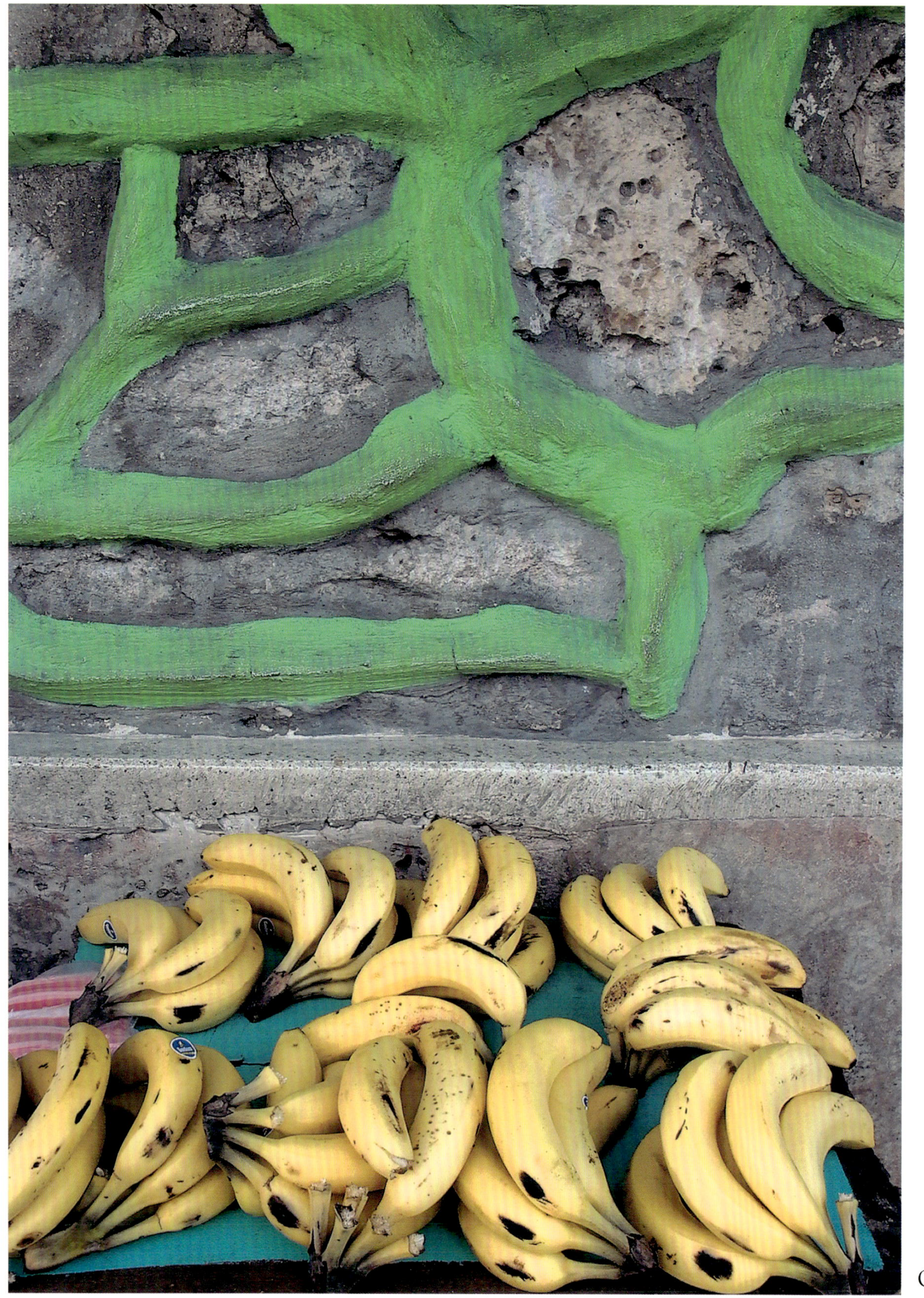

Charles Traub

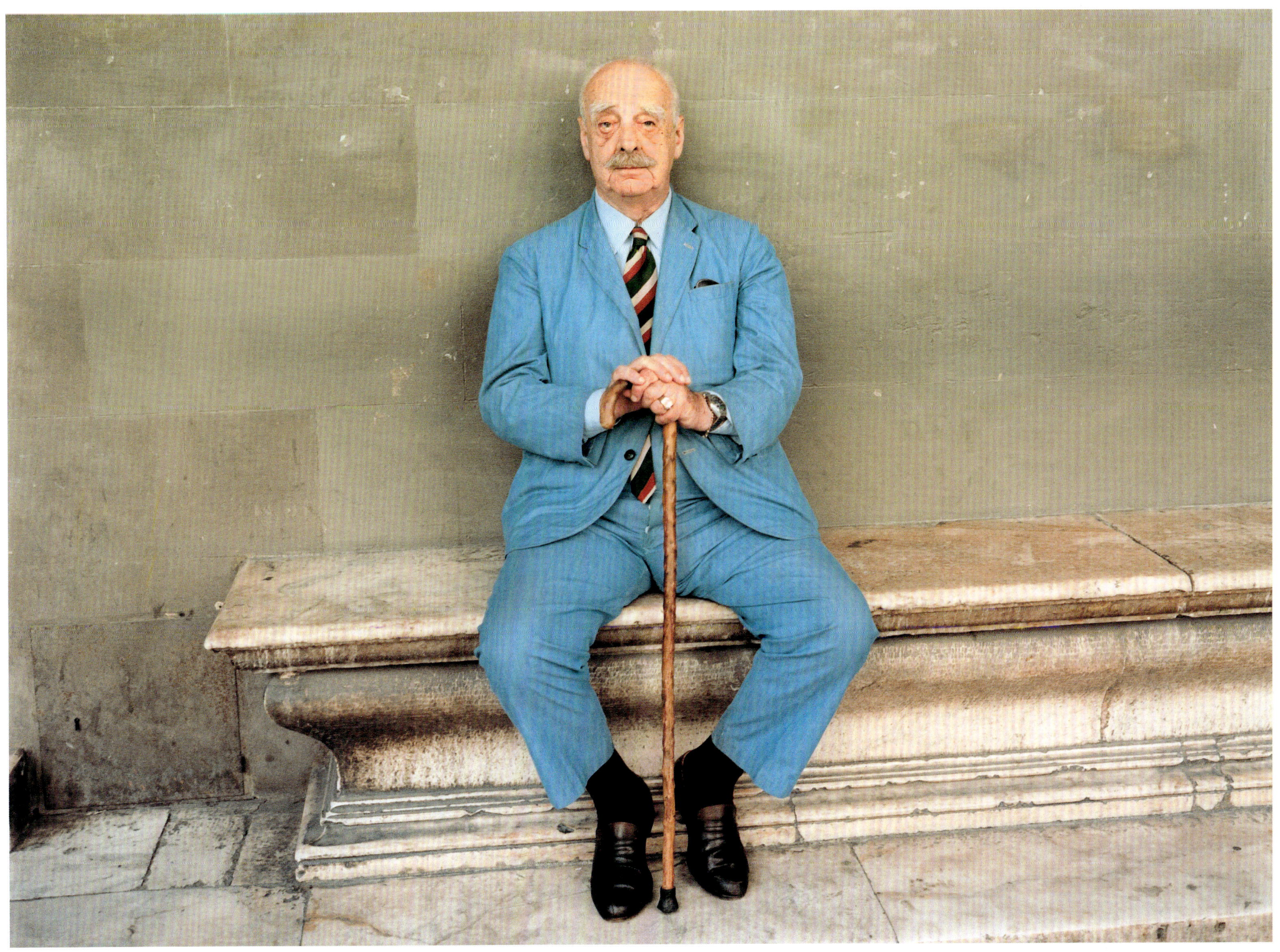

Charles Traub

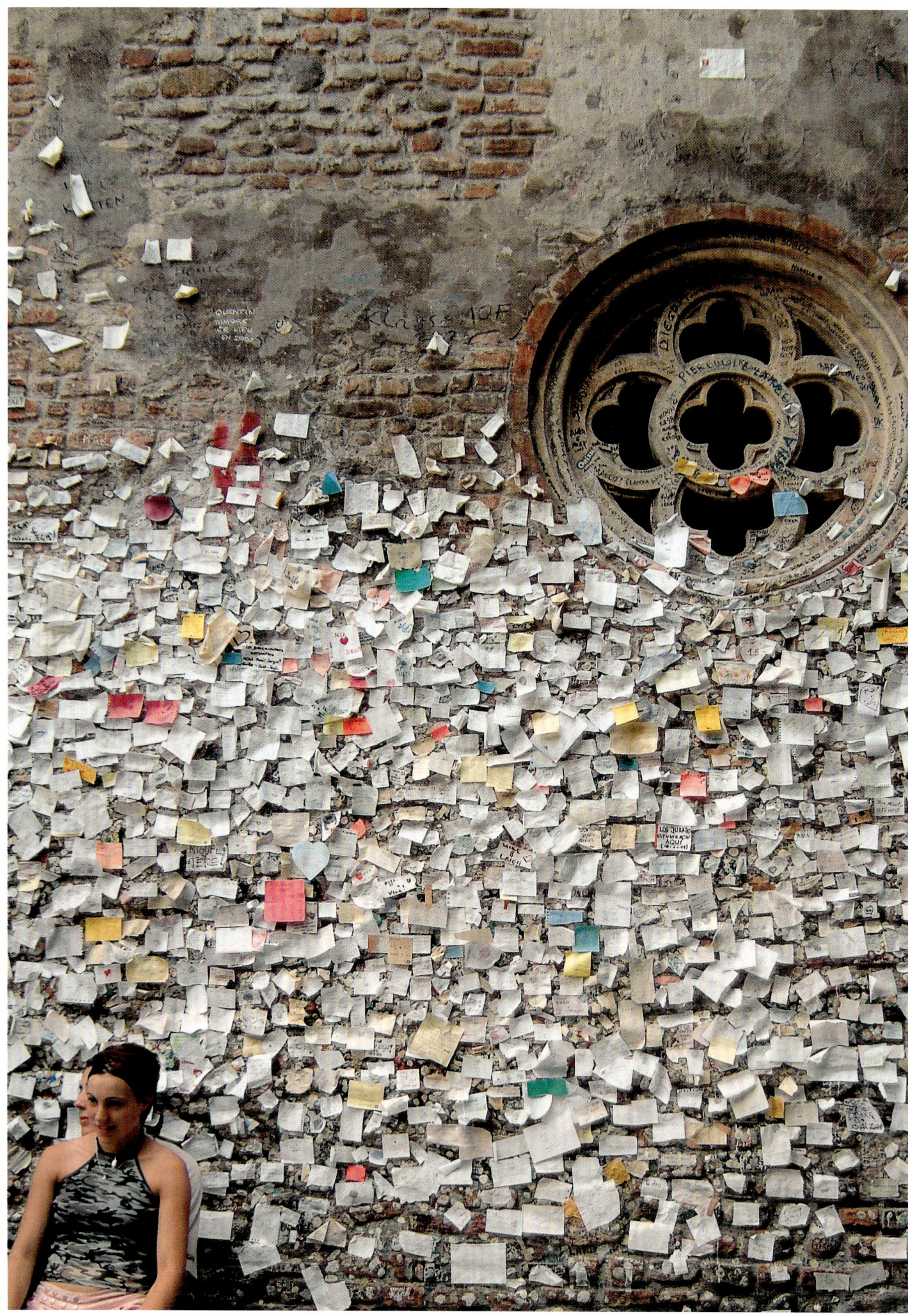

The whole secret to the study of life lies in learning to use one's eyes. – George Sand

The photographs, herein, were made from the early 1980's to the present throughout the world. They reflect my continual interest in observing our passing through and our inseparability from the fictions we create about ourselves. These are the silly falsehoods from reality. For me, serendipity, coincidence, and chance are more interesting than any preconceived construct of our human encounters.

The past twenty years have been quite significant for the history of imagery. Photographic documentary practice was waning as the prominent discipline of the photographic arts. The constructs of post-modernism and the advent of computer practice rallied the interest of photographers, distracting them from traditional real world witness.

Throughout a good deal of this period, I had moved myself away from my own creative documentary practice to take on assignments for editorial and corporate publications as well as becoming an educator. The notion of pursuing a project or a body of work for the purpose of exhibition, for which I felt most at ease as a creative person, was in conflict with the pressures of having to perform to someone else's expectations other than my own. This is not an unusual conflict, though it is rarely resolved to the satisfaction of the artist. Thus, when making pictures for myself, I made a decision to give up the conventional paradigms of the artist and any others that apply to the various hats a photographer might wear. I would be free from all constraints. The photographs taken in this period are those that were made on the fly; taken to and from the assignment and in route to that place where one kills time on the job. They come from the back streets, from the spoils of working travel – the sights of a crowded life. In these pictures there is no preconceived idea, no intention of purpose, often as not, they are the last frames shot to finish the roll. Though they are made out of years of wandering and looking.

For years, I saved these pictures because I liked them, but threw them in a plastic box to save them for I know not what. They had no context as they were made piece meal without a project in mind. The inherent relationship of this eclectic work came to me recently and ironically, through my attempts to paint. I discovered still life – the inanimate setting of fruit on a table. The possibilities of shape, form, color and space fascinated me without limit. The inanimate became live moving images of possibilities in gauche. When I happened to examine my plastic box full of transparencies, it struck me that the moving drama of the ordinary crowded life was an arrangement to be held in time by the still making shutter of the camera. This realization was a kind of reverse: the camera stops the animate and makes it inanimate while paint gives meaning thus life to the inanimate. It was all so simple, and hence I realized that herein was the stuff made from the stills in the life that constituted in the still life.

In this post historical time, the depiction of physical space becomes a culture-scape full of meaning. All images transcend their original reasons for being made. And are ascribed new roles via their ability to stimulate the viewer's memory or fantasy of their own passing through the cultural landscape. One must be ever mindful of the many masks an image might hold. It served different guises for different people, though it is always a relic of the period of which it is made. We cannot divorce the illusion of the photograph from that something in the real world that we think we know.

Private faces in public places are wiser and nicer than public faces in private places.
– W.H. Auden

Charles Traub

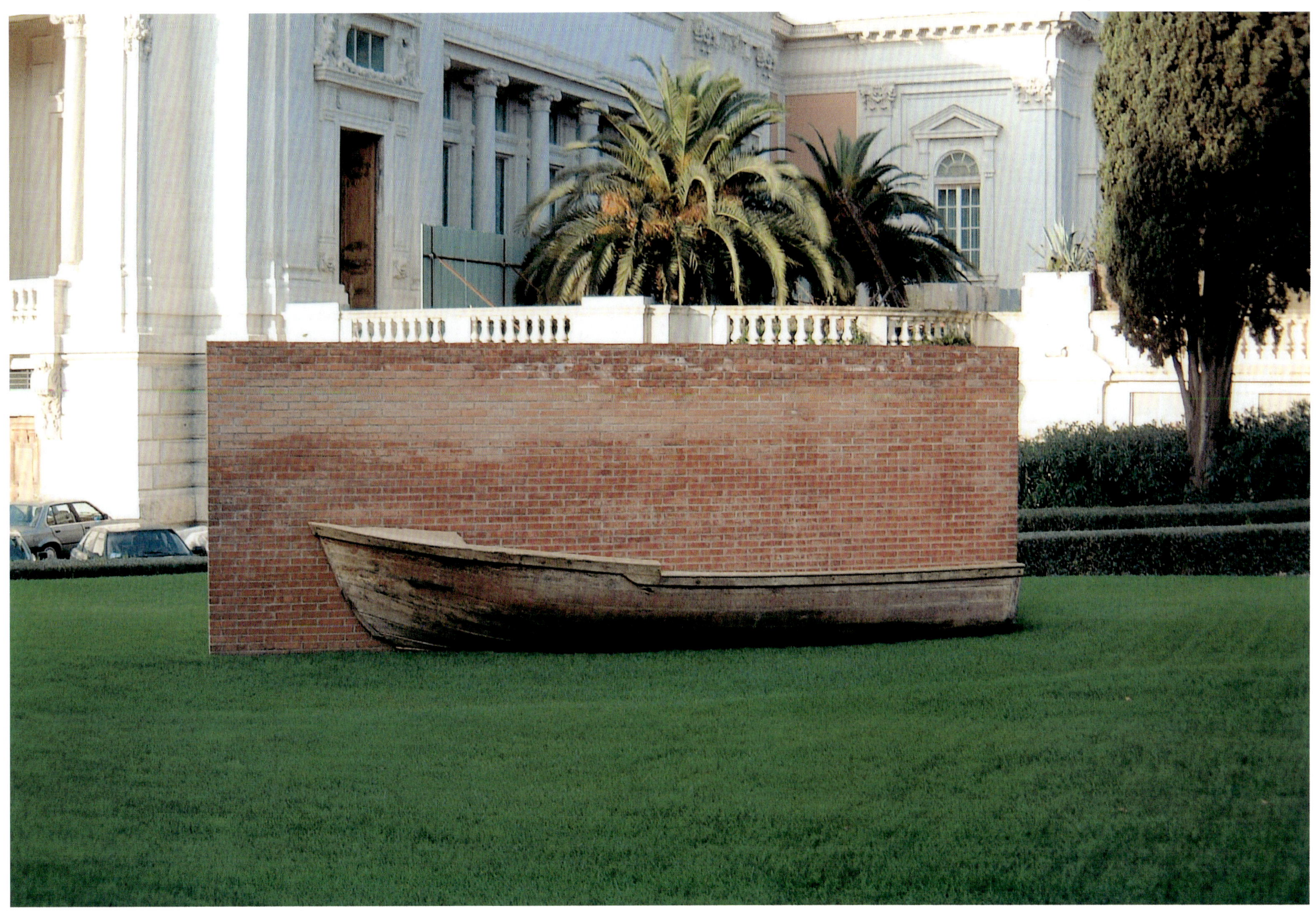

Charles Traub

Blue Sky Gallery
Oregon Center for the Photographic Arts
1231 NW Hoyt Street
Portland OR 97209

The front cover image is by Adrain Chesser.
Check out our website at http://www.blueskygallery.org

Blue Sky is a non-profit gallery supported by our members, the Paul G. Allen Charitable Foundation, the Autzen Foundation, Digi-Craft, the M.J. Murdock Charitable Trust, the National Endowment for the Arts, and Portland's Regional Art & Culture Council.
Two images from each of these exhibitions are now part of the "Blue Sky Collection" within the Portland Art Museum's permanent photography collection thanks to the generous support of James and Susan Winkler and the artists.
All images by Berenice Abbott are the property of the Museum of the City of New York.
Charles Cohen's work is courtesy of Bonni Benrubi Gallery, New York.
Jim Cooke and Martina Mullaney's work was supported by the British Council.
Jeffrey Milstein would like to thank Dr. Elliot Kornberg and Jewish Solidarity for helping facilitate his travels to Cuba.
Martina Mullaney's work is courtesy of Yossi Milo Gallery, New York.
Simon Norfolk's work is courtesy of Gallery Luisotti, Santa Monica.
Magali Nougarède's work is courtesy of Rosenberg & Kaufman Fine Art, New York.
Paul Seawright's work is courtesy of Kerlin Gallery, Dublin.
Bob Thall's work was supported by the John Simon Guggenheim Foundation and Columbia College Chicago.
Charles Traub's work is courtesy of Gitterman Gallery, New York.
19th Century photographs used by Annu Palakunnathu Matthew are courtesy of The Library of Congress, Washington, DC, except "Hattie Tom. Chiricahua Apache" by F. A. Rinehart, Omaha 1899 ("with dot on face") which is courtesy of University of Pennsylvania Museum of Archeology and Anthropology, Philadelphia, Pennsylvania.
ISBN 0-931194-08-3

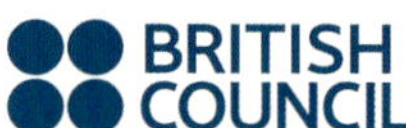

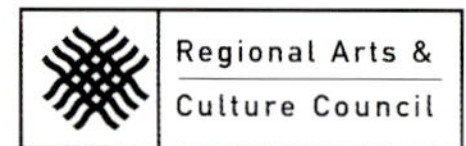

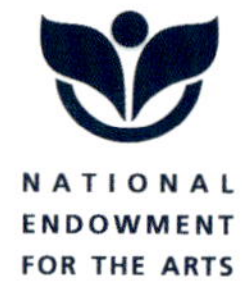